WITHDRAWN

THE
Character, Claims and Practical Workings

OF

FREEMASONRY

By Rev. C. G. Finney
Late President of Oberlin College, Ohio

ᏣᎬᏩ

Jon Kregel, Inc., dba JKI Publishing
P.O. Box 131480
Tyler, Texas 75713
1998

D0916244

IMPORTANT NOTE TO THE READER

As you begin this book, it is essential that you have a clear understanding of what is meant by the Gospel of Jesus Christ. The Gospel (or Good News) is extremely relevant since the forgiveness of sin, the gift of eternal life, and eternity in heaven are based on this simple, yet profound message.

This "Good News" is understood only when we realize the really bad news of what sin has done. The Bible says, "For all have sinned and come short of the glory of God." (Rom. 3:23) Again we read, "for the wages of sin is death, but the gift of God is eternal life through Jesus Christ, our Lord." (Rom. 6:23)

In other words, we can not possibly save ourselves! Yet, some try. To them Jesus says, "Verily, verily, I say unto you, He that entereth not by the door into the sheepfold, but climbeth up some other way, the same is a thief and a robber... I am the door of the sheep... by me if any man enter in, he shall be saved... I am the way, the truth, and the life: no man cometh unto the Father, but by me." (John 10:1, 7, & 9; 14:6).

Still, some believe their good works are enough to get them to heaven. But, the Bible says, "For by grace are ye saved through faith; and that not of yourselves: it is the gift of God: Not of works, lest any man should boast." (Eph. 2:8-9).

Simply put, the Good News of Jesus Christ means that God has provided the means to bridge the gap between sinful man and holy God through the life, death, burial, and resurrection of His Son, Jesus Christ. When Almighty God rose Christ from the grave, He offered us the same eternal life if we turn from our sin of rebellion, and trust in Christ alone to save us.

Don't be too proud, or ashamed at what your lodge buddies might think if you accept Jesus Christ as your Savior. The Bible says, "For I am not ashamed of the gospel of Christ; for it is the power of God unto salvation to everyone that believeth; to the Jew first, and also to the Greek." (Rom 1:16).

It is the prayer of all involved in the publication of this book that many will come to a saving faith in our Lord and Savior, Jesus Christ, and that revival will come to His Church.

Charles G. Finney

President Charles G. Finney died in 1875, at the age of eighty-three years.

He began his public life as a lawyer and a freemason; he closed it as one of the greatest evangelists this country and Europe had ever known; as an author and theological teacher of renown; as president of a great college, which had grown up under his administration. He was widely known as an abolitionist and as a seceding Mason.

The practical results of his life-work increasingly commend themselves, and give testimony to that work as a remarkable uplifting and spiritualizing force. His best-known published writings are: Lectures on Revivals of Religion; Lectures to Professing Christians; Lectures on Theology; Character, Claims and Practical Workings of Freemasonry; Memoirs — An Autobiography.

CR8O

What Freemasonry Says About

Charles G. Finney

from *10,000 Famous Freemasons*
by William R. Denslow, 1958

Anti-Mason, clergyman, abolitionist and president of Oberlin College (Ohio) from 1851-65. He received his degrees in Meridian Sun Lodge No.32, Warren, Conn. in 1816, and in June, 1818, made his first visit to Rising Sun Lodge No. 125 at Adams, N.Y. Although not a member of the latter lodge at the time, he was voted to serve as secretary, pro tem at a meeting on Feb. 24, 1820. On Dec. 14, 1820 he was admitted a member of the lodge and named secretary at the same meeting. On May 6, 1824, he was discharged by his own request. It was in this year that he was licensed as a minister by the St. Lawrence Presbytery, and two years later he began conducting religious revivals throughout the Middle and Eastern states. He wrote and preached anti-Masonry wherever he was, and with Jonathan Blanchard, a Presbyterian minister and president of Wheaton College, published an anti-Masonic newspaper called *The Christian Cynosure*. He was active with Blanchard and Bishop David Edwards in the formation of the National Christian Association in 1868, whose purpose was to oppose all secret societies. This grew into the American Party in 1872, and this short-lived organization ran candidates in the 1876 and 1880 elections. Eventually dissension and petty jealousies in the anti-Masonic ranks caused the movement to die. As one biographer stated: "Were he alive today, how surprised he would be to learn that there are more Masons among the undergraduates and graduates of Oberlin College than existed during the Morgan affair in the entire state of New York. ■

CONTENTS

END FINNEY

CR&

FOREWORD

Freemasonry's Attempted Murder Of Ed Decker

I lay on the floor of the bathroom, retching. I was sure I was going to die. I had a TV show to do in just a few hours and I was certain that I wouldn't live to see it. I pulled myself up, leaning against the wall next to the toilet, trying to pull away from the pain I was in and sort out what was happening.

I supposed that I had contracted food poisoning during the Pastors' lunch earlier, but then, my table companions, sharing the same pizza, were not in here fighting for space at this receptacle. I remembered the two out-of-town visitors, whose attendance made our host concerned. "This is a dangerous business, and I don't know these fellows," he warned.

"Don't give it another thought," I answered. "God is our protector."

Then I recalled that one of them had offered to refresh my drink and I had consented. A half hour later, I was convulsing in pain.

Reflecting back I guess I ought to have questioned the wisdom of going to Inverness, Scotland to do a TV program on "The Occult Origins of Scottish Rite Masonry." My host was correct in his concern, yet God truly was my protector.

I rose up that evening by His strength and did that program standing up. Yet, by the morning I was too ill to continue my tour. The next day I began a terrible journey back to Seattle. I arrived home 25 pounds lighter and barely able to walk. The poison had effected my involuntary muscle system and it was difficult to use my hands and feet and hold my head steady.

Tests showed that I had sustained a high, lethal dose of arsenic, enough to have killed me a few times over. It took months to recover from the incident. Not only had the poison done serious damage to my digestive system, but I would lay in bed, sleeping fitfully while my body twitched continually. Later, the heavy metal began to work its way out through

i

vicious sores on the tops of my hands and my head, making a terrible odor that smelled like dog urine.

Even just recently, while I was undergoing lung surgery caused by a bus accident, several blood vessels in my lower back broke spontaneously for no apparent reason. The doctors puzzled over the phenomenon for the better part of the day until a nurse asked my wife if I had been exposed to metallic poison in a work environment. When Carol told them about the Scotland incident, they had their answer. Tests showed that pockets of arsenic still in my system [lower back area] had been the cause and the vessels broke while I was in severe trauma.

In Scotland, I suppose I could have pointed out the man who poisoned me. Maybe he would have gone to prison, but as one Scottish friend warned, our host would have paid the price at the hands of the Masons. I determined it wasn't worth it.

I am sure there are more than a few Masons in Scotland that can't understand why I am still alive. But, it's no puzzle to me. God intended for me to live so I could continue to speak out on the awful truth of Freemasonry.

The trip to Scotland wasn't by chance. I had been studying, writing and lecturing on Freemasonry for a number of years. Somehow, I had become an expert.

It wasn't an easy transition, because it meant that I had to look back at my own father, grandfather and their fathers before them for almost two hundred years. They were honest men — church men who took our faith, our family and our country seriously, fighting in its many wars. Generation after generation, each son followed after his father and entered into lodge membership. That line ended when I stepped out of the DeMolay to join the Mormon Church.

The Mormons told me that Masonry was a society of "secret combinations" and "works of darkness." I was forbidden to continue membership in the DeMolay. As an active Mormon, I would *not* seek to follow my father into the Lodge.

After I became a born again Christian, I began to speak at churches on the Mormon Temple ritual. At one such service in a Baptist church, I discovered from an angry Deacon that the ritual of the Masonic Lodge was the actual foundation of the LDS temple ritual. I knew that if what he said was true, I would also have to expose the roots of Masonry to the same light of truth that I was bringing to bear on Mormonism. That was easier said than done.

Within a month of that experience, I found myself at the funeral of a friend's father and once seated, discovered I was about to witness a Masonic funeral. By the time those men in their somber clothes walked down the church aisle, I knew that this was birthed in the very pit of hell and it had become rooted within the church itself. I knew there was work to do.

It wasn't like the work hadn't been done before. Great men like Charles Finney had discovered its evil core and brought this information to the church. But the church soon forgot the danger, choosing instead not to rile the Masons who ran their boards and paid their salaries. Only a few lone pastors over the next century would study Masonry and bring out its darkness from the pulpit. Many times this resulted in their removal. Sometimes their careers were destroyed in the process. This mattered not to the Masons, for their goal had been accomplished. With the pastor's dismissal, the preaching of the truth about the lodge was removed from their ears.

There will be a day of reckoning. A Mason's ignorance of the Luciferian roots and dark secrets of the Lodge will be no defense on that day of judgment. As for the Mason who calls himself a Christian — woe be unto him [Luke 13:24-28]. As for the pastor who is a Mason — woe, woe be unto him [Mathew 7:21-23 and 23:13-14]!

Well, Finney's words are still the fire of truth today, as they were in 1869. As you shall see, Freemasonry and Christianity are as far removed from each other as are the North and South poles. And like Finney, godly pastors are still speaking out in spite of threats from the Masons and their odious acts of ignominy in defying the very Word of God. You shall hear from four of these couragous pastors at the end of this book.

Ed Decker

INTRODUCTION

History of the Murder of Capt. William Morgan and the Anti-Masonic Movement it Spawned
© 1998 by John Daniel

Revival In America

Early in 1831, Alexis de Tocqueville (1805-1859), a famous French statesman, received official permission from the French government to travel to the United States to study the reason behind America's greatness. After having spent nine months in our land, he returned and delivered the following report to the French Parliament:

> I went at your bidding and passed through their thoroughfares of trade; I ascended their mountains and went down their valleys; I visited their manufactories, their commercial markets and emporiums of trade; I entered their judicial courts and legislative hall; but I sought everywhere in vain until I entered the Church. It was there as I listened to the soul-elevating principles of the Gospel of Christ, as they fell from Sabbath to Sabbath upon the masses of the people, that I learned why America was great and free and why France was a slave.
>
> America is great because America is good, and if America ever ceases to be good, America will cease to be great.[1]

Tocqueville visited America during our nation's Second Great Awakening, when pulpits were aflame with the gospel of repentance and salvation. Very significant were the thousands of Masons who flocked to church altars to renounce their Masonic oaths and receive Christ as Savior. Evangelist Charles Finney specifically included repentance from Freemasonry in his preaching and saw this action as a precursor to revival. America was experiencing revival amidst the Anti-Masonic Movement.

Little or no mention is made in our history books of the Anti-Masonic Movement, which formed the Anti-Masonic Party in 1827. *The Random House Dictionary of the English Language* gives a sketchy definition:

> **Anti-Masonic party**, *U.S. Hist.* a former political party (1826-35) that opposed Freemasonry in civil affairs.

> **Anti-Mason**, *U.S. Hist.* a member of the Anti-Masonic party or a supporter of its principles.

The *Encyclopaedia Britannica* gives a broader view of the Anti-Masonic Movement than do the dictionaries, yet it, too, holds to the media standard of reporting only part of the facts. We shall let the *Britannica* speak for itself before we tell the complete story.

> In U.S. history, the Anti-Masonic Movement reflected a long-standing suspicion of secret fraternal orders, culminating in the political activities of the Anti-Masonic Party (1827-36). The movement was touched off in 1826 in western New York by the mysterious disappearance of William Morgan, a Freemason who had prepared for publication a book revealing the secrets of the Order of the Masons. Charged with stealing and indebtedness, Morgan was imprisoned and then reportedly kidnapped shortly after his release. He was never heard from afterward, and it was widely thought that he had been murdered. After prolonged investigation of the case, the press, churches, temperance and antislavery elements joined in condemning the apparent "murder."

When 15 Anti-Masonic candidates were elected to the New York Assembly in 1827, the dynamic political nature of the issue was recognized and the Anti-Masonic Party was organized. National conventions met at Philadelphia in 1830 and at Baltimore in 1831, the latter to nominate [renounced Mason] William Wirt, former U.S. attorney general, as a presidential candidate. By this time the movement had spread across the Middle Atlantic states and into New England, usually through church, temperance, and anti-slavery channels.

The Anti-Masonic national nominating convention in Baltimore, with 13 states represented by 116 Anti-Masons, was the first of its kind in the history of U.S. politics. The convention required a special three-fourths majority rather than a simple majority to nominate, a precedent followed by the Democrats in subsequent national conventions for more than a century. The convention system has been used since by the major U.S. political parties.

The Anti-Masonic Party won a large number of Congressional seats in 1832, but thereafter internal improvements and the protective tariff became the major issues. By late in the decade, Anti-Masonic agitation had been largely superseded by antislavery activities, and remnants of the party merged with the newly formed Whig Party in 1838.[2]

Freemasonry In Early America

A brief history of the activity of Masonry in young America, both politically and militarily, must be understood before we can fully comprehend the appalling truth behind the censored story that spawned the Anti-Masonic Movement.

FREEMASONRY

First, we must recognize that there were, and still are, two separate Masonic forces in the world — one in London and one in Paris. The one in Paris is of Templar origin. Its founders were the Knights Templar, who fled to Scotland during their 14th century persecution. While in Scotland they developed an esoteric form of worship they carried into workingman lodges. Most working men in those days built cathedrals and castles out of stone. As stone masons, they quartered in mason lodges close to their work. Apprentices quartered in "entered apprentice" lodges; craftsmen in "fellow craftsmen" lodges; and task masters in "master mason" lodges. The Templars attached their form of mystic worship to these three degrees of labor. Hence, masonic lodges were turned into centers of esoteric worship.

This form of secret worship was carried to London in the 17th century during the Scottish Stuart reign of King James I. During the 1640s, when civil war erupted against the Stuart dynasty, the freedom fighters were of the working class. Naturally, they planned their secret strategy against the throne behind the walls of their masonic lodges. After they won their freedom, they became known as free masons.

In 1660, the Stuarts were back on the throne. In 1688, the Glorious Revolution permanently dethroned them. In 1717, the Stuart remnant were exiled to France along with their Scottish-flavored Freemasonry. By 1755, French Freemasonry acquired the name Scottish Rite Freemasonry with thirty-two degrees. The Scottish Rite was brought to America during the French and Indian War (1754-1760), and settled at Charleston, S.C.

In 1786, the Southern Jurisdiction of Scottish Rite Freemasonry used the French Masonic constitution as a basis for its constitution and is therefore Templar and republican in origin. In 1801, the 33rd degree was created at Charleston. Today the Masonic world is ruled from that city with that final degree. Lodges with French Constitutions end their prayers in the name of the Great Architect of the Universe.[3]

The other force of Freemasonry is of Rosicrucian origin headquartered in London. After the exile of the Stuarts to France, the remnant of Freemasonry in England was united in 1717 by seven Rosicrucians under a Grand Lodge. Placed at its head was the King of England. From then until now, English Freemasonry has remained royalist and Rosicrucian. The British kept the original three degrees of Freemasonry until 1860, when they acquired the additional thirty degrees of the Scottish Rite, but for competitive reasons dropped the name "Scottish."[4]

Before the French and Indian War, American lodges were of British origin under British constitutions. Within the lodges were two factions vying for control — Moderns and Ancients. The Moderns wanted to modernize the ancient rituals. Under their control, prayers ended in the Name of Jesus Christ. When the Ancients merged with the Moderns in 1813, the lodges became purely deistic and prayers in Christ's name gradually died out as the ancient rituals returned. Under the Ancients prayers were offered in the name of the Great Architect of the Universe, as in French Freemasonry.[5]

A few Ancient lodges existed in America before 1813. For example, St. John's Lodge in Philadelphia went Ancient in 1761, as did one in Boston in 1751.[6] The Philadelphia lodge, the earliest known in the North American colonies, was founded by the British in 1730. One of its first initiates was Ben Franklin, who received his degrees in February of 1731.[7]

As stated earlier, French lodges did not appear in America until the French and Indian War, where young George Washington first learned soldiering. These lodges were called "military" or "traveling lodges," and were exclusively for soldiers and diplomates. French military lodges became famous during our War of Independence. George Washington officiated at several of these traveling lodges, as we shall see.[8]

George Washington is an important figure, both in Masonic history and in understanding the story of William Morgan. Morgan, a Royal Arch Mason, renounced Freemasonry, and in 1826 planned to expose the dangers of its secrets in a book. Washington likewise warned the whole country on the eve of his death to beware of secret societies. Both men were specific in their warning — American Freemasonry had been infiltrated by the European Illuminati.[9]

FREEMASONRY

Washington's Boycott of English Masonic Lodges

Washington was an adhering Mason from age 21 to his death. His Masonic credentials begin at Fredericksburg, Va. in Lodge No. 4, where he was initiated 1st degree on November 4, 1752; passed to 2nd degree on March 3, 1753; and raised to 3rd degree on August 4, 1753.[10] Lodge No. 4 was a British constituted lodge, which offered only three degrees. At that time, Washington was as high as he could go in colonial Freemasonry. A year after initiation, he visited the lodge once again, and after that never returned. In fact, he never set foot in any British lodge after the Revolution began.[11]

Washington, however, was not alone in breaking connections with the mother lodge of England. Freemason Albert G. Mackey informs us that "Soon after the beginning of the Revolution, a disposition was manifested among American Freemasons to dissever their connection, as subordinates, with the Masonic authorities of the mother country, and in several of the newly erected States the Provincial Grand Lodges assumed an independent character.[12]

Another record of Washington's affiliation with a lodge was in 1788. That year, Lodge No. 39 of Alexandria, Va., which had previously been working under the Grand Lodge of Pennsylvania, transferred its allegiance to Virginia and became Lodge No. 22. (Virginia was one of the states that dissevered it lodges from English control.) On April 28 of that year, President Washington was made Charter Master in absentia and reelected Dec. 20, 1788. He is pictured in *Life Magazine,* Oct. 8, 1956, wearing his Masonic apron while presiding over the lodge as Worshipful Master. There is record that he did officiate there.[13]

There is no record that Washington renounced his Masonic oaths, resigned from any lodge, be it British or French, or protested his leadership role in a lodge in absentia. Our first President was an active Mason his entire life, writing cordial letters to, and receiving letters from lodges until his death.[14]

Throughout his political career he visited a number of French lodges and officiated in some, but always boycotted English lodges.

President Washington also enjoyed attending public Masonic functions. On Sept. 18, 1793, he was pictured in his Masonic apron laying the cornerstone of the Capitol Building.[15] In 1795, he assisted in laying out the streets of the Capitol in the shape of Masonic symbols.[16]

Washington constantly gave a Masonic idiom. When speaking of Providence, which was our founding father's term when referencing God, he frequently used the phrase "Grand Architect of the Universe." He believed the success of the Revolution was due to the "Grand Architect of the Universe," and ended his frequent prayers in that deity's name. In short, writes Masonic scholar William H. Stemper, "Freemasonry was Washington's political theology. It enabled him to project a political sacrality.... Washington's usage of Freemasonry as a political theology was to reconcile and harmonize democracy...with...the providential moral workings of the foundation of the Republic.... Yet, there is little or no 'sacred' mystery [in Washington's lifestyle]."[17]

Washington was so revered by American Masons that some started a movement to make him national Grand Master of all U.S. Masons. To create a national Grand Lodge, all state Grand Lodges would be required to relinquish their authority. Massachusetts Masons did not consent, and the idea died.[18]

Most of General Washington's hands-on Masonic activity occurred during our War of Independence. Before that, Freemasonry grew slowly in America. War increases Masonic membership, because Masonic oaths demand that Masons, whether friend or foe, protect each other from harm. The Mason swears:

> ، I will not give the grand hailing sign of distress, except I am in real distress...and should I ever see that sign given, or the word accompanying it, and the person who gave it appearing to be in

distress, I will fly to his relief, at the risk of my life, should there be a greater probability of saving his life than of losing my own....[19]

This oath was practiced at least twenty years before the Revolution. Consequently, it was a great incentive for a soldier to join Freemasonry. According to Masonic records, "Members of the Craft were among the highest in command of all armies...."[20]

Masonic Partiality

Here we discover an extreme partiality among Masonic soldiers that gives privileges not afforded the average soldier. When the war was over, this partiality was extended to their private and public lives. For example, a Mason often found it easier to find work than a non-Mason. If venturing into business, a Mason was assured a loan simply by giving the proper handshake to a Masonic banker.[21] Should a Mason choose politics as a career, he was guaranteed the votes of all Masons who had reached the Royal Arch degree (13th degree in Scottish Rite and 7th degree in York Rite), which oath reads as follows:

I will promote a companion Royal Arch Mason's political preferment, in preference to another of equal qualifications.[22]

Once in political office, the Mason must vote the dictates of his Masonic superiors. In the Masonic book, *Webb's Monitor*, we read:

Right or wrong his very existence as a Mason hangs upon obedience to the powers immediately set above him. The one unpardonable crime in a Mason is contumacy [insubordination] or disobedience.[23]

Masonic partiality also permits Master Masons to commit criminal acts and find protection among Masons. The Master Mason swears:

> A Master Masons's secrets given to me in charge as such, and I knowing him to be such, shall remain as secure and inviolable in my breast as in his own...murder and treason excepted.[24]

If a Mason is a defendant in court, Masonic partiality extends to the witness stand. For example, if a fellow Mason is called as a witness, he is bound by Masonic oath to protect the defendant. In the *Masonic Hand Book* we read:

> You must conceal all the crimes of your brother Masons, except murder and treason, and these only at your own option, and should you be summoned as a witness against a brother Mason be always sure to shield him. Prevaricate, don't tell the whole truth in this case, keep his secrets, forget the most important points. It may be perjury to do this, it is true, but you're keeping your obligations, and remember if you live up to your obligations strictly, you'll be free from sin.[25]

Masonic partiality extends to the jury box. The Blue Lodge degrees read:

> Whenever you see any of our signs made by a brother Mason, and especially the grand hailing sign of distress, you must always be sure to obey them, even at the risk of your life. If you're on a jury, and the defendant is a Mason, and makes the grand hailing sign, you must obey it; you must disagree with your brother jurors, if necessary, but you must be sure not to bring the Mason

guilty, for that would bring disgrace upon our order. It may be perjury, to be sure, to do this, but then you're fulfilling your obligation, and you know if you live up to your obligations you'll be free from sin.[26]

Once a Mason reaches the Royal Arch degree, he is to conceal all crimes of brother Masons, including murder and treason. The Royal Arch Mason swears:

> I will aid and assist a companion Royal Arch Mason, when engaged in any difficulty, and espouse his cause, so far as to extricate him from the same, if in my power, whether he be right or wrong.... A companion Royal Arch Mason's secrets, given me in charge as such, and I knowing him to be such, shall remain as secure and inviolable, in my breast as in his own, murder and treason not excepted.[27]

Although there is an upside to being a Mason, which is preferential treatment of each other in every walk of life, including protection should a Mason himself commit crimes, there is also a downside. A Mason must agree to maintain silence of knowledgeable crimes committed by brother Masons, including murder. If summoned to court as a juror or a witness, he must perjure himself on behalf of a brother Mason being prosecuted.

Preferential treatment, partiality, and hiding crimes are contrary to the Holy Scriptures that lay open on the Masonic altar. The Apostle Paul wrote in I Tim. 5:21-22, "I charge thee before God, and the Lord Jesus Christ, and the elect angels, that thou observe these things without preferring one before another, doing nothing by partiality. Lay hands suddenly on no man, neither be partaker of other men's sins: keep thyself pure."

INTRODUCTION

When John Quincy Adams learned of these odious Masonic obligations and partialities during his Presidency, he united his National Republican Party with the Anti-Masonic Party, which union became the Whig Party in 1838.[28] In 1845, he wrote of Freemasonry, "A more perfect agent for the devising and execution of conspiracies against church or state could scarcely have been conceived."[29]

Partiality Increases Masonic Membership During War

Preservation of life was the bait that enabled Freemasonry to grow rapidly during our War of Independence. A soldier had a greater chance of returning home if he joined a military lodge.[30] In *Life Magazine* (Oct. 8, 1956), we read: "During the Revolutionary War, Washington...favored creation of military Lodges for soldiers. There were at least 11 such Lodges, the most famous being American Union Lodge Number One. At Valley Forge, Washington helped initiate Lafayette into Masonry."

By the time we won our revolution, Masons occupied every dominant position that militarily protected or politically governed this fledgling nation. Freemasonry confirms this. According to a 1951 Masonic edition of the Holy Bible (page 6), twenty-four of Washington's major generals were Masons, as were thirty of his thirty-three brigadier generals. And of the fifty-six signers of the Declaration of Independence, fifty-three were claimed by Freemasonry to be Master Masons. In fact, there is ample evidence to show that we won the revolution because of complicity among American, French and British Masons.[31]

After the war, Masonic partiality helped pave the road to the White House. George Washington, an able candidate, was elected first President of the United States. His Vice President was Freemason John Adams, who is reported to have been the founder of the Masonic Lodges in New England. John Adams was the father of President John Quincy Adams (1825-1828), who for twenty years following his presidency, played an important role in the Anti-Masonic Movement.

FREEMASONRY

At George Washington's inauguration, Masonic involvements continued to prevail. The Oath of Office was administered by Robert Livingston, Grand Master of New York's Grand Lodge. Marshal of the day was Freemason General Jacob Morton. Washington's escort was Freemason General Morgan Lewis. The Bible used for the oath of office was a Masonic Edition from St. John's Lodge No. 1 of New York.[32]

Again, near the end of Washington's second term as President, when he announced that he would not seek a third term, the President received a letter from the Grand Lodge of Pennsylvania congratulating him for his many years of Masonic and public service. Washington's cogent response brings into focus the subtlety and importance of this stage in American Masonic development:

> Fellow citizens and brothers...I have received your address with all Brotherly affection... [T]o have been, in any degree, an instrument in the hands of Providence to promote orders and union, and erect upon a solid foundation, the true principles of government, is only to have shared with many others in a labour, the result of which, let us hope, will prove through all ages a sanctuary for Brothers, and a lodge for the virtues... Permit me to reciprocate your prayers, and to supplicate that we all may meet thereafter in the eternal Temple whose Builder is the Great Architect of the Universe.[33]

One year before his death, Washington was informed by letter that Masonic partiality had enabled evil to enter the Lodge. His beloved Freemasonry had been infiltrated by agents of the European Illuminati for the express purpose of subverting our government. The letter also accused the President of "presiding over the English lodges in this country."[34] (See pages lxi-lxvii at the end of this "Introduction" for a brief history of the Order of Illuminati in early American history).

Washington responded by letter dated "Mt. Vernon, September 25, 1798": "I have little more to add than thanks for your wishes, and favorable sentiments, except to correct an error you have run into of my presiding over the English lodges in this country. The fact is I preside over none, nor have I been in one more than once or twice within the last thirty years. I believe, notwithstanding, that none of the lodges in this country are contaminated with the principles ascribed to the society of the Illuminati."[35]

The accusation made of Washington that he presided "over the English lodges in this country" was to apparently suggest he was a secret agent for the British. As Masonic history records, and as we have revealed, he was careful not to set foot in an English lodge after the Revolution began. His Masonic activity after that time was in lodges that had "dissevered" from the "mother country." The military lodges Washington officiated in were founded by the French, whose great assistance in military arms, funds, and soldiering is a matter of historic record to the success of our Revolution.[36]

However, Washington's answer to the question of Illuminati activity in American lodges is indeed interesting. It certainly reveals his knowledge of this European order. Therefore, we must consider this here, since it likewise was the concern of Captain William Morgan, whose 1826 book was not only intended to reveal the awful blood oaths of Freemasonry, but to likewise expose Illuminati activity in American lodges.

John M. Roberts, in *The Mythology of Secret Societies*, states, "the Illuminati were the first society to use for political subversion the machinery of secret organization offered by free masonry.... [T]hrough the craft they began to spread."[37]

According to Salem Kirban in *Satan's Angels Exposed*, the Illuminati had already infiltrated fifteen lodges in America long before Washington wrote this letter in 1798. In 1785, the Columbian Lodge of the Order of the Illuminati was established in New York City. Its members included George Clinton, Governor of New York and his nephew DeWitt Clinton, who was destined to be Governor of New York during the Morgan Affair. Another member of the Columbian lodge was Clinton Roosevelt, ancestor of Franklin D. Roosevelt. And Thomas Jefferson was identified with an Illuminati lodge in Virginia.[38] According to Professor Charles Eliott Norton (1827-1908), lecturer at Harvard from 1874 to 1898, the Illuminati were planning to use the USA as a catalyst for their one-world government. If it could be proven that thirteen states could successfully unite under one federal government, then all governments of the world could likewise unite under a one-world federation.[39]

But, how was George Washington to know all this? Although a Mason, he never frequented English lodges, and rarely was active in the reconstituted American Grand Lodges. He certainly was knowledgeable of the existence of the Illuminati, but was obviously ignorant of the inroads it had made into our society.

His ignorance did not last long. During the summer or fall of 1799, just months before his death, Washington was informed by John Adams that indeed the Illuminati had infiltrated American Freemasonry, and that this order was a danger to our new Republic.[40] Because of his faith in Adams, the President immediately warned the whole country to beware of all secret societies — not that he believed secret societies were bad, but rather that he recognized how their structure enabled easy penetration by the Illuminati, who had designs for America not in step with his own.

Thomas Jefferson and John Adams later disagreed over the use of American Freemasonry by the Illuminati. In fact, "John Adams...accused Jefferson of using the lodges that he himself had founded, for subversive Illuminati purposes. The three letters of Adams which deal with this problem are in the Wittenburg Square Library in Philadelphia."[41]

As stated earlier, since the founding of the United Grand Lodge of England in 1717, there has been a struggle between Moderns and Ancients for the internal control of all Masonic lodges. The Moderns were Rosicrucians who reigned from 1717 to 1813. Their prayers in lodge ended in the Name of Jesus Christ. In 1813, when the Illuminati completed their takeover of American Freemasonry, they put in power the Ancients, who were deists. From 1813 until our day, the Name of Jesus Christ has been forbidden to be uttered in Masonic lodges.

History suggests that from our nation's birth, Satan has had a plan for America — use the United States of America as the catalyst for a United Nations of the World.[42] But the God of the Bible slowed Satan's plan with two Great Awakenings: 1739-1750 and 1824-1835. The Second Great Awakening took place amidst the Anti-Masonic Movement, which put American Freemasonry to flight for nearly a century.

Two Great Awakenings

> So shall they fear the name of the Lord from the west, and his glory from the rising of the sun. When the enemy shall come in like a flood, the Spirit of the Lord shall lift up a standard against him. (Isaiah 59:19)

This may be a prophecy of the Church, for the name of the Lord has only been carried around the globe ("from the west, and...from the rising of the sun) by the Church.

In Hebrew, the phrase "lift up a standard" can be translated "put to flight." God's Word has always been the standard that put the enemy to flight. "Enemy" can be translated "adversary." Satan is also translated "adversary."[43] He is the enemy of the Church who is put to flight by the preaching of the gospel.

In Scripture, when a direction on the compass is given, its reference point is usually Jerusalem. Therefore, the direction "west" is anywhere west of Jerusalem. Significantly, in Hebrew "west" carries the idea of "extreme west," for it can be translated "the region of the evening sun." West, from the vantage point of Jerusalem is Europe, and finally America.

Western history records that the "standard" lifted up in the "west" was the gospel of Christ preached by the evangelical

Church. Western history also records that the enemy (Satan) employed the use of western governments to openly persecute the Church, first the Roman Empire, then the Holy Roman Empire. The settling of America was by Christians fleeing the latter persecution.

When Satan followed the Church to America, he could not persecute her through government, because our Constitution provided for freedom of religion. He therefore went underground in the form of secret societies to infiltrate our government. One day he would have the Constitution reinterpreted by a Supreme Court stacked with Masons.[44] Meanwhile, Isaiah 59:19 was fulfilled in America by the preaching of the gospel during two Great Awakenings.

The First Great Awakening
"When the enemy shall come in like a flood..."

God first lifted up His standard of evangelism in America in 1739, nine years after the first Masonic Lodge was planted on our soil. For the next decade, George Whitefield (1714-1770) became a popular preacher in both England and the American colonies. With the Wesley brothers, he worked for revival in the church. His preaching tours in America helped kindle the first Great Awakening.

During that same period, Jonathan Edwards (1703-1758), a Congregational minister, became one of the most influential theologians and evangelists in American history. His preaching was an important factor in the Great Awakening in New England. As the most learned scholar of his generation, Edwards became president of a college known today as Princeton University.

So powerful were these revivals that by the time our constitution was written and passed by Congress in 1787, two-thirds of the three million citizens in the United States were professing Christians.

INTRODUCTION

Where Christ's Standard is Lifted Up

When a democratic nation is dominated by a majority of citizens who are Bible-believing and Spirit-led Christians, pagans work their mystic arts in secret. And so it was in America following the first Great Awakening. Christians controlled the vote and therefore, biblical standards were written into our civil laws. As a consequence, illuminated Freemasonry was compelled to commence its anti-Christian program for America more slowly than the 33rd degree Supreme Council desired.

Previous evidence submitted and subsequent evidence will reveal that the Fraternity's conspiracy took the following three phases: (1) the Constitution of the United States of America was written as a wholly deistic instrument; (2) Masons would hold every political post of importance in the budding federal, state, and local governments; and (3) Freemasonry would take over all media resources. This not only would include the press, but schools and pulpits as well. By 1826, Masons dominated the majority of these positions and were ready to broadcast their successes.

The Complete Story behind
the Anti-Masonic Movement

Before the year 1826, nothing slowed the progress of Freemasonry to occupy every seat of political and religious importance in America. By 1826, so confident had the Fraternity become that it began to congratulate itself in broad speeches at their public festivals. That year a Mr. Bainaird (no first name available) announced that "Masonry was exercising its influence in the sacred desk, in the legislative hall, and on the bench of justice."[45]

William Morgan, who was a captain during the War of 1812 under the command of Freemason Andrew Jackson, heard Bainaird's speech. Morgan was a Royal Arch Mason, who had been practicing the craft for thirty years. When he accepted

Christ as Savior and Lord of his life, he renounced Freemasonry and resigned from the Lodge. Charles Finney writes of Morgan's opinion of Freemasonry: "He regarded it as highly injurious to the cause of Christ, and as eminently dangerous to the government of our country."

Morgan was aware that the Illuminati had infiltrated American Freemasonry and knew of their plan to take over our government. He could not let Mr. Bainaird's speech stand without revealing these facts. Morgan began to voice his intent to publish a book exposing the Illuminati, as well as revealing the Masonic rituals and vile oaths of the first three degrees.[46]

Morgan contracted with a local printer, David C. Miller, who had likewise renounced Freemasonry after salvation. No sooner had the ink dried on the contract than trouble began. Morgan disappeared. His badly decomposed body was found a year later in Oak Orchard Harbor and identified by his wife and dentist. Miller was abducted, but escaped to print the book.

Masonic Oaths and Masonic Partiality were behind the Murder of William Morgan and the subsequent cover-up

Masonry is as old as government. It constitutes a government in itself. Its origin, principles, organization and administration are to be found in loyalty, obedience, hope charity and love. It is operative everywhere, because its foundation can be laid among mankind wherever mankind exist. Resistance to, or disobedience of, any of these principles is not permitted in Masonic sovereignty. Masonry could not exist a moment, it would not have lived longer than languages, races, and empires, if it had tolerated insubordination or rebellion against its authority.

Committee of Correspondence,
Grand Lodge of Pennsylvania
June 13, 1861.[47]

A heavy burden is placed on the shoulders of a Mason when he joins the lodge. He is no longer his own man. He must obey unseen powers set above him, whether he agrees with them or not, or else he pays the penalty. Yet, there is a reward for those who obey — Masonic partiality.

As documented earlier, Masonic partiality means success in this present world. To a soldier it means protection during war. To an applicant it means work. To an employee it means a promotion. To a businessman it means customers and/or a loan. To a politician it means a vote. To a civil servant it means an appointment. To a criminal it means protection from the law.

Simply put, Masonic partiality can get a Mason where he wants to go in life, whether he be honorable or dishonorable. If he fails to obey the rules in this game of partiality, he is not successful. If he blatantly breaks the oath, or disobeys Masonic authority, he meets the most gruesome death, so say the words he pronounces against himself when he takes the oaths.

These oaths are critical, because behind them lies the reason for the murder of William Morgan and the subsequent cover-up of the crime. First, a Blue Lodge Mason (degrees 1-3), agrees to ever conceal and never reveal any of the secret arts, parts or points of the hidden mysteries of Ancient Freemasonry. Second, he promises to always be ready to obey all Masonic authority set above him, and never cheat, wrong, nor defraud a fellow Mason. Then he takes the following blood oath:

> All this I most solemnly and sincerely promise and swear, with a firm and steadfast resolution, to keep and perform the same without any equivocation, mental reservation or secret evasion of mind whatever, binding myself under a no less penalty than that of having my throat cut across, my tongue torn out by its roots and buried in the rough sands of the sea at low water mark, where the tide ebbs and flows twice in twenty-four hours...

having my breast torn open, my heart plucked out and given as a prey to the beasts of the field and the fowls of the air... having my body severed in twain, my bowels taken from thence and burned to ashes, and the ashes scattered to the four winds of heaven, that no trace or remembrance may be had of so vile and perjured a wretch as I, should I ever knowingly violate this my solemn obligation of an Entered Apprentice Mason...Fellow Craft Mason...Master Mason. So help me, God, and keep me steadfast in the due performance of the same.[48]

William Morgan broke his Masonic code of silence and paid the penalty with his life. On Wednesday, September 20, 1826, he was murdered by three Masons. Twenty-two years later, one of the three made a deathbed confession. That confession is printed in Finney's book on pages 6-10.

In 1826, and the year following, there was a general consensus among Masons that Morgan was indeed killed as penalty for his crimes against the Brotherhood. How or when Morgan was killed, and what Mason or Masons were honored with the task, was not known by the majority of lodge brothers. But, like the Niagara River in which he was drowned, rumors flowed endlessly among them. Following are four such rumors.

Elias Wilder of Elba, New York, himself not a Mason, said that "two or three weeks before William Morgan was carried from Batavia, I had a conversation with Freemason Cyrus Grout on the subject of Morgan's attempt to publish the secrets of Masonry. Mr. Grout told me that the Masons had sent to the Grand Lodge of New York for instructions, and when they got word from them there would be something done." After the abduction of Morgan, Mr. Wilder had another conversation with Cyrus Grout on the subject of what had become of Morgan, and Grout said to him, "Morgan was gone a fishing on the Niagara River of Lake Ontario."[49]

INTRODUCTION

A Mason by the name of William Terry of Niagara county was told by a fraternity brother that Morgan was "taken and carried away, had been killed, and sunk in Lake Ontario." Mr. Terry also stated that word came from the New York Grand Lodge that those engaged in the murder of Morgan, if indicted, were "to be kept harmless, and that all expense requisites to pay any fines that might be imposed was to be defrayed by the Grand Lodge; and that the actors in the affair of the abduction of Morgan so acted in obedience to orders coming from Grand Lodge."[50]

Mason Sylvester R. Hathaway of Niagara county was told by another Mason that "two ruffians had taken him [Morgan] out and cut his throat and tied his body to a rope and stone and threw it into the lake."[51]

Dr. Samuel Taggart, a Freemason from Byron, New York, told two other Masons, John Southworth and Luther Wilder of the same city, that he would "not be afraid to bet a thousand dollars that Morgan was not in the land of the living; that he had taken a voyage on Lake Ontario without float or boat and would never be seen again by any human being."[52]

Many decent men of the order of Masons justified the murder of Morgan by saying, "that efforts to learn the fate of Morgan would be useless — that if they had done anything with him, it was no one's business but their own."[53]

These quotes are taken from depositions made on March 9, 1827 by Justice of the Peace Andrew Dibble of Genesse County, New York. Mr. Dibble was one of several J.P.'s to whom 38 law-abiding citizens took witnesses after forming committees to conduct an independent investigation into the abduction and murder of Morgan.

Citizens of the land of the free and the home of the brave were forced to take action, because the proper authorities delayed, botched, or hid evidence. To the man, these "proper authorities" were Masons, obeying orders from the Grand Lodge of New York, while disobeying the laws of the land.

FREEMASONRY

Seven citizen committees in as many counties were established to investigate these crimes. For nearly a year they took leave of their jobs and paid their own expenses to return justice to our land. In stark contrast, Freemasonry used civil servants and public funds to obstruct justice. Upon completion of their investigations, the citizens presented their evidence and demanded action.

The number of Masons directly involved in the abduction, murder, and cover-up of these crimes was at least 136. They were not all from the same locality, but scattered along a hundred miles of countryside. They worked in perfect concert a daring and criminal scheme without incurring the risk of full conviction or punishment. Many were of respectable character, yet their reputation came second to their primary obligation of obeying their diabolical Masonic oaths.

All that was necessary to conceal Morgan's kidnapping and murder was the Masonic partiality found in oaths taken in the first three degrees of Freemasonry, as well as the oaths taken in the Royal Arch and Knights Templar degrees. In the first three degrees, the oaths forbid Blue Lodge Masons from divulging criminal acts of brother Masons, with the exception of murder and treason. The Royal Arch and Knights Templar oaths forbid Masons from divulging all criminal acts of their brother Masons, including murder and treason. The 136 Masons involved in the crime were of the latter degrees.

Evidence against Freemasonry was so compelling that it precipitated a mass exodus from the Lodge. Of 50,000 Masons in the United States at that time, 45,000 withdrew their membership and renounced their oaths, forcing the closure of 2,000 lodges.[54]

The Crime in more Detail

When William Morgan contracted with printer David C. Miller of Batavia to publish *Illustrations of Masonry*, the Masonic fraternity went into action to form a conspiracy to stop them.

One group of sixty-nine Masons moved against Morgan, while another group of sixty-seven Masons moved against Miller. Their intrigues were carried out in six stages from August 9 through September 20, 1826. Stages 3-6 began on Sunday, September 10 and ended Monday, September 20.[55]

1. An anonymous Mason denounced Morgan as an impostor in New York newspapers published at Canandaigua, Batavia and Black Rock. Although these places were of some distance from each other, all were within the limits of the region in which the subsequent acts of violence were committed.
2. Masons employed a spy to infiltrate the meetings between Morgan and Miller for the express purpose of betraying the manuscripts of the proposed work to the Masonic Lodges in an attempt to frustrate the printing of the book.
3. Masons employed an agent to secretly prepare materials for torching the printing office.
4. Several Masons from various locales rendezvoused at the home of a high-degree Mason to plan the forcible seizure of the manuscripts and the destruction of the printing press.
5. Masons abused laws by hunting up small debts or civil offenses with which to carry out harassment suits against Morgan and Miller. Once arrested, these men were in the hands of Masons for easy abduction.
6. The Masonic hierarchy planned the capture and murder of both Morgan and Miller by abusing the due processes of the law. Officers of justice, who themselves were Masons, were involved in the conspiracy. Their efforts failed in the case of Miller, but succeeded against Morgan.

FREEMASONRY

Newspaper Article Denouncing Morgan
is a coded Masonic call-to-arms

On August 9, 1826, the following newspaper article was published in Canandaigua, New York exactly as you see printed here. The print was immediately picked up by other newspapers throughout the state, including "Spirit of the Times" and the "People's Press" in Batavia, Morgan's home town.

NOTICE AND CAUTION

If a man calling himself William Morgan should intrude himself on the community, they should be on their guard, particularly the MASONIC FRATERNITY. Morgan was in this village in May last, and his conduct while here and elsewhere, calls forth this notice. Any information in relation to Morgan can be obtained by calling at the MASONIC HALL in this village. *Brethren* and *Companions* are particularly requested to *observe, mark* and *govern* themselves accordingly.

☞ Morgan is considered a swindler and dangerous man.

☞ There are people in this village who would be happy to see this Capt. Morgan.[56]

A two-part coded message (one written; one visual) is in the above article calling to arms Master Masons and Royal Arch Masons. Master Masons swear: "I promise and swear, that I will obey all regular signs, summonses, or tokens given."

Written message: "*Brethren* and *Companions* are particularly requested to *observe, mark* and *govern* themselves accordingly."

Visual message: two right hands with index fingers pointing to both the coded problem and the coded command.

Message decoded: Master Masons are called "Brothers." Royal Arch Masons are known as "Companions." We shall once again quote the obligations of these two degrees before we decipher the coded message.

INTRODUCTION

During the initiation of the Master Mason, he is told, "You must conceal all the crimes of your <u>brother</u> Masons, except murder and treason, and these only at your own option...." The Royal Arch Mason swears, "A <u>companion</u> Royal Arch Mason's secrets, given me in charge as such, and I knowing him to be such, shall remain as secure and inviolable, in my breast as in his own, murder and treason not excepted."

The first portion of the written code identifies which degree of Mason is to respond to the call-to-arms. The second portion of the written code informs Brothers and Companions "to *observe, mark* and *govern* themselves accordingly."

In context, *observe* means to "vigilantly observe Morgans movements." *Mark*, in Masonic parlance, refers to a "token," "debt," or "favor" that must be returned when asked. A favor is returned when a command is obeyed. *Govern* means, "to organize a strategy for the capture of William Morgan."

The command handed down is found in the visual coded message of two "pointing right hands."

A right hand is one of the most important symbols in Freemasonry. It both identifies and commands. It identifies with a particular and peculiar "grip" of a "brother" or "companion," even in the dark. We read how it commands in *Mackey's Encylopedia of Freemasonry*: "The right hand has in all ages been deemed an important symbol to represent the virtue of fidelity...to an obligation." In another place we read, "the right hand was naturally used instead of the left, because it was...the instrument by which superiors give commands to those below them."[57]

The two pointing right hands give a reason and a command: (1) "Morgan is considered a swindler and dangerous man," meaning "he has broken his oath of silence by exposing Masonic secrets"; and (2) "There are people in this village who would be happy to see this Capt. Morgan," meaning "Morgan is to be captured and brought before the lodge tribunal."

Simply stated, Master Masons and Royal Arch Masons were ordered to observe and report the movements of Morgan, plan a strategy for his capture, and when commanded, meet out just punishment to this Masonic traitor.

FREEMASONRY

The Plot to Kidnap and Murder William Morgan
(next few pages are actual deposition taken from court records)

On Sunday, Sept. 10, 1826, the Ontario county coroner, Nicholas G. Chesebro, himself the Master of the Lodge at Canandaigua, applied for and obtained from Jeffrey Chipman, justice of the peace, a warrant to arrest Morgan, who lived fifty miles away at Batavia. Morgan's alleged offense was larceny for neglecting to return a shirt and tie that had been borrowed the previous May. Armed with the warrant, the coroner hired a carriage at the public's expense to pick up ten Royal Arch Masons along the fifty-mile route. Their names and occupations were: Holloway Hayward - constable, Henry Howard - merchant, Asa Nowlen and James Ganson - innkeepers, John Butterfield - storekeeper, Samuel S. Butler - physician, Ella G. Smith, Harris Seymour, Moses Roberts, and Joseph Scofield - occupations unknown. All ten men were anxious and willing to share in avenging the insulted majesty of their Masonic law.

The party stopped for the night at the tavern of James Ganson, six miles from Batavia. Early Monday morning on September 11, five of the Masons were led by the constable to rent another coach at public expense. They proceeded from Ganson's tavern to Batavia. At daybreak, they seized Morgan.

Near sunset on September 11, the Masons arrived back in Canandaigua. The prisoner was immediately taken before the justice of the peace who had issued the warrant. The futility of the complaint was established and Morgan was set free, since the person from whom he had borrowed the shirt and tie had not shown up at court. In fact, this person was unaware of the actions against Morgan and had not sought a prosecution for the so-called offense. The idea originated in the mind of the coroner, who executed the plan by using the law to serve the vindictive purpose of Freemasonry.

Morgan's release posed a problem for the conspirators. They needed him in jail to give them ample time to complete their schemes against him. Out of jail, Morgan could elude them. Consequently, no sooner had the hapless prisoner been released than he found the same coroner tapping him on the shoulder again, this time armed with a writ for a debt of two dollars to a tavern keeper of Canandaigua. Without the ability to pay, Morgan was returned to the county jail.

With Morgan secure, the Masons could concentrate on making arrangements to complete the remainder of their plot. On Tuesday evening of the next day (Sept. 12), the same coroner made his appearance at the jail. After some negotiation, Morgan was once more released. No sooner was he on the street dreaming of escape from these annoyances, when upon a given signal a yellow carriage and gray horses were seen by three witnesses rolling toward the jail in the bright moonlight with extraordinary speed. A few minutes passed. Morgan was seized, gagged, and bound, then thrown into the carriage filled with Masons. Without turning, the carriage sped away. Morgan was now completely in the power of his enemies. With the veil of law removed, the arm of the flesh would now be employed.

Drawing below is found in *Life* magazine, Oct. 8, 1956, p.122

GREAT KIDNAPING FUROR took place in 1826 over disappearance of William Morgan, a renegade Mason who was supposedly abducted and then killed by Masons. *Harpers* drawing shows Masons forcing Morgan into coach.

FREEMASONRY

The carriage moved along night and day, over a hundred miles of well-settled country. Fresh horses and carriage drivers were supplied at six different places, with corresponding changes of men guarding Morgan to carry on the conspiracy. With one exception, every individual involved was a Mason bound by secret oaths "to conceal and never reveal the crime of a brother Mason." The inadvertent exception was Corydon Fox, a last minute carriage driver on one of the routes to Lewiston. Fox was later initiated by unanimous vote of the Masons in Lewiston. Officiating in the ceremony to initiate Fox was a reverend clergyman from Rochester. This clergyman was the only Mason in the carriage with Morgan on the leg from Rochester to Lewiston. The driver of the carriage on that leg was Freemason Jeremiah Brown, a member of the New York state legislature.

It afterward appeared in the evidence gathered by the citizen investigators that the Lodge at Buffalo was also involved in the plot, as were the lodges at LeRoy, Bethany, Covington, Lockport, and Rochester. Each Lodge had contributed to the conspiracy with either manpower, horses, or other preparation made along the route traveled by the party. Nowhere was there delay, or hesitation, or explanation, or discussion. Everything was carried out in silence as planned, up to the hour of the evening of Sept. 14, when the prisoner was taken from the carriage at Fort Niagara and lodged in the place originally designed for a powder magazine.

Fort Niagara was an unoccupied military post near the mouth of the Niagara River. During the War of 1812, the jurisdiction of the Fort had been turned over by the State to the Federal Government. At the end of the war, the federal government had entrusted the Fort to a Mason. It was this Mason who opened the gates to the conspirators.

On the same evening the carriage arrived at Fort Niagara, there was an installation ceremony at the Masonic Lodge "Benevolent" in the neighboring town of Lewiston, at which the arch conspirator, Nicholas G. Chesebro (the coroner), was to be made Grand High Priest. The ceremony was actually a cover for planning the next move against Morgan. An invitation was given to Masons from distant points to come together at the ceremony and consult upon what to do next with this Masonic traitor.

At the "ceremony" several Masons hesitated at the idea of murder. Messengers were dispatched to Rochester for advice. At Rochester they did not proceed hastily, nor adopt their ultimate decision without long and painful reluctance. They earnestly deliberated upon their Masonic obligation. Their final conclusion was that Masonic oaths were binding. Morgan had certainly and essentially violated them. The Masons at Rochester made a unanimous decision that Morgan must die.

In understanding Masonic thought, as well as Masonic common sense — if their obligations are binding, Masons are righteous in their decision to execute Morgan. Hence, it was not a sin, but rather an honor for the eight Masons who volunteered to draw lots to carry out the penalty. Three of the lots were marked. The eight executioners were not to look at their lots until they arrived home. The three with marked lots were to rendezvous at a predetermined location and carry out their Masonic duty.

The meeting was adjourned in prayer by the same clergyman who had accompanied Morgan from Rochester to Lewiston. He blasphemously invoked God's blessing upon the planned violation of His most solemn law — "Thou shalt not kill."

At midnight September 19, the three executioners took their victim from the fort, rowed him by boat to the middle of the Niagara River, fastened weights around his body and pushed him overboard. In 1848, one of the three confessed on his death-bed the evil deed he had done. That confession is printed in detail in Finney's book, pages 6-10.

That such a tragedy could be executed in a land that guarantees freedom of speech, and security of life and liberty; that it could enlist citizens of good reputation from so many quarters; that it could secure the cooperation of legislators, judges, sheriffs, constables, coroners, clergymen, generals, physicians, and lawyers; that with impunity it could involve all these possibilities and more, turned the current of popular indignation from the guilty individuals towards the Masonic institution itself. Thus, the Anti-Masonic Movement turned into a political movement, which opposed all secret societies at the polls.

Freemasonry did not repent of its murder of William Morgan. Instead, it reinforced its diabolical obligations by reminding Masons of what happened to Morgan when he broke his Masonic oath. From the *Masonic Hand Book* we read:

> When a brother reveals any of our great secrets; whenever, for instance, he tells anything about Boaz, or Tubalcain, or Jachin, or that awful Mahhah-bone, or even whenever a minister prays in the name of Christ in any of our assemblies, you must always hold yourself in readiness, if called upon, to cut his throat from ear to ear, pull out his tongue by the roots, and bury his body at the bottom of some lake or pond.
>
> Of course, all this must be done in secret, as it was in the case of that notorious man Morgan, for both law and civilization are opposed to such barbarous crimes, but then, you know you must live up to your obligation, and so long as you have sworn to do it, by being very strict and obedient in the matter, you'll be free from sin.[58]

The Plot to Kidnap and Murder David C. Miller

While coroner Nicholas Chesebro led one group of sixty-nine Masons in deliberating the fate of Morgan, constable Jesse French led another group of sixty-seven in an attempted destruction of Miller's print shop, as well as his kidnapping and planned murder. Like Morgan, Miller was a Mason, albeit only an Entered Apprentice (1st degree). Yet, the attitude of Masons toward Miller was the same as that toward the high-degree Morgan. Miller must also be killed. Following are some quotes of Masons concerning the fate of Miller:

In Buffalo, a politician said that he was astonished Miller had been permitted to go so far in printing the book; that if he should come to Buffalo, there were twenty Masons willing to take his life in less than half an hour.

In Leroy, a physician and former sheriff of the county declared at a public table that, "The book should be suppressed, if it cost every one of us our lives."

In Batavia, a Mason holding a respectable office declared that "Miller's office would not stand there long."

Also in Batavia two justices of the peace, both of whom were Masons, left town on the day Miller's print shop was to be leveled. As they boarded the stage, one justice turned to a citizen and said in the presence of the other justice, "I should not be surprised if when I return to Batavia I find Miller's office leveled with the ground." The citizen asked them, "Do you two, being justices of the peace, think such proceedings against Miller right?" The second justice answered with a smirk, "If you found a man abusing your marriage bed, would you have recourse to the law, or take a club and beat his brains out?"[59]

The conspiracy against Miller actually began before the conspiracy against Morgan. In the early summer of 1826, rumors began to spread in the town of Batavia that Miller, a newspaper publisher in town, was planning to print Morgan's book. The rumor excited no one but Masons, who avowed that the suppression of the work was determined at all costs.

Their first attack was an attempt to bankrupt Miller. A large number of subscribers to his paper suddenly withdrew their subscriptions, followed by numerous lawsuits against Miller to enforce the payment of small debts. The collection of these debts was done in a manner so as to embarrass Miller.

This failing, Freemasonry's second attempt was to infiltrate his business and steal the manuscript to Morgan's book. The

FREEMASONRY

Mason selected for the task was well known for his skill in deception. His name was Daniel Johns, a Knights Templar who lived about fifty miles from Batavia.

About the middle of August, Mr. Johns appeared in Batavia and lodged at one of the public houses. The next morning he presented himself before Miller, proposing that he assist the printer in the publication of the book, offering to advance any sum of money that might be needed in the venture. Johns was accepted and received into Miller's confidence. Within days he absconded with the manuscript.

Miller, a shrewd man himself, had prepared for such an occasion. When he contracted with Morgan, he had him write four copies of the manuscript. Two were to remain at the Captain's home — one visible and one hidden in a straw mattress. Two were to be held at Miller's office, one visible and the other likewise hidden. Johns absconded only with the visible copy.

When Miller proceeded to print Morgan's book, only then did the Masons learn that there was another manuscript. They supposed it to be hidden either at Morgan's house, or at the printing office, and made plans to get it.

One Saturday evening in August, when Captain Morgan was away, three Masons (Johnson Goodwill, Daniel H. Dana, and Thomas McCully) were sent to his home to find the manuscript. As Mrs. Morgan opened the door, Goodwill and Dana, without permission or ceremony, brushed her aside and proceeded upstairs to rummage among the trunks, boxes, drawers and every other place where it was probable the manuscript might be found. McCully remained downstairs to keep Mrs. Morgan from sounding an alarm. They left without the papers, unaware they were hidden in the straw mattress.

Upon hearing of the unwelcome intrusion on Mrs. Morgan, Miller anticipated the Masons might attack his office, so he set up a fortification. When the Masons learned of the printer's defense, they planned to burn the building to the ground, capture Miller and kill him along with Morgan.

Miller's office was in a wooden building, with the ground floor occupied by a family of ten. The print shop was upstairs, with sleeping quarters for six employees. The reckless determination of Freemasonry to burn out Miller gave no concern for these sixteen souls, nor for the souls of the villagers, for had the fire made much headway, a considerable portion of the town would have been consumed.

The arsonist was Freemason Richard Howard of Buffalo, a book-binder by trade. Howard's plan was to implicate John Mann, a blacksmith from Buffalo, by having him purchase the ingredients to torch Miller's office. The blacksmith declined, so Howard purchased a keg of turpentine himself, which purchase later tied him to the crime.

Howard took a late stage to Batavia and arrived in the city on Sunday night, September 10, the evening before Morgan was captured. He went immediately to Miller's office, splashed turpentine on the siding directly under the stairs leading to the printing apartment above, then soaked cotton balls and straw with turpentine and scattered them around the foundation.

Miller had anticipated trouble and previously set a watch on the print shop. Almost immediately after the flame was lit it was discovered and quickly extinguished. Howard was chased by one of the lookouts and barely escaped. When he was later implicated in the crime, he never stood trial, for he mysteriously disappeared. It was believed he had been spirited out of the country by Freemasons and lived the rest of his life in a foreign land, leaving behind his wife and children.

Failing in their attempt to burn out Miller, the Masons planned to take the print shop by force, level the building, destroy the printing press, capture Miller and kill him. The Lodge at Batavia informed the Lodge at Buffalo that Tuesday, Sept. 12 would be the perfect day, since the two justices of the peace in town were scheduled to stand as witnesses before a justice of the peace in a neighboring town. The only official left in Batavia was the sheriff, and he was one of them.

Meanwhile, on Monday, September 11, Captain William Morgan failed to return home to his 23-year-old wife and two small children. Early Tuesday morning, September 12, Mrs.

FREEMASONRY

Morgan sent for Sheriff William R. Thompson to inquire of her husband's whereabouts. The sheriff informed her that Morgan had been arrested for stealing a shirt and tie, that he believed it was a pretense to spirit him out of town and kill him. Mrs. Morgan, knowledgeable of the manuscript hidden in the straw mattress, offered to give it up in return for the release of her husband. The sheriff accepted and took the manuscript to a Mason named George Ketchum, who in turn took the papers to the Masons in Rochester. Morgan, however, was not released.

At about high noon that same day, while the sheriff was visiting with Mrs. Morgan over her husband's fate, and while the two justices of the peace were officiating in a neighboring village, a crowd of sixty-seven men suddenly appeared from all directions in the little town of Batavia. Nearly all were carrying clubs or sticks newly cut. Each was dressed alike so as not to be easily recognized. Leading them was constable Jesse French.

French selected six of the ruffians and together they went to Miller's office, and in a rude and violent manner arrested him under the pretense of having a warrant. They carried Miller to a neighboring village where he was illegally confined in a Masonic lodge room, assaulted and threatened with the fate of Morgan. By the assistance of friends and his own intrepidity, Miller escaped. Meanwhile, the citizens at Batavia, hearing of Miller's capture, surrounded his office with weapons in hand. Gradually, the crowd of Masons disbursed.

Citizen Investigators

These outrages extended over six counties. In this alarming emergency, the agents of government were paralyzed. The public institutions and provisions for the preservation of tranquility and the repression of crime seemed worthless. Therefore, in a move unprecedented in our nation's history, and in defiance of the most malignant, persevering, and ingenious counteraction by Freemasons, the citizens of New York took the matter into their own hands. At great expense of their own time and money, they suspended their private concerns and gave themselves up to all the labors of a complicated investigation. At every turn they met obstruction to justice. They could obtain no involuntary testimony; they received no assistance from public office; and in their travels their lives were endangered. Still they went on fearlessly and successfully — inquiring cautiously but persistently into all the circumstances of these most revolting crimes. Their sole purpose was to obtain enough evidence to be effective for the judicial exposure and punishment of the offenders. Yet, all the while their motives were venomously slandered and their conduct belied in the Masonic-controlled press. Such tenacity on the part of these citizens is indicative of the safety, and prophetic of the perpetuity of our free institutions.

In the end the citizen investigators uncovered enough evidence to bring charges against individual Masons and the Masonic Institution as a whole. However, the sheriffs in all the counties in which the deeds of violence against Morgan had been committed, whose duty it was under the laws of New York to select and summon the grand juries, were one and all Freemasons. Several had themselves been party to the crime. Hence, they did not hesitate to make use of their power as officers of justice to screen the criminals from conviction. The jurors were most of them Masons, with some of them participants in the crimes into which it became their civil duty to inquire.

Five years were consumed in attempting to obtain a legal conviction of the various offenders, but to no avail. Some of the suspected persons indeed stood trial. But it was a mockery of justice, for the secret obligation prevailed in the jury box. Consequently, they were one and all rescued in the moment of their utmost need. Others vanished from the scene and eluded pursuit even to the farthest limits of the United States. The Masonic coroner, the one most guilty of perpetuating these offenses, was tracked to a Lodge in New York City. From there the citizen investigators discovered that Masons in that city secreted him aboard a vessel below the harbor and sent him to a foreign land, leaving his wife and children behind.

Important witnesses were carried off at the moment when their evidence was indispensable, and placed beyond the jurisdiction of the State. Those who were called to testify, and actually did sit on the stand, stood doggedly mute; or else they placed themselves entirely under the guidance of legal advisers employed to protect them from incriminating themselves. All the while, distant Lodges responded favorably to the call for aid in the defense of their endangered brethren by forwarding sums of money for the relief of the accused.

The sixty-nine Masons who actually participated in the abduction and murder of Captain William Morgan gradually dropped out of sight. So well hidden were they that it was the belief of all who were knowledgeable of these events that they lived and died outside of the United States, secure from every danger of legal punishment. Twenty-two years after the fact, one of the three who actually murdered Morgan made a deathbed confession, which is printed in detail in Finney's book on pp. 6-10.

All persons engaged in these outrages were either Royal Arch Masons at the time of their crimes, or made so immediately after their crimes. As such, they were obligated by oath to conceal and never reveal the crimes of a brother Mason, treason and murder not excepted. They knew full well the consequences should they disobey. Therefore, many Masons called as witnesses perjured themselves. Others were excused from testifying by alleging they would incriminate themselves. And yet, all those who were guilty of participating in the offenses were held up by the Fraternity as heroes of fidelity to their duty, and victims to the prejudices of their fellow citizens. To their dying day, they were still retained as worthy and cherished members of their beloved Fraternity.

One faithful and able state officer, whose lawful duty it was to investigate these offences, officially reported on the proceedings in which he had been in charge:

Difficulties which never occurred in any other prosecution, have been met at every step. Witnesses have been secreted: they have been sent off into Canada, and into different states of the Union. They have been apprised of process being issued to compel their attendance, and have been thereby enabled to evade its service. In one instance, after a party implicated had been arrested and brought into this state, he was decoyed from the custody of the individual having him in charge, and finally escaped. These occurrences have been so numerous and various as to forbid the belief that they are the result of individual effort alone; and they have evinced the concert of so many agents as to indicate an extensive combination to screen from punishment those charged with a participation in the offences upon William Morgan.[60]

The irony of all ironies is that shortly following the ransacking of Mrs. Morgan's house by three Masons, and the murder of her husband by three others, benevolent Freemasonry came to her financial aid. James Ganson, who was directly involved with the abduction of her husband, visited Mrs. Morgan, assuring her that Freemasonry was making arrangements for her support, that she would be well-provided for, that her children would be sent to school as soon as they were old enough.

After Freemasonry determined how they were going to care for Mrs. Morgan and her children, they appointed Thomas McCully to deliver the message. McCully, you recall, was one of the three Masons who had bullied their way into her house, ransacking it in their attempt to find the manuscript to her husband's book. McCully informed Mrs. Morgan that "Freemasonry had raised support for her family, and had provided board for them at a public tavern in the village." The tavern was the same at which her husband had been detained after his arrest.

Six months after the murder of her husband, Henry Brown of Batavia, who was Grand Commander of the Knights Templar at LeRoy, New York, called on Mrs. Morgan and handed her a bag containing silver dollars that had been collected from the various Lodges throughout the state.

Her distress of mind and unprotected situation did not sway her to bow to their hypocritical benevolence. Without hesitation she said, "I shall accept no assistance from the Masons."

The ends of justice were defeated by the oath of Freemasonry, which came in conflict with the duty to society and to God, and succeeded in setting it aside. Gradually, the opposition to Masonry became more and more political and the Anti-Masonic Party was formed.

The Second Great Awakening

Before these Masonic outrages, Almighty God had once again set up His standard in America to put the Masonic enemy to flight, and bring revival to our land. At the turn of the 19th century, men such as Francis Asbury, the first bishop of the Methodist Church in America, and Peter Cartwright, Timothy Dwight, and Lyman Beecher, led the way to the Second Great Awakening. The most eminent figure and symbol of the revival was former Mason Charles G. Finney (1792-1875), who, after becoming a Christian in 1824, renounced his affiliation with the Lodge and two years later began preaching, bringing great revival to the Eastern States. His meetings were characterized by deep and open mourning over sin. After Morgan's murder, Finney included repentance from Masonry wherever he went, and thousands of Masons renounced their oaths and received Christ as Savior. It was Finney who wrote the textbook on revival during the Second Great Awakening.[61]

Recall Christ's promise to the evangelical Philadelphia Church, "Behold, I will make them of the synagogue of Satan, which say they are Jews, and are not, but do lie; behold, I will make them to come and worship before thy feet, and to know that I have loved thee." (Rev. 3:9).

This promise suggests a submission of a "synagogue of Satan" to the preaching of the evangelical church. Such submission can only be God-sent and God-controlled, causing the synagogue of Satan (those who say they are Jews and are not), to bow in shame before the work of evangelism.

What group during the Second Great Awakening might be identified as the synagogue of Satan? The answer comes from three sources: (1) Two Masonic authorities; (2) Holy Scripture; and (3) theologians.

From the first Masonic authority we can document that rituals in the Scottish Rite, from 4-33, were acquired from the Jewish Cabala. Thirty-third degree Mason Albert Pike, the most important Masonic figure of the 19th century, confirms this in his 1871 Masonic publication, *Morals and Dogma:*

> All truly dogmatic religions have issued from the Kabalah and return to it: everything scientific and grand in the religious dreams of all the illuminati...is borrowed from the Kabalah; all the Masonic associations owe to it their secrets and their symbols.
>
> The Kabalah alone consecrates the alliance of the Universal Reason and the Divine Word; it establishes, by the counterpoises of two forces apparently opposite, the eternal balance of being; it alone reconciles Reason with Faith, Power with Liberty, Science with Mystery; it has the keys of the Present, the Past, and the Future.
>
> Masonry is a search after Light. That search leads us directly back, as you see, to the Kabalah. In that ancient and little understood medley of absurdity and philosophy, the Initiate will find

the source of many doctrines; and may in time come to understand the Hermetic philosophers, the Alchemists, all the Anti-papal Thinkers of the Middle Ages....

Thus was a second Bible born, unknown to, or rather uncomprehended by, the Christians....[62]

Since the Scottish Rite rituals come from the Jewish Cabala, the Scottish Rite is known as the Jewish Rite of Freemasonry. Because of this, the second Masonic authority, *Mackey's Encyclopedia of Freemasonry*, explains the Jewish character of Gentile Masons: "Each Lodge is and must be a symbol of the Jewish Temple; each Master in the chair representing the Jewish King; and every Freemason a personation of the Jewish Workman."[63]

If gentile initiates, who make up the bulk of membership in the Scottish Rite, claim to be Jews and clearly are not, does this not support the first portion of the three-source equation, that the Masonic Lodge is a counterfeit synagogue?

Source two of the three-source equation prompts the question, "Is this counterfeit synagogue a Satanic order?"

The answer is found in Scripture, the source of our second confirmation that Freemasonry is indeed a synagogue of Satan.

Jesus Christ, speaking in Matthew 5:33-37, informs us from where sworn oaths come:

Again, ye have heard that it hath been said by them of old time, Thou shalt not forswear thyself, but shalt perform unto the Lord thine oaths: But I say unto you, Swear not at all; neither by heaven; for it is God's throne: Nor by the earth; for it is his footstool: neither by Jerusalem; for it is the city of the great King. Neither shalt thou swear by thy head, because thou canst not make one hair white or black. But let your communication be, Yea, yea; Nay, nay: for whatsoever is more than these cometh of evil.

In Greek, the word "evil" can be translated "the devil."[64] Therefore, the taking of oaths, according to Jesus Christ, comes from the devil, or Satan.

James, the brother of Jesus, wrote in James 5:12: "But above all things, my brethren, swear not, neither by heaven, neither by the earth, neither by any other oath: but let your yea be yea; and your nay, nay; lest ye fall into condemnation."

In Greek, the word "condemnation" can also be translated "deceit" or "hypocrisy." It comes from a primitive root word, which means "to be covertly placed in an inferior position."[65] Fairly translated, Christians who take Masonic oaths are hypocrites, who permit themselves to be deceived.

Conclusion: If Freemasonry requires the taking of oaths, which it does, then according to Scripture these oaths are of Satan. And if Freemasonry claims to pattern its lodges after the Jewish temple, which it does, then there can be little doubt that Masonic Lodges qualify as synagogues of Satan.

Source three of the three-source equation comes from theologians. In 1961 the Roman Curia, the supreme government of the Vatican, published a book entitled, *The Plot Against The Church*, in which a warning to Catholics stated that the Scottish Rite of Freemasonry is the synagogue of Satan spoken of by Jesus Christ, and that its agents were planning to infiltrate the Catholic Church during Vatican II. The book also states that in 1738 Pope Clement XII declared that the Masonic lodge is "the synagogue of Satan."[66]

Finally, former 33rd degree Mason Dr. Jonathan Blanchard became a preaching companion with Finney. During the mid-1800s, Dr. Blanchard was president of Wheaton College. Following Morgan's example of exposing the Blue Lodge degrees, Blanchard exposed all 33 degrees of Freemasonry in a two-volume work entitled, *Scottish Rite Masonry Illustrated* In that work he stated that "Every lodge is a Synagogue of Satan and its ritual is Sorcery."[67]

Jesus said to the evangelical Philadelphia Church, "Behold, I will make them of the synagogue of Satan, which say they are Jews, and are not, but do lie; behold, I will make them to come and worship before thy feet, and to know that I have loved thee."

In Greek, the phrase "worship before thy feet," can be translated, "to prostrate oneself in homage." Did Freemasonry submit to the preaching of the gospel of Jesus Christ following the Morgan Affair? Did Masons come and worship before the feet of evangelicals? Charles G. Finney gives the answer, which can be read in more detail on page 179 in his book:

> Before the publishing of Morgan's book, the Baptist denomination...had been greatly carried away by Freemasonry. A large proportion of its eldership and membership were Freemasons. A considerable number of ministers and members of other branches of the Christian Church had also fallen into the snare. The murder of Wm. Morgan and the publication of Masonry... broke upon the churches...like a clap of thunder from a clear sky. The facts were such, the revelations were so clear, that the Baptist denomination backed down, and took the lead in renouncing and denouncing the institution. Their elders and associated churches, almost universally, passed resolutions disfellowshipping adhering Masons. Now it is worthy of all consideration and remembrance, that God set the seal of His [approval] upon the action taken by those churches at that time, by pouring out His Spirit upon them.
>
> Great revivals immediately followed.... In 1830 the greatest revival spread over this [land] that had ever been known in this or any other country.

As you shall read in Finney's book, as God's Word was delivered, Masons by the thousands rushed to the altars, repented and bowed before the feet of evangelicals and worshipped God. This was in fulfillment of Christ's prophecy to the Philadelphia Church in America: "Behold, I will make them of the synagogue of Satan...to come and worship before thy feet, and to know that I have loved thee." (Rev. 3:9).

As a result of these revivals, great conventions were called by thousands of repentant Masons, who made public confessions of their relation to the institution, and openly renounced Freemasonry. The proceedings of these conventions, part of which you have just read, were published everywhere, and Masons attending the conventions returned home and made public their Masonic oaths.

As revival swept the northern states, so ashamed were the Masons of the institution that Freemasonry was almost universally renounced. Of the 50,000 Masons throughout our land in 1830, 45,000 turned their backs on the lodge, the result of which was the suspension of 2,000 lodges.

This was the America visited in 1831 by French statesman, Alexis de Tocqueville, after which he returned to France and reported, "It was there [in the Churches] as I listened to the soul-elevating principles of the Gospel of Christ, as they fell from Sabbath to Sabbath upon the masses of the people, that I learned why America was great and free.... America is great because America is good, and if America ever ceases to be good, America will cease to be great."

America was good because repentance and salvation was preached from the pulpits during two Great Awakenings. America has lost that goodness because evangelism is a dying art. Instead of winning our nation to Christ through evangelism, we carry picket signs in protest against evil. This causes the wicked to hate us all the more. On the other hand, evangelism will bring them to Christ and change their heart.

Christ calls the lukewarm Church in America to repentance in Revelation 3:19. The reprinting of Finney's book is dedicated to that cause — to provoke the Church in America to evangelism before we are chastised by our Savior.

FREEMASONRY

Introduction Notes

1. John A. Stormer, *The Death of a Nation* (Florissant, MO: Liberty Bell Press, 1968) pp. 20-21.
2. "Anti-Masonic Movement," *Encyclopaedia Britannica: Micropaedia*, 15th ed., 1984.
3. John Daniel, *Scarlet and the Beast*, vol.1 (Tyler, Tx.: JKI Publishing, 1995) chaps. 1-5 (detailed documentation).
4. Daniel.
5. H.L. Haywood, *Supplement to Mackey's Encyclopedia of Freemasonry*, vol. 3 (Chicago: The Masonic History Co., 1946) p. 1159; also Daniel, vol.1, pp. 112-113..
6. William R. Denslow, *10,000 Famous Freemasons*, vol. 2 (Trenton, Mo.: Missouri Lodge of Research, 1958) p. 73.
7. Denslow.
8. Allen E. Roberts, *House Undivided: The Story of Freemasonry and the Civil War* (Richmond, Va.: Macoy Publishing and Masonic Supply Co., 1961) p. 65; also Denslow, vol. 4, pp. 300-301.
9. See p. lxi for a brief history of the Illuminati.
10. Albert G. Mackey, *Mackey's Encyclopedia of Freemasonry*, vol. 2 (Chicago: The Masonic History Co., 1946) p. 647.
11. Finney, p. 150 this book.
12. Mackey, vol. 2, p. 1094.
13. "Busy Brotherly World of Freemasonry," *Life Magazine* (8 Oct. 1956), p. 122. Also see Masonic bio of Washington at the end of this "Introduction."
14. Read Washington's letters in his Masonic biography at the end of this "Introduction."
15. Print of this painting is in the library of John Daniel.
16. J. Edward Decker, *Freemasonry: Satan's Door to America?* (Issaquah WA: Free the Masons Ministries, n.d) n.p.
17. William H. Stemper, "Conflicts and Development in Eighteenth-Century Freemasonry: The American Context" (London: Transactions of Quatuor Coronati Lodge, 1961) vol. 104, n.p.

18. "Busy Brotherly World."
19. Printed in *The Proceedings Of The United States Anti-Masonic Convention* held in Philadelphia, September 11, 1830, and in John Quincy Adams' *Letters On The Masonic Institution,* 1846. Both these documents can be purchased in their original form from Acacia Press, PO Box 656, Amherst MA 01004.
20. Roberts, p. vii. Roberts gives many detailed examples of soldier enemies protecting Masonic brothers who displayed the grand hailing sign of distress; also see *Mackey's Encyclopedia of Freemasonry,* vol. 2, p. 667.
21. Martin Short vividly exposes this partiality among Masonic bankers in his book, *Inside The Brotherhood: Further Secrets of the Freemasons* (New York: Dorset Press, 1989) pp. 165-168, 367.

A banker, who was the only non-Mason in the bank, told a Mason that he was unable to advance him a loan because of the financial instability of his business. The banker said, "I knew him quite well and let him appeal to the ultimate authority — the general manager's assistant for advances. I added that he was a fellow Mason and that he was to be sure to give him the proper handshake! I introduced them and left them together. He called at my office on the way out, wreathed in smiles, giving a thumbs-up sign to indicate total success. His borrowings are now at unprecedented levels and are in the 'doubtful' category — meaning they will inevitably be written off and deducted from the shareholders' funds. In the meantime, many worthy applications have been turned down — including one for the importation of ethical drugs for the hospital."

John Daniel, author of this "Introduction," as well as author of the trilogy, *Scarlet and the Beast,* tells a story of his earlier years in business, which took place during the "fuel crisis" of the 1970s. To "weather the storm," he needed a business loan. At that time, he was five years into his Masonic research. He knew all the grips and passwords of Freemasonry. He tells the story:

"I'm not a Mason, nor have I ever been a Mason. I am, however, a child of God, through the redemptive work on Calvary's cross by my Lord and Savior, Jesus Christ. I'm not proud of what I'm about to tell you. At the time it happened, I was spiritually weak with little faith. This is not an excuse, simply a fact.

"My banker of seven years was a Mason. I had shaken his hand many times, but never had I returned his Masonic handshake.

"During the fuel crisis in the '70s, I asked my banker for a $50,000 loan. He knew I had no collateral, so he recommended I apply for an SBA loan, stating that this government agency was liberal in guaranteeing loans to small businesses. I went through the SBA process, but was turned down.

"In desperation I returned to my banker. When he extended the Masonic handshake this time, I returned it. At first he looked puzzled, then shook my hand again. I responded to his satisfaction. He smiled and said, 'Lets fill out an application and see how far it goes.'

"Throughout this process he asked me questions that I recognized were tests to see if I was truly a Mason. I responded correctly each time. Finally, he smiled and said, 'Brother Daniel, I'll have the papers ready in two days. I want to meet with you and your accountant Wednesday for lunch. Meanwhile, go ahead and write checks. I'll cover them.'

"At the Wednesday luncheon the banker said something to this effect, 'What are brothers for, but to assist in time of need.' He advanced me $50,000 on my signature. I repaid it on schedule."

Another example of success in business is found in a 4-volume Masonic publication entitled *10,000 Famous Freemasons*, written by William R. Denslow, and published in 1957 through 1961 by the Missouri Lodge of Research. It reads like "Who's Who" in American corporate business. This does not suggest that these men were not able businessmen. It only suggests that Masonic partiality may have given them an edge over equally able non-Masons.

22. *Proceedings.*

23. C.F. McQuaig, *The Masonic Report* (Norcross, GA: Answer Books and Tapes, 1976) p. 4; quoting *Webb's Monitor*, p. 169.

24. *Proceedings.*

25. McQuaig, p. 9, quoting the *Masonic Hand Book*, p. 183.

26. *Proceedings.*

27. *Proceedings.*

28. See bio of John Q. Adams on p. L,

29. John Quincy Adams, *Letters On The Masonic Institution* (Boston: T.R. Marvin, 1847) Preface. See bio of Adams at the end of this "Introduction."

30. Roberts, entire.

31. John Daniel, *Scarlet and the Beast: A History Of The War Between English And French Freemasonry* (Tyler, TX: JKI Publishing, 1995) vol. I, chap. 27, with detailed documentation from many sources, including Masonic.

32. Michael Baigent et al, *The Temple and the Lodge* (New York: Arcade Pub., 1989) p. 261.

33. Stemper quoting "Sachse," Coil, *Freemasonry*, vol. II, p. 227.

34. Finney, p. 150 this book.

35. Finney.

36. Daniel, *Scarlet and the Beast*, vol. 1, chap. 27. This entire chapter deals with the early Masonic history in America. Ample documentation is given of the involvement of French and European Freemasons in our War of Independence, many of whom were generals leading the fight against England. They were one and all Templar Scottish Rite Masons opposed to British

Rosicrucian Freemasonry. These Templar Mason made it understood they were fighting a "Masonic War" to create the world's first Masonic republic.

37. J.M. Roberts, *The Mythology of Secret Societies* (New York: Charles Scribner's Sons, 1972) pp. 123-124.

38. Salem Kirban, *Satan's Angels Exposed* (Rossville, Ga.: Grapevine Book Distributors, 1980) p. 151.

39. J.R. Church, *Guardians of the Grail* (Oklahoma City: Prophecy Publications, 1989) p. 177.

40. Church, pp. 163-164.

41. Church.

42. See "Illuminati" on p. lxi.

43. James Strong, *Strong's Exhaustive Concordance of the Bible* (1890; Nashville: Abingdon, 1980) Selected words from the King James Version, "west" in Hebrew #4628; "standard" in Hebrew #5127; "enemy" in Hebrew #6862; "Satan" in Hebrew #7854.

44. See "Epilog" of this book. For a historic study of the infiltration of secret societies into the Church during the last 2,000 years of Church history, see John Daniel's, "Secret Societies and Their Infiltration into the Seven Churches of Revelation," 7 audio cassette tapes. rec. 1997 (JKI Publishing, POB 131480, Tyler TX 75713). For the period of prophesied Church history relating to the "Introduction" of this book, see tape #6, "The Secret Society at the Church of Philadelphia." For the period of prophesied Church history relating to the "Epilog" in this book, see tape #7, "The Secret Society at the Church of Laodicea."

45. *Proceedings.*

46. A copy of Morgan's book, which is in the possession of the author, has no reference to the Illuminati. We understand that Freemasonry bought all Illuminati editions long ago and republished a spurious edition. Finney alludes to this as well. If anyone reading this has an original of Morgan's book, which references the activity of the Illuminati, please contact JKI Publishing.

47. Roberts, pp. 33-34.
48. Edmond Ronayne, *Handbook of Freemasonry* (1943; Chicago: Powner Co., 1973) p. 45.
49. D.C. Miller, *History of the Morgan Abduction: Facts and Circumstances Relating to the Kidnaping and Murder of Captain William Morgan* (Batavia: D.C. Miller, 1827) p.10 Note: This publication contains most of the depositions and other court documents to substantiate the statements made, and discloses many particulars of the transactions. Also included is the Supplementary Report of the Committee containing the Report of the Coroner's Inquest on the body of Wm. Morgan.
50. Miller, p. 72.
51. Miller, p. 73.
52. Miller.
53. Miller, p.10.
54. 45,000 is the number quoted in Finney's book.
55. Adams, *Letters*, Preface.
56. Miller, pp. 70, 123, 173.
57. Mackey. Look up key words in the Index of vol. 3 under the following headings: mark, token, debt, favor, govern, hand, right hand, etc.
58. McQuaig, p. 3, quoting the *Masonic Hand Book*, p. 74.
59. Miller, p. 45.
60. *Proceedings.*
61. Michael Smythe, "1800s ushered in U.S. 'Era of Good Feelings,'" *The National Educator* (Dec. 1996) p. 13.
62. Albert Pike, *Morals and Dogma* (1871: Richmond, VA: L. Jenkins, 1942) pp. 741, 744-745.
63. Mackey, vol. 2, pp. 1022-1023.
64. Strong. Greek #4090.
65. Strong. Greek #5272, 5271, 5259.
66. Maurice Pinay, *The Plot Against The Church* (1967; Los Angeles: St. Anthony Press, 1982) Introduction.
67. J. Blanchard, *Scottish Rite Masonry Illustrated*, Vol. I, (1944: Chicago: Charles T. Powner Co., 1979) p. 462.■

FREEMASONRY

JOHN QUINCY ADAMS (1767-1848)

President of the United States from 1825 to 1829, Adams was one of the most famous figures in the Anti-Masonic Movement. He joined the Movement shortly after his inauguration. Up to that point his career had been almost uniformly successful. But when he joined the Anti-Masons, his presidency was in most respects a political failure because of the virulent opposition of the Jacksonians. In 1828, Andrew Jackson, who was himself a Mason, was elected President over Adams. It was during Jackson's administration that irreconcilable differences developed between the followers of Adams, who were anti-Masons, and the followers of Jackson, who were Masons.

Adams' political party was known as the National Republicans, who with the Anti-Masons, were the precursors of the Whigs. Supported largely by members of the Anti-Masonic Movement, Adams was elected a member of the national House of Representatives in 1830. He served in the House from 1831 until his death on the House floor in 1848.

To the day he died, Adams never abandoned his hopes for a reelection to the presidency — whether as nominee of the Anti-Masonic Party, or of the National Republican Party, or of a union of both, which became the Whig Party in 1838. The Whigs became the Republican Party in 1854, and remain so today.

In 1846, two years before his death, and twenty years after the mysterious disappearance of William Morgan and the founding of the Anti-Masonic Movement, John Quincy Adams published a book entitled, "Letters on the Masonic Institution." The Preface to his book summarizes the findings of the citizens' Anti-Masonic Movement and discusses the results of the Movement and the political party it spawned. The information gleaned for the Introduction of Finney's book comes partly from John Q. Adams letters, as well as from "The Proceedings of the United States Anti-Masonic Convention," held in Philadelphia, September 11, 1830.■

INTRODUCTION

GEORGE WASHINGTON'S MASONIC RECORD
as written by William R. Denslow's
10,000 Famous Freemasons
vol. 4, pp. 300-301

George Washington (1732-1799). First President of the United States; supreme commander of Continental forces in American Revolution and "father of his country." b. Feb. 22, 1732 (by present calendar) at Bridges Creek, Westmoreland Co., Va. Inasmuch as his biography is readily available, this sketch will deal only with the Masonic facets of his life. He was initiated in 1752 in the lodge at Fredericksburg, Va., and the records of that lodge, still in existence, show that on the evening of Nov, 4 "Mr. George Washington was initiated as an Entered Apprentice: and the entrance fee of 2 pounds 3 pence was acknowledged. On March 3, 1753 he received the Fellow Craft degree, and on Aug. 4, same year, was raised to Master Mason. Each of the above days fell on Saturday and he was last in the Fredericksburg lodge on Saturday, Sept. 1, 1753. It is possible that he received some additional degree, or was reobligated during the French War in a military lodge attached to the 46th Regiment. It might have been the Mark Master degree. It is also speculated that he received the Royal Arch degree in Fredericksburg Lodge as it was being worked by that lodge at the time Washington was raised. This claim is aided by the fact that in Aug., 1784 Lafayette presented Washington with a Masonic apron which had been embroidered by Madame Lafayette, and contained emblems of the Royal Arch with the letter H.T.W.S.S.T.K.S. in a circle and a beehive within the circle to indicate that it was the wearer's mark. In 1777 a convention of Virginia lodges recommended Washington to be Grand Master of the Independent grand lodge of that commonwealth. Washington, however, declined. Soon after the start of the Revolution, there was a movement to throw off the authority of the mother country, and several of the provincial grand lodges assumed an independent character. The idea of a grand master for all the colonies also became popular. On Feb. 7, 1780, a convention of delegates from Army lodges met at Morristown, N.J. and suggested to several grand lodges that "one Grand Lodge in America" be established. On Jan. 13, 1780, the Grand Lodge of Pennsylvania held a session, and declaring that Freemasonry would benefit by "a Grand Master of Masons throughout the United States," they elected Washington for the position. They then sent minutes of the election to the different grand lodges, but when Massachusetts failed to come to any determination on the question, the matter was dropped. The next Masonic record of Washington is in 1788 when Lodge No. 39 of Alexandria, Va., which had previously been working under the Grand Lodge of Pennsylvania, transferred its allegiance to Virginia. On May 29 of that year the lodge adopted the following resolution: "The Lodge proceeded to the appointment of Master and Deputy master to be recommended to the Grand Lodge of Virginia when George Washington, Esq., was unanimously chosen Master; Robert McCrea, Deputy Master; Wm. Hunter, Jr., Senior Warden; John Allison, Junior Warden. The charter to the lodge was issued by Edmund Randolph, then governor of Virginia and grand master of the Grand Lodge of Virginia, and named Washington as master. It also designated the lodge as Alexandria Lodge No. 22. In 1805 the lodge was permitted to change its name to that of Washington Alexandria Lodge in honor of its first master. Washington served in the capacity of master a total of 20 months. Throughout his career, Washington visited a number of lodges and attended many Masonic functions. His correspondence has many references to Freemasonry. In 1797 he wrote the Grand Lodge of Massachusetts, "My attachment to the Society of which we are members will dispose me always to contribute my best endeavors to promote the honor and prosperity of the Craft." In an earlier letter to the same body he expressed his idea that the Craft's "grand object is to promote the happiness of the human race." In answering a letter from the Grand Lodge of South Carolina in 1791, he said: "I recognize with pleasure my relation to the Brethren of your Society," and "I shall be happy, on every occasion, to evince my regard for the Fraternity." He also referred to the fraternity as "an association whose principles lead to purity of morals, and are beneficial of action." Writing to the officer and members of St. David's Lodge at Newport, R.I. in 1791 he stated: "Being persuaded that a just application of the principles on which the Masonic fraternity is founded must be promotive of private virtue and public prosperity, I shall always be happy to advance the interests of the Society, and to be considered by them as a deserving Brother." In November, 1798, only 13 months before his death, he wrote to the Grand Lodge of Maryland; "So far as I am acquainted with the doctrines and principles of Freemasonry, I conceive them to be founded in benevolence, and to be exercised only for the good of mankind. I cannot, therefore, upon this ground, withdraw my approbation [approval] from it." ■

GEORGE WASHINGTON'S MASONIC RECORD
as written by Albert G. Mackey in
Mackey's Encyclopedia of Freemasonry
vol. 2, pp. 1093-1096

WASHINGTON, GEORGE. ....[T]he opponents of Freemasonry...have sought to deny the premises [that Washington was a Mason in good standing], and, even if compelled to admit the fact of Washington's initiation, have persistently asserted that he never took any interest in it, disapproved of its spirit, and at an early period of his life abandoned it. The truth of history requires that these misstatements should be met by a brief recital of his Masonic career.

Washington was initiated, in 1752, in the Lodge at Fredericksburg, Virginia, and the records of that Lodge, still in existence, present the following entries on the subject. The first entry is this: "Nov. 4th. 1752. This evening Mr. George Washington was initiated as an Entered Apprentice"; and the receipt of the entrance fee, amounting to 2 pounds 3 pence, was acknowledged."

FREEMASONRY

On March 3 in the following year, "Mr. George Washington" is recorded as having been passed a Fellow Craft; and on August 4, same year, 1753, the record of the transactions of the evening states that "Mr. George Washington," and others whose names are mentioned, have been raised to the Sublime Degree of Master Mason.... [H]e was last in the Lodge at Fredericksburg on Saturday, September 1, 1753.

For five years after his initiation, he was engaged in active military service, and it is not likely that during that period his attendance on the communications of the Lodge could have been frequent. Some English writers have asserted that he was made a Freemason during the old French War [French and Indian War, 1754-1760], in a military Lodge attached to the 46th Regiment.

The records of the Lodge are, or were, extant, and furnish the evidence that Washington was there, and perhaps received some Masonic Degree...as it was then the custom to confer the Mark Degree as a side Degree in Master's Lodges, and as it has been proved that Washington was in possession of that Degree, he may have received it in Lodge No. 227, attached to the 46th Regiment.

In that Virginia Lodge on August 4, 1753, [when] George Washington was raised a Master Mason, the Royal Arch Degree [was] being worked four months and eighteen days previously. When he was initiated Washington was twenty years old; six feet three inches tall; a Major and Adjutant-General for the Colony. By the time he had taken the Master Mason's Degree he had been appointed a Colonel. He was Commander of the Northern Military District of Virginia at the outbreak of the French and Indian War, in May, 1754. Brother Cyrus Field Willard points out that an examination of this record would indicate that this wealthy young man must have gone on and taken his Royal Arch Degree as others did who were initiated in the Lodge with him and appear later as officers of the Royal Arch. Naturally Washington would follow this example so far as receiving the Degree was concerned in order that he might be fully prepared for his military career, many Brethren having done exactly the same thing for a like purpose, as one may readily call to mind in thinking over the initiation in the days of War.

[Publisher's note: refer to the "Introduction," p.x for a rendering of the oath taken in the Royal Arch Degree that protects the initiate from treason and murder, both of which are important to a soldier during war.]

There is ample evidence that during the Revolutionary War, while he was Commander-in-Chief of the American armies, he was a frequent attendant on the meetings of military Lodges. Years ago, Captain Hugh Maloy, a revolutionary veteran, then residing in Ohio, declared that on one of these occasions he was initiated in Washington's marquee, the chief himself presiding at the ceremony. Brother Scott, a Past Grand Master of Virginia, asserted that Washington was in frequent attendance on the Communications of the Brethren.

In 1777, the Convention of Virginia Lodges recommended Washington as the most proper person to be elected Grand Master of the Independent Grand Lodge of that Commonwealth ["independent" meaning it was no longer under the Masonic jurisdiction of English Freemasonry]. Brother Dove has given in his *Text-Book* the complete records of the Convention; and there is therefore no doubt that the nomination was made. It was, however, declined by Washington.

Soon after the beginning of the Revolution, a disposition was manifested among American Freemasons to dissever their connection, as subordinates, with the Masonic authorities of the mother country [England], and in several of the newly erected States the Provincial Grand Lodges assumed an independent character.

On January 13, 1780, [at the Grand Lodge of Pennsylvania], it had held a session, and it was unanimously declared that it was for the benefit of Freemasonry that "a Grand Master of Masons throughout the United States" should be nominated; where upon, with equal unanimity, General Washington was elected to the office. It was then ordered that the Minutes of the election be transmitted to the different Grand Lodges in the United States, and their concurrence therein be requested. The Grand Lodge of Massachusetts, doubting the expediency of electing a General Grand Master declined to come to any determination on the question and so the subject was dropped.

This will correct the error into which many foreign Grand Lodges and Masonic writers have fallen, of supposing that Washington was ever a Grand Master of the United States.

We next hear of Washington's official connection in the year 1788. Lodge No. 39, at Alexandria, which had hitherto been working under the Grand Lodge of Pennsylvania, in 1788 transferred its allegiance to Virginia. On May 29 in that year the Lodge adopted the following resolution: "The Lodge proceeded to the appointment of Master and Deputy Master to be recommended to the Grand Lodge of Virginia, when George Washington, Esq., was unanimously chosen Master....

The evidence, then, is clear that Washington was the master of a Lodge. Whether he ever assumed the duties of the office, and, if he assumed, how he discharged them, we know only from the testimony of Timothy Bigelow, who, in a Eulogy delivered before the Grand Lodge of Massachusetts, two months after Washington's death, and eleven [months] after his [Bigelow's] appointment as Master, made the following statement: "The information received from our Brethren who had the happiness to be members of the Lodge over which he presided for many years, and of which he died the Master, furnishes abundant proof of his persevering zeal for the prosperity of the Institution. Constant and punctual in his attendance, scrupulous in his observance of the regulations of the Lodge, and solicitous, at all times, to communicate light and instruction, he discharged the duties of the Chair with uncommon dignity and intelligence in all the mysteries of our art."

[Publisher's note: Bigelow's speech was made two months after Washington's death. If Bigelow was a blatant liar in this speech, which speech was made to fellow Masons, the entire membership of that lodge would have had to participate in the lie. If that were the case, it would seem logical that this lie would

have been discovered by other Masons, who all would conceal the lie. This would be highly improbable. Therefore, it is our opinion that George Washington did indeed actively preside as Master of the Alexandria Lodge No. 22 as stated by Bigelow].

On repeated occasions he [Washington] has announced, in his letters and addresses to various Masonic Bodies, his profound esteem for the character, and his just appreciation of the principles, of that Institution into which, at so early an age, he had been admitted. And during his long and laborious life, no opportunity was presented of which he did not avail himself to evince his esteem for the Institution.

Thus, in the year 1797, in reply to an affectionate address from the Grand Lodge of Massachusetts, he says: "My attachment to the Society of which we are members will dispose me always to contribute my best endeavors to promote the honor and prosperity of the Craft." Five years before this letter was written, he had, in a communication to the same Body, expressed his opinion of the Masonic Institution as one whose liberal principles are founded on the immutable laws of "truth and justice," and whose "grand object is to promote the happiness of the human race."

Answering an address from the Grand Lodge of South Carolina in 1791, he says: "I recognize with pleasure my relation to the Brethren of your Society," and "I shall be happy, on every occasion, to evince my regard for the Fraternity." And in the same letter he takes occasion to allude to the Masonic Institution as "an association whose principles lead to purity of morals, and are beneficial of action."

Writing to the officers and members of Saint David's Lodge at Newport, Rhode Island, in the same year, he uses this language: "Being persuaded that a just application of the principles on which the Masonic fraternity is founded must be promotive of private virtue and public prosperity, I shall always be happy to advance the interests of the Society, and to be considered by them as a deserving Brother."

And lastly, for we will not further extend these citations, in a letter addressed in November, 1798, only thirteen months before his death, to the Grand Lodge of Maryland he has made this explicit declaration of his opinion of the Institution: "So far as I am acquainted with the doctrines and principles of Freemasonry, I conceive them to be founded in benevolence, and to be exercised only for the good of mankind. I cannot, therefore, upon this ground, withdraw my approbation from it."

So much has been said upon the Masonic career and opinions of Washington because American Freemasons love to dwell on the fact that the distinguished patriot, whose memory is so revered that his unostentatious grave on the banks of the Potomac has become the Mecca of America, was not only a Brother of the Craft, but was ever ready to express his good opinion of the Society. They feel that under the panoply of his great name they may defy the malignant charges of their adversaries. They know that no better reply can be given to such charges than to say, in the language of [DeWitt] Clinton, [governor of New York during the Morgan Affair], "Washington would not have encouraged an Institution hostile to morality, religion, good order, and the public welfare."

Julius F. Sachse, for the Grand Lodge of Pennsylvania, dealt with the *Masonic Correspondence of Washington*, 1915, as found among the papers in the Library of Congress...."■

Will The Real George Washington Please Stand

There are many Christians who would like to think George Washington turned his back on the Lodge. Charles G. Finney is no exception. Therefore, to be fair to the reader, we shall quote Finney on Washington, then make our analysis:

"Freemasons have paraded the fact that Gen. Washington was a Mason before the public. The following conclusion of a letter from him will speak for him, and show how little he had to do with Masonry. Before his death he warned the whole country to beware of secret societies. The letter alluded to is dated "Mt. Vernon, September 25, 1798." Here we have its conclusion. It needs no comment:

'I have little more to add than thanks for your wishes, and favorable sentiments, except to correct an error you have run into of my presiding over the English lodges in this country. The fact is I preside over none, nor have I been in one more than once or twice within the last thirty years. I believe, notwithstanding, that none of the lodges in this country are contaminated with the principles ascribed to the society of the Illuminati.'
Signed, George Washington

Publisher's analysis: George Washington did not tell a lie, nor did he try to deceive. As John Daniel brought out in the "Introduction," for obvious reasons our first President never presided over an English lodge, nor set foot in one after the Revolution began. England was his enemy.

This is probably the intent of Washington's respone above. However, evidence from many sources other than Masonic confirm that Gen. Washington did preside over military lodges during the Revolution. These were French, not English. And he presided over Alexandria, Va. Lodge No. 22 beginning in 1788. This lodge was strictly American. Virginia was one of several colonies that "dissevered" their lodges from the mother country just as the Revolution began, long before 1788.

We have presented facts that confirm Washington remained an active Mason all his life, spoke highly of Freemasonry in speeches and letters, and was fond of using the Masonic idiom, "Grand Architect." There is no record that he resigned from a lodge, renounced his oaths, or objected to his appointment to Master of a lodge in absentia. He never objected to his appointment of Grand Master over all American lodges. He simply declined that position. It is our opinion that he declined because it would have been a full-time job — that he had more important things to do, such as presiding over our nation as President.

Yet, Washington was a praying man. And he believed in Almighty God. But was his Almighty God the incarnate God of

Christians? Or was his god the deistic god of Freemasonry, the Grand Architect of the Universe, to whom he attributed the success of the Revolution, and to whom he prayed?

As for his knowledge of the Illuminati — obviously, in the above letter, Washington had not yet learned of the extent of Illuminati penetration into American lodges. He only heard rumors and answered the enquiry by what knowledge he possessed. Later he was informed by a reputable source, John Adams, that the Illuminati had indeed penetrated fifteen lodges. It is believed that Adams, Franklin, and Jefferson were manipulated by the Illuminati until Adams alerted them.

After hearing of the Illuminati design for America from Adams, Washington not only warned America to "beware of secret societies," he also warned the Masonic Lodge in America of the dangers of the Illuminati. [J.R. Church, *Guardians of the Grail* (Oklahoma City: Prophecy Publications, 1989) p.163].

It is our opinion that this warning does not reflect Washington's sudden opposition to secret societies. It simply reveals his wise understanding of their penetration by an evil Illuminati with designs for his beloved America not in step with his own.

In 1802, three years following Washington's death, John Wood exposed the Illuminati in America in a work entitled, "A Full Exposition of the Clintonian Faction and the Society of the Columbian Illuminati," (Newark: Printed for the author, 1802). Wood quoted the oath of the organization, and traced its existence in its present American form, "The Theistical Society", to the German Illuminati from John Robison. He singles out Thomas Jefferson, Thomas Paine and the two Clintons (DeWitt and George) as members, and accuses it of the rankest Jacobinism with the vilest deism.

According to William Stemper, whose research has already been quoted in this "Introduction", the Illuminati thrived unabated until exposed by William Morgan in 1826.

Publisher's Conclusion: Freemasonry during Washington's day did indeed have the same blood-curdling oaths as printed in this "Introduction." Yet, it may not have been evil in the odious sense as it later became when infiltrated by the Illuminati. Illuminated Freemasonry is the Freemasonry Morgan paid with his life to expose. It was not the Freemasonry known to George Washington. Not until Washington was informed by John Adams of the evil intent of the Illuminati did he fully understand and warn America and its lodges. The Morgan Affair, however, confirms that no one heeded our first President's warning. After the Morgan Affair, when the Church was of the opinion Freemasonry was dead, the Church dropped its guard. Finney admits this in his book.

After you read Finney, you will be hard-pressed to believe Freemasonry is harmless — and even more hard pressed after you read John Daniel's "Epilog" and the four testimonies of the SBC pastors who suffered unjust persecution at the hands of Freemasons in our day.

CR80

THE ILLUMINATI

The Illuminati is a secret society that penetrated and ultimately transformed French Freemasonry on the Continent into a revolutionary power and shaped the creation of a new world power in North America.

The world's first exposure of the Illuminati came in 1798 by way of Scotland, when John Robison, a professor of Natural Philosophy at Edinburgh University, published *Proofs of a Conspiracy against all the Religions and governments of Europe.*

Robison was a Master Mason of unquestionable character in English Freemasonry. He travelled Europe prior to the French Revolution and frequented many Continental Lodges. Being a Scotsman, he naturally wanted to receive the high degrees in the Scottish Rite. It was there that he learned of the Illuminati. Appearing sympathetic to their cause, Robison was entrusted with Illuminati documents. After the French Revolution and its atrocities, he studied the documents. For the first time he realized that republican French Masonry was in total opposition to the designs and directions set forth by monarchist English Masonry. He therefore felt he was not infringing on his Masonic obligation of silence by unmasking this clandestine Order.

For the same reason George Washington warned Americans of the dangers of the Illuminati, Robison warned the British. He exposed the Illuminati as an order housed within French Freemasonry bent on the destruction of the Catholic Church, the dethroning of all monarchies, and the confiscation of businesses and land. Its ultimate aim was to inaugurate a New World Order based upon *Plato's Republic*, which called for world government ruled by an initiated few and backed by a military world power. Robison went so far as to recommend that English lodges be suspended to avoid penetration into the British government by the Illuminati.[1]

Mackey's Encyclopedia of Freemasonry describes Robison's book as "a history of the introduction of Freemasonry on the Continent, and of its corruptions, and...to a violent attack on the Illuminati. But while recommending that the Lodges in England should be suspended, he [Robison] makes no charge of corruption against them...." In Mackey's judgment of Robison, he seems to concur with the professor's evaluation of French Freemasonry during the Revolution, "So that, after all, his charges are not against Freemasonry in its original constitution, but against its corruption in a time of great political excitement."[2]

After two world wars in Europe, a 1946 "Supplement" to *Mackey's Encyclopedia of Freemasonry* revised its opinion of the Illuminati: "The Order of the Illuminati was the greatest single misfortune ever to befall European Freemasonry because it became at once the pattern and the point of departure for a succession of secret, underground, political conspiracies which divided Masonry and brought disgrace upon its name."[3]

Mackey also gives a brief biography of the founder of the Illuminati: "A secret society, founded on May 1, 1776, by Adam Weishaupt, who was Professor of Canon Law at the University of Ingolstadt. Its founder at first called it the Order of the Perfectibles; but he subsequently gave it the name by which it is now universally known.... Weishaupt, though a reformer in religion and a liberal in politics, had originally been a Jesuit.... To give to the Order [of the Illuminati] a higher influence, Weishaupt connected it with the Masonic Institution, after whose system of Degrees, of esoteric instruction, and of secret modes of recognition, it was organized.... The character [a point within a circle], now so much used by Freemasons to represent a Lodge, was invented and first used by the Illuminati.... It cannot be denied, that in process of time abuses had crept into the Institution and that by the influence of unworthy men the system became corrupted."[4]

May 1st, the day the Illuminati was founded, has become known as May Day, the universal holiday of communist countries. Weishaupt's Illuminati Colors were "red" to represent the human blood to be shed in all future revolutions. Every May Day the former Soviet Union flaunted its military might under thousands of red banners, as the Red Army marched down Red Square behind awesome weapons of war created to spill man's blood into rivers of red.

May 1st was such a catastrophic day in the revolutionary history of the world, that it has since been interwoven into our societal conscience as "May-day! May-day!" when transmitted along radio waves as the international signal for distress.

The Luciferian Connection

Adam Weishaupt used symbolism to conceal both the god and the assignment of the Illuminati. For example, the word "illuminati" is simply a Latin plural noun meaning "enlightened ones." By itself it appears quite harmless. Yet, when we research its use in mystery religions, and make a thorough examination of its etymology, we discover the disturbing truth that "Illuminati" means "those who emulate Lucifer," or "followers of Lucifer." For example, the ancients called Lucifer the "enlightened one," or the "light-bearer." Venus, goddess of love, was also known as the "light-bearer." The planet Venus is to this day called the "morning star." In antiquity Venus was known as "Lucifer." In Hebrew "Lucifer" is translated "morning star," or the "shining one."[5]

The first Masonic Lodge into which Weishaupt superimposed the Illuminati was the Grand Orient Lodge in Paris, France. The Grand Orient was previously organized in 1772, fours years before Weishaupt founded the Illuminati. The name "Grand Orient," like the name "Illuminati," has a sinister paternity. We turn to the story of Julian the Apostate to explain.

Before Julian became emperor of Rome (361-363 A.D.), he was initiated into one of the Babylonian mysteries by the theurgist, Maximus of Ephesus. As the subterranean ceremony progressed, Maximus directed his initiate, asking:

> "Wouldst thou see the Rebel? Look!"
> Above the head of the spectre shone the Morning Star, the Star of Dawn; and the Angel said:
> "In my name deny the Galilean." (Thrice demanded and thrice denied.)
> "Who art thou?"
> "I am the Light, I am the Orient, I am the Morning Star!
> "How beautiful thou art!"
> "Be as I am."
> "What sadness in thine eyes!"
> "I suffer for all living; there must be neither birth nor death. Come to me, I am the shadow, I am peace, I am liberty! Rebel, I will give thee force. Break the law, love, curse Him and be as I am."[6]

Notice that the apparition of Lucifer said, "I am the Orient." So, too, in the veiled language of Masonry, Orient actually means Lucifer! This fact was crucial to Weishaupt's success. He could indoctrinate his initiates by degrees under the cloak of Grand Orient Freemasonry. In time they would be Luciferian operatives.

INTRODUCTION

The Seal of the Illuminati:
Unfinished Pyramid and All-Seeing Eye

The Seal of the Illuminati is esoterically important in that it symbolically communicates to the initiated the assignment given this Luciferian order. Likewise, the founding date on the Seal (1776), has significant esoteric and numeric implications.

The Seal is pictured as a 13-layered unfinished pyramid with its capstone missing. Hovering above the pyramid is a sun-rayed triangle, as if waiting to be lowered to complete the structure. Inside the sun-rayed triangle is a single eye.

Strangely, the Seal of the Illuminati was adopted by American Freemasonry two months after it was created. Stranger still, it became part of the Great Seal of the United States. The Illuminati Seal and the Flying Eagle Seal both make up the whole of the Great Seal of the United States of America. Both seals can be viewed on the reverse side of our $1 bill. In Washington, DC both seals are laminated back to back. It is therefore apparent that the Illuminati was founded in 1776 to coincide with the American Revolution. Weishaupt was instructed, most likely by Thomas Jefferson, to design the Seal of the Illuminati as part of the Great Seal of the United States of America.[7]

The sun-rayed triangle in pagan religions symbolizes power, such as a throne or an empire, and is sometimes pictured as a horn. The triangle is also a symbol of the dwelling place of the pagan gods, represented by a mountain top in hilly country, a pyramid in Egypt, or a ziggurat in Mesopotamia. The ancients called the ziggurat "Hill of Heaven," or "Mountain of God."[8] Numbers 22:41 and Deuteronomy 12:2 refer to these pagan mountain top shrines as "high places."

Ezekiel 28:14-15 is possibly in reference to Lucifer's dwelling place in heaven prior to his fall. God, speaking to the King of Tyrus as a symbol for a greater personality, Lucifer,[9] said, "Thou art the anointed cherub that covereth; and I have set thee so: thou wast upon the holy mountain of God...Thou wast perfect in thy ways from the day that thou was created, till iniquity was found in thee."

lxix

FREEMASONRY

Satan is never original. He is a counterfeiter. As Lucifer he was cast to earth and became Satan. Satan then replicated the "holy mountain of God" on earth as an unholy pyramid.

When Weishaupt designed the sun-rayed "mountain of God" as a capstone hovering above an unfinished pyramid, he placed within the triangle an eye like the eye of man — known to Masons as the "Eye of Providence," or the "All-Seeing Eye." According to Freemasonry, the All-Seeing Eye is "an important symbol of the Supreme Being." It is a rendition of the "Egyptian eye of Osiris."[10]

(We suggest that pastors study Daniel 7:8. The "little horn" is believed by many prophecy scholars to represent the end-time Antichrist. Look up "horn" and "eyes" in the Hebrew text and you will recognize the "little horn" as the Seal of the Illuminati).

Above the pyramid are the Latin words "Annuit Coeptis," meaning "Announcing the Birth." Below is "Novus Ordo Seclorum," meaning "New Secular Order," which can also be translated "New World Order." Superimposed in Roman numerals on the bottom layer of bricks is the year 1776, the year the Illuminati was founded, and the year the American colonies declared independence. The coded message in the year 1776 is 666, which is the number of Beast.[11]

Thus, in the Illuminati Seal we find both the Antichrist and the forbidden number of the Beast! Together, they make up the Mark of the Beast. Scripture says that a day will come when no man can buy or sell without that Mark, or some rendition of that Mark, either in the palm of his hand or in his forehead (Rev. 13:16-18).

Hidden within each of the two seals are coded messages originally known only to the initiated. Most messages have since been decoded, but not all. Each seal's message is distinctly different from the other, except for the All-Seeing Eye and the 13 stars above the Flying Eagle. You will notice that the stars are arranged to shape a hexagram (six-pointed star). The Eye and the hexagram both represent the same deity. In occult theology, the All-Seeing Eye represents the Eye of Lucifer, whereas the hexagram represents Lucifer himself.[12]

INTRODUCTION

The coded symbology in the Seal of the Illuminati, when incorporated as part of the Great Seal of the United States, put the world of secret societies on notice that illuminated Freemasonry was beginning to build in America the base of its long-desired New World Order. When the one-world government becomes a reality, the capstone will rest atop the pyramid as Antichrist is inaugurated.

Professor Charles Eliott Norton (1827-1908) lectured at Harvard from 1874 to 1898 concerning the coded message of the Illuminati. He said, "Not only were many of the founders of the United States Government Masons, but they received aid from a secret and august body existing in Europe, which helped them to establish this country for a peculiar and particular purpose known only to the initiated few."[13]

A message to Masons: Most of you are unaware that the coded message within the 13-stepped unfinished pyramid contains instructions on how you are to play a part in completing the New World Order under the watchful eye of Lucifer. Satan could care less whether you know this or not, or believe this or not. As a member of the Craft, you will play your part in the inauguration of Antichrist when you pay your dues, when you go to lodge, and when you obey all orders handed down to you by your superiors. You cannot shirk your responsibility to the lodge simply by walking away from it, for you are still bound by the oaths. You must take three steps to escape the clutches of this Satanic order. First, you must quit the lodge. Second, you must renounce your oaths (see pp. 265-272). And third, you must accept Jesus Christ as your Savior and Lord. This book is dedicated to encourage you to this end.■

Illuminati Notes

1. John Robison, *Proofs of a Conspiracy* (1798; Boston: Western Islands, 1967) entire.
2. "Robison, John," *Mackey's Encyclopedia of Freemasonry,* vol. II.

3. "Knigg, Baron Von," *Mackey's Encyclopedia*, vol. III.
4. "Illuminati of Bavaria," *Mackey's Encyclopedia*, vol. I.
5. *Strong's Concordance*, Hebrew #1966 & #1984
6. Julian's ceremony is found in, *La Mort des Dieus*, by Russian historian Dmitri Merejkovsky. It is quoted by Miss (Inquire Within) Stoddard, *Light-bears of Darkness* (1930; Hawthorne, CA: Christian Book Club of America, 1969) p. 170.
7. Stan Deyo, *The Cosmic Conspiracy* (Kalamunda, Aust.: West Australian Texas Trading, 1978) pp. 64-79.
8. Merrill F. Unger, Archaeology and the Old Testament (Grand Rapids, MI: Zondervan, 1954) pp. 102, 104.
9. Bible, KJV, Pilgrim Edition (1948; New York: Oxford University Press, 1976) Ezekiel 28:12, FN 2.
10. "All-Seeing Eye," *Mackey's Encyclopedia*, vol. I.
11. Explanation is too lengthy for this work. See *Scarlet and the Beast*, vol. I, end of chap. 26 and all of chap. 27 for a detailed explanation.
12. Mark Spaulding, *The Heartbeat of the Dragon*, (Sterling Heights, MI: Light Warrior Press, Ltd., 1992) p. 91.
13. Mustafa El-Amin, *Freemasonry, Ancient Egypt, and the Islamic Destiny* (Jersey City, NJ: New Mind Production, 1988) p. 10.

CR℘

PREFACE

by Charles G. Finney

In few words I wish to state what are not and what are my reasons for writing this book.

1.   It is not that I have any quarrel or controversy with any member of the Masonic Order. No one of them can justly accuse me of any personal ill-will or unkindness.

2.   It is not because I am fond of controversy—I am not. Although I have been compelled to engage in much discussion, still I have always dreaded and endeavored to avoid the spirit and even the form of controversy.

3.   It is not because I disregard the sensibility of Freemasons upon the question of their pet institution, and am quite willing to arose their enmity by exposing it. I value the good opinion and good wishes of Freemasons as I do those of other men, and have no disposition to capriciously or wantonly assail what they regard with so much favor.

4.   It is not because I am willing, if I can dutifully avoid it, to render any member of the Fraternity odious. But my reasons are:

1.   I wish, if possible, to arrest the spread of this great evil, by giving the public, at least, so much information upon this subject as to induce them to examine and understand the true character and tendency of the institution.

2.   I wish, if possible, to arouse the young men who are Freemasons, to consider the inevitable consequences of such a horrible trifling with the most solemn oaths, as is constantly practiced by Freemasons. Such a course must, and does, as a matter of fact, grieve the Holy Spirit, sear the conscience, and harden the heart.

3.   I wish to induce the young men who are not Freemasons "to look before they leap," and not be deceived and committed, as thousands have been, before they were at all aware of the true nature of the institution of Freemasonry.

4.   I, with the many, have been remiss in suffering a new generation to grow up in ignorance of the character of Free-

masonry, as it was fully revealed to us who are now old. We have greatly erred in not preserving and handing down to the rising generation the literature upon this subject, with which we were made familiar forty years ago. For one, I must not continue this remissness.

5.   Because I know that nothing but correct information is wanting to banish this institution from wholesome society. This has been abundantly proven. As soon as Freemasons saw that their secrets were made public, they abandoned their lodges for very shame. With such oaths upon their souls, they could not face the frown of an indignant public, already aware of their true position.

6.   Freemasons exhort each other to maintain a dignified silence and are exhorted not to enter into controversy with opposers of Freemasonry. The reasons are obvious to those who are informed. We know why they are silent if they are so, and why they will not enter the field of controversy and attempt to justify their institution. Let anyone examine the question and he will see why they make no attempt to justify Free-masonry as it is revealed in the books from which I have quoted. I greatly desire to have the public, and especially the church of Christ, understand what Freemasonry is. Then let them act as duty requires.

7.   Should I be asked why I have not spoken out upon this subject before, I reply that until the question was sprung upon us in this place a year ago, I was not at all aware that Freemasonry had been disinterred and was alive, and stalking abroad over the face of the whole land.

8.   This book contains the numbers published in the *Independent* last year. These are revised, enlarged and rear-ranged. To these are added eight numbers not heretofore pub-lished.

9.   I have said in the body of the work, and say also in this preface, that I have no pecuniary intent in the sale of this work. I have not written for money, nor for fame. I shall get neither for my pains. I desire only to do good.   C. G. FINNEY

CHAPTER I

INTRODUCTORY

It is high time that the Church of Christ was awake to the character and tendency of Freemasonry.

Forty years ago we supposed that it was dead, and had no idea that it could ever revive. But, strange to tell, while we were busy in getting rid of slavery, Freemasonry has revived, and extended its bounds most alarmingly. I propose to write a series of articles, giving my views of the character and tendency of the institution.

I know something about it, for I have been a Freemason myself. Soon after I was twenty-one years of age, and while in Connecticut at school, an old uncle of mine persuaded me to join the Freemasons, representing that, as I was from home and much among strangers, it would be of service to me, because if a Freemason I should find friends everywhere. The lodge in that place was but a Master's lodge. I therefore took three degrees, or as far as what they call "the sublime degree of Master Mason." When I returned to the State of New York, to enter upon the study of law, I found at Adams, where I resided, a Masonic lodge and united with them. I soon became secretary of the lodge, and met regularly with the lodge. When I took especially the Master's degree I was struck with one part of the obligation, or oath, as not being sound either in a political or moral point of view.

However, I had been brought up with very few religious privileges, and had but slight knowledge on moral subjects; and I was not, therefore, greatly shocked, at the time, with the immorality of anything through which I passed. The lodge where I took my degrees was composed, I believe, mostly of professed Christians. But when I came to join the lodge at Adams I found that the Master of the lodge was a deist. At this distance of time I can not be certain whether the deist to whom

1

FREEMASONRY

I refer, Eliphalet Edmunds, was Master of the lodge when I first joined. My best recollection is that Captain Goodell was Master when I first joined the lodge at Adams, and that Judge Edmunds was Master at the time of my conversion to Christ. I am certain that deism was no objection to any man becoming a member or a Master of the lodge. There were in that lodge some as thoroughly irreligious men as I have ever associated with anywhere, and men with whom I never would have associated had they not been Freemasons. I do not recollect that any Christian men belonged to that lodge at the time I joined it. There were some very profane men who belonged to it, and some men of very intemperate habits.

As I paid the strictest attention to what they called their lectures and teachings, I became what they call "a bright Mason;" that is, as far as I went, I committed to memory their oral teaching—for they had no other.

The oaths, or obligations, were familiar to me, as was everything else that belonged to those three degrees that I had taken.

I had belonged to the lodge in Adams nearly four years when I was converted to Christ. During the struggle of conviction of sin through which I passed, I do not recollect that the question of Freemasonry ever occurred to my mind. The season that I called properly my conviction of sin was short. My exercises were pungent, and I very soon obtained hope in Christ.

Soon after my conversion the evening came for attendance upon the lodge. I went. They of course, were aware that I had become a Christian, and the Master of the lodge called upon me to open the lodge with prayer. I did so, and poured out my heart to the Lord for blessings upon the lodge. I observed that it created a considerable excitement. The evening passed away, and at the close of the lodge I was requested to pray again. I did so, and retired, but much depressed in spirit. I soon found that I was completely converted from Freemasonry to Christ, and that I could have no fellowship with any of the proceedings of the lodge. Its oaths appeared to me to be monstrously profane and barbarous.

At that time I did not know how much I had been imposed upon by many of the pretensions of Masonry. But upon reflection and examination, and after a severe struggle and earnest prayer, I found that I could not consistently remain with them. My new life instinctively and irresistibly recoiled from any fellowship with what I then regarded as "the unfruitful works of darkness."

Without consulting any person, I finally went to the lodge and requested my discharge. After manifesting considerable reluctance, they granted my request. My mind was made up. Withdraw from them I must, with their consent if I might, without their consent if I must. Of this I said nothing; but some way it came to be known that I had withdrawn from them. This created some little feeling among them. They, therefore, planned a Masonic celebration or festival. I do not recollect exactly what it was. But they sent a committee to me, requesting me to deliver an oration on the occasion. I quietly declined to do so; informing the committee that I could not conscientiously in anywise do what would manifest my approval of the institution, or sympathy with it. However, at that time, and for years afterward, I remained silent and said nothing against the institution; for I had not then so well considered the matter as to regard my Masonic oaths as utterly null and void. But from that time I never allowed myself to be recognized as a Freemason anywhere. This was a few years before the revelations of Freemasonry, by William Morgan, were published. When that book was published, I was asked if it was a true revelation of Freemasonry. I replied that it was, so far as I knew anything about it; and that, as nearly as I could recollect, it was a verbatim revelation of the first three degrees as I had myself taken them. I replied in this way because I saw, of course, that as the thing was published, and no longer a secret, I could not be under any obligations to keep it a secret, unless I could be under an obligation to lie, and to lie perpetually, by denying that that which had been published was truly Freemasonry.

FREEMASONRY

I knew that I could be under no obligations to be guilty of a perpetual falsehood, and that I really made no revelation of any secret when I frankly acknowledged that that which had been published was a true account of the institution, and a true exposé of their oaths, principles and proceedings.

Afterward I considered it more thoroughly, and was most perfectly convinced that I had no right to adhere to the institution, or to appear to do so; and that I was bound, whenever the occasion arose, to speak my mind freely in regard to it, and to renounce the horrid oaths I had taken.

On reflection and examination, I found that I had been grossly deceived and imposed upon. I had been led to suppose that there were some very important secrets to be communicated to me. But in this respect I found myself entirely disappointed.

Indeed, I came to the deliberate conclusion, and could not avoid doing so, that my oaths had been procured by fraud and misrepresentations, and that the institution was in no respect what I had been previously informed it was.

And, as I have had the means of examining it more thoroughly, it has become more and more irresistibly plain to my convictions that the institution is highly dangerous to the State, and in every way injurious to the Church of Christ.

This I expect to show in detail should I be spared to finish the articles which I contemplate writing. But in my next it will be in place to inquire, How are the public to know what Freemasonry really is?

After this inquiry is settled, we shall be prepared to enter upon an examination of its claims, its principles, and its tendency.

CR&O

CHAPTER II

SCRAP OF HISTORY

In this number I must remind readers of some facts that occurred about forty years ago; which, as matters of history, though then well-known to thousands, are probably now unknown to the great majority of our citizens. Elderly men and women, especially in the Northern States, will almost universally remember the murder of William Morgan by Freemasons, and many facts connected with that terrible tragedy. But, as much pains have been taken by Freemasons to rid the world of the books and pamphlets, and every vestige of writing relating to that subject, by far the larger number of young people seem to be entirely ignorant that such facts ever occurred. I will state them as briefly as possible.

About forty years ago, an estimable man by the name of William Morgan, then residing in Batavia, N.Y., being a Freemason, after much reflection, made up his mind that it was his duty to publish Freemasonry to the world. He regarded it as highly injurious to the cause of Christ, and as eminently dangerous to the government of our country, and I suppose was aware, as Masons generally were at that time, that nearly all the civil offices in the country were in the hands of Freemasons; and that the press was completely under their control, and almost altogether in their hands. Masons at that time boasted that all the civil offices in the country were in their hands. I believe that all the civil offices in the county where I resided while I belonged to them, were in their hands. I do not recollect a magistrate, or a constable, or sheriff in that county that was not at that time a Freemason.

A publisher by the name of Miller, also residing in Batavia, agreed to publish what Mr. Morgan would write. This, coming to be known to Freemasons, led them to conspire for his destruction. This, as we shall see, was only in accordance with

5

their oaths. By their oaths they were bound to seek his destruction, and to execute upon him the penalty of those oaths.

They kidnapped Morgan and for a time concealed him in the magazine of the United States Fort — Fort Niagara, at the mouth of Niagara River, where it empties into Lake Ontario. They kept him there until they could arrange to dispatch him. In the meantime, the greatest efforts were made to discover his whereabouts, and what the Masons had done with him. Strong suspicions came finally to be entertained that he was confined in that fort; and the Masons, finding that those suspicions were abroad, hastened his death. Two or three have since, upon their death-bed, confessed their part in the transaction. They drowned him in the Niagara River. The account of the manner in which this was done will be found in a book published by Elder Stearns, a Baptist elder. The book is entitled "Stearns on Masonry." On page 311, of that work, you will find that confession. But as many of my readers have not access to that work, I take the liberty to quote it entire, as follows:

CONFESSIONS
THE MURDER OF WILLIAM MORGAN,
CONFESSED BY THE MAN WHO, WITH HIS
OWN HANDS, PUSHED HIM OUT OF THE BOAT
INTO NIAGARA RIVER!

The following account of that tragical scene is taken from a pamphlet entitled, "Confession of the murder of William Morgan, as taken down by Dr. John L. Emery, of Racine County Wisconsin, in the summer of 1848, and now (1849) first given to the public;"

This "Confession" was taken down as related by Henry L. Valance, who acknowledges himself to have been one of the three who were selected to make a final disposition of the ill-fated victim of masonic vengeance. This confession it seems was made to his man was to draw one at the same moment. After drawing we were all to separate, without looking at the paper that each held in his hand. So soon as we had arrived at certain distances from the place of rendezvous, the tickets were to be examined, and those who held blanks were to return instantly to their homes; and those who should hold marked tickets were to proceed to the fort at midnight, and there put Morgan to death, in such a manner as should seem to themselves most fitting." Mr. Valance was one of the three who drew the ballots on which was the signal letter. He returned to the fort, where he was joined by his two companions, who had drawn the death tickets. Arrangements were made immediately for executing the sentence passed upon their prisoner, which was to sink him in the river with weights; in hope, says Mr. Valance, "that he and our crime alike would thus be buried beneath the waves." His part was to proceed to the magazine where Morgan was confined, and announce to him his fate — theirs was to procure a boat and weights with which to sink him. Morgan, on being informed of their proceedings against him, demanded by what authority they had condemned him, and who were his judges. "He commenced wringing his hands, and talking of his wife and children, the recollections of whom, in that awful hour, terribly affected him. His wife, he said, was young and inexperienced, and his children were but infants; what would become of them were he cut off, and they even ignorant of his fate?" What husband and father would not be "terribly affected" under such circumstances — to be cut off from among the living in this inhuman manner?

Mr. V.'s comrades returned, and informed him that they had procured the boat and weights, and that all things were in readiness on their part. Morgan was told that all his remonstrances were idle, that die he must, and that soon, even before the morning light. The feelings of the husband and father were still strong within him, and he continued to plead on behalf of his family. They gave him one half hour to prepare for his "inevitable fate." They retired from the magazine and left him. "How Morgan passed that time," says Mr. Valance, "I cannot tell, but everything was quiet as the tomb within." At the expiration of the allotted time, they entered the magazine, laid hold of their victim, "bound his hands behind him, and placed a gag in his mouth." They then led him forth to execution. "A short time," says this murderer, "brought us to the boat, and we all entered it — Morgan being placed in the bow with myself, along side of him. My comrades took the oars, and the boat was rapidly forced out into the river. The night was pitch dark, we could scarcely see a yard before us, and therefore was the time admirably adapted to our hellish purpose." Having reached a proper distance from the shore, the oarsmen ceased their labors. The weights were all secured together by a strong cord, and another cord of equal strength, and of several yards in length, proceeded from that. "This cord," says Mr. V., "I took in my hand [did not that hand tremble?] and fastened it around the body of Morgan, just above his hips, using all my skill to make it fast, so that it would hold. Then, in a whisper, I bade the unhappy man to stand up, and after a momentary hesitation he complied with my order. He stood close to the head of the boat, and there was just length enough of rope from his person to the weights to prevent any strain, while he was standing. I then requested one of my associates to assist me in lifting the weights from the bottom to the side of the boat, while the others steadied her from the stern. This was done, and, as Morgan was standing with his back toward me, I approached him, and gave him a strong push with both my hands, which were placed on the middle of his back. He fell forward, carrying the weights with him, and the waters closed over the mass. We remained quiet for two or three minutes, when my companions, without saying a word, resumed their places, and rowed the boat to the place from which they had taken it."

They also kidnapped Mr. Miller, the publisher; but the citizens of Batavia, finding it out, pursued the kidnappers, and finally rescued him.

The courts of justice found themselves entirely unable to make any headway against the wide-spread conspiracy that was formed among Masons in respect to this matter.

These are matters of record. It was found that they could do nothing with the courts, with the sheriffs, with the witnesses, or with the jurors; and all their efforts were for a time entirely impotent. Indeed, they never were able to prove the murder of Morgan, and bring it home to the individuals who perpetrated it.

But Mr. Morgan had published Freemasonry to the world. The greatest pains were taken by Masons to cover up the transaction, and as far as possible to deceive the public in regard to the fact that Mr. Morgan had published Masonry as it really is.

Masons themselves, as is affirmed by the very best authority, published two spurious editions of Morgan's book, and circulated them as the true edition which Morgan had published. These editions were designed to deceive Masons who had never seen Morgan's edition, and thus to enable them to say that it was not a true revelation of Masonry.

In consequence of the publication of Morgan's book, and the revelations that were made in regard to the kidnapping and murdering of Mr. Morgan, great numbers of Masons were led to consider the subject more fully than they had done; and the conscientious among them almost universally renounced Masonry altogether. I believe that about two thousand lodges, as a consequence of these revelations, were suspended.

The ex-president of a Western college, who is himself a Freemason, has recently published some very important information on the subject, though he justifies Masonry. He says that, out of a little more than fifty thousand Masons in the United States at that time, forty-five thousand turned their backs upon the lodge to enter the lodge no more. Conventions were called of Masons that were disposed to renounce it. One was held at Leroy, another at Philadelphia, and others at other places, I do not now remember where. The men composing these conventions made public confession of their relation to the institution, and publicly renounced it. At one of these large conventions they appointed a committee to superintend the publication of Masonry in all its degrees. This committee was composed of men of first-rate character, and men quite generally known to the public. Elder Bernard, a Baptist elder in good standing, was one of this committee; and he, with the assistance of his brethren who had been appointed to this work, obtained an accurate version of some forty-eight degrees. He published also the proceedings of those conventions, and much concerning the efforts that were made by the courts to search the matter to the bottom, and also several speeches that were made by prominent men in the State of New York. This work was entitled "Light on Masonry." In this work any person who is disposed may get a very correct view of what Freemasonry really is. This and sundry other reliable works on Freemasonry may be had at Godrich's, and Fitch & Fairchild's bookstores, in Oberlin. In saying this, it is proper to add that I have no direct or indirect pecuniary interest in the sale of those or of any book on Freemasonry whatever, nor shall I have in the sale of this which I am now preparing for the press. Freemasons shall not with truth accuse me of self-interest in exposing their institution.

Before the publication of "Bernard's Light on Masonry," great pains were taken to secure the most accurate knowledge of the degrees published by the committee, as the reader of that work will see, if he reads the book through. An account of all these matters will be found in "Light on Masonry," to which I have referred. In the Northern or non-slaveholding States Masonry was almost universally renounced at that time. But it was found that it had taken so deep a root that in all New England there was scarcely a newspaper in which the death of William Morgan, and the circumstances con-nected therewith, could be published. This was so generally true throughout all the North that newspapers had to be every-where established for the purpose of making the disclosures that were necessary in regard to its true character and ten-dency. The same game is being played over again at the present day. The "Cynosure," the new anti-masonic paper published at Chicago, is constantly intercepted on its way to subscribers. Four of its first six numbers failed to reach me, and now in December, 1868, I have received no number later than the sixth. The editor informs me that the numbers are constantly intercepted. The public will be forced to learn what a lawless and hideous institution Freemasonry is. But at present I refrain from saying more on this point.

It was found that Masonry so completely baffled the courts of law and obstructed the course of justice that it was forced into politics; and for a time the anti-masonic sentiment of the Northern States carried all before it. Almost all Masons become ashamed of it, felt themselves disgraced by having any connection with it, and publicly renounced it. If they did not publish any renunciation, they suspended their lodges, had no more to do with it, and did not pretend to deny that Masonry had been published.

Now these facts were so notorious, so universally known and confessed, that those of us who were acquainted with them at the time had no idea that Masonry would have the impudence ever again to claim any public respect. I should just as soon expect slavery to be re-established in this country, and become more popular than ever before—to take possession of the Government and of all the civil offices, and to grow bold, impudent, and defiant—as I should have expected that Masonry would achieve what it has. When the subject of Freemasonry was first forced upon our churches in Oberlin, for discussion and action, I can not express the astonishment, grief and indignation that I felt on hearing professed Christian Freemasons deny either expressly or by irresistible implication that Morgan and others had truly revealed the secrets of Freemasonry. But a few years ago such denial would have ruined the character of any intelligent man, not to say of a professed Christian.

But I must say, also, that Masonry itself has its literature. Many bombastic and spread-eagle books have been published in its favor. They never attempt to justify it as it is revealed in "Light on Masonry," nor reply by argument to the attacks that have been so successfully made upon it; neither have they pretended to reveal its secrets. But they have eulogized it in a manner that is utterly nauseating to those that under-stand what it really is. But these books have been circulated among the young, and have no doubt led thousands and scores of thousands of young men into the Masonic ranks, who, but for these miserable productions, would never have thought of taking such a step.

CHAPTER III

HOW KNOWN

We are prepared in this number to take up the question, How are the public to know what Freemasonry really is? This we may answer.

1. Negatively. (1.) Masonry cannot be known from a perusal of the eulogistic books which adhering Masons have written. Of course they are under oath in no way whatever to reveal the secrets of Masonry. But it is their secrets that the public are concerned to know. Now their eulogistic books, as any one may know who will examine them, are silly, and for the most part little better than twaddle. If we read their orations and sermons that have been published in support of Masonry, and the books that they have written, we shall find much that is silly, much that is false, and a great deal more that is mere bombast and rho domontade. I do not say this rashly. Any person who will examine the subject for himself must admit that this language is strictly true. But shall have occasion hereafter when we come to examine the character of the institution, to show more clearly the utter ignorance or dishonesty of the men who have eulogized it.

Let it be understood, then, that adhering Masons do not profess to publish their secrets. And that which the country and the church are particularly interested to understand they never publish — their oaths, for example; and, therefore, we cannot tell from what they write what they are under oath to do.

(2.) We cannot learn what Masonry is from the oral testimony of adhering Masons.

Let it be pondered well that every one of them is under oath to conceal and in no way whatever to reveal the secrets of the order. This Freemasons do not deny. Hence, if they are asked if the books in which Masonry has been published are

15

true, they will either evade the question or else they will lie; and they are under oath to do so.

Observe, adhering Masons are the men who still acknowledge the binding obligation of their oaths. Now, if they are asked if those books truly reveal Masonry, they consider themselves under an obligation to deny it, if they say anything about it. And, as they are well aware that to refuse to say anything about it is a virtual acknowledgment that the books are true, and would therefore be an indirect revelation of Masonry; they will almost universally deny that the books are true. Some of them are ashamed to say anything more than that there is some truth and a great deal of falsehood in them.

(3.) As they are under oath to conceal the secrets of Masonry, and in no wise whatever to reveal any part of them, their testimony in regard to the truthfulness or untruthfulness of those books is of no value whatever. It is mere madness to receive the testimony of men who are under oath, and under the most horrid oaths that can be taken — oaths sustained by the most terrific penalties that can be named to conceal their secrets and to deny that they have been published, and that those books contain them — I say it is downright madness to receive the testimony of such men, it matters not who they are. Masons have no right to expect an intelligent person to believe their denials that these books have truly revealed Masonry. Nor have they a right to complain if we reject their testimony. What would they have us do? Shall we believe the testimony of men who admit that they are under oath to conceal and never in any way reveal the secrets of their order, when they deny that their secrets are revealed in certain books, and shall we ignore the testimony of thousands who have conscientiously renounced those horrid oaths, at the hazard of their lives, and declared with one accord, and many of them under the sanction of judicial oaths lawfully administered, that Morgan, Bernard and others have truly revealed the secrets of Freemasonry? There are at this day thousands of most conscientious men who are ready to testify on oath that those books contain a substantially correct exposition of Freemasonry as it was and is. I say again that Freemasons have no right to expect us to believe their denials; for while they adhere to Masonry they are under oath to "conceal and never reveal" any part of its secrets and of course they must expressly or impliedly deny every revelation of its secrets that can be made. Would they have us stultify ourselves by receiving their testimony?

2. Positively. How, then, are we to know what Masonry is? I answer: (1.) From the published and oral testimony of those who have taken the degrees; and afterward, from conscientious motives, have confessed their error, and have publicly renounced Masonry. But it has been said that these are perjured men, and therefore not at all to be believed. But let it be remarked that this very accusation is an admission that they have published the truth; for, unless they have published the secrets of Masonry truly, they have violated no Masonic oath. Therefore, when Masons accuse them of being perjured, the very objection which they make to the testimony of these witnesses is an acknowledgment on the part of Masons themselves that they have truly published their secrets.

But again. If to reveal the secrets of Masonry be perjury, it follows that to accuse the revealers of Masonry of perjury, is itself perjury; because by their accusation they tacitly admit that that which has been published is truly a revelation of Masonry, and therefore their accusation is a violation of their oath of secrecy. Let it then be understood that the very objection to these witnesses, that they have committed perjury, is itself an acknowledgment that the witnesses are entirely credible, and have revealed Masonry as it is. And not only so — but in bringing forward the objection, they commit perjury themselves, if it be perjury to reveal their secrets; because, as I have said, in accusing the witnesses of perjury, they add their testimony to the fact that these witnesses have published

FREEMASONRY

Masonry as it is. So that by their own testimony, in bringing this charge of perjury, they themselves swell the number of witnesses to the truthfulness of these revelations.

(2.) Renouncing Masons are the best possible witnesses by whom to prove what Masonry really is. (a.) They are competent witnesses. They testify from their own personal knowledge of what it is. (b.) They are in the highest degree credible witnesses. First, because they testify against themselves. They confess their own wrong in having taken those terrible oaths, and in having had any part in sustaining the institution. Secondly, their testimony is given with the certainty of incurring a most unrelenting persecution. Adhering Freemasons are under oath to persecute them, to destroy their characters, and to seek to bring them to condign punishment. This we shall see when we come to examine the books. Adhering Masons have persecuted, and still persecute, those that reveal their secrets, just as far as they dare. They are in the highest degree intolerant, and this every Mason knows. In a recent number of their great Masonic organ, published in New York, they advise the Masons in Oberlin in no way to patronize those who oppose them. Those who renounce Masonry are well aware of their danger. But, not withstanding, they are constrained by their consciences, by the fear and love of God, and by regard to the interests of their country, to renounce and expose it. Now, surely, witnesses that testify under such circumstances are entitled to credit; especially as they could have had no conceivable motive for deceiving the public. Their testimony was wrung from them by conscience. And the authors of the books that I have named, together with several others — such as Richardson, Stearns, and Mr. Allyn, and I know not how many others — are sustained by the testimony of forty-five thousand who publicly renounced Masonry, out of a little more than fifty thousand that composed the whole number of Freemasons then in the United Sates. Now, it should be well remembered that the five thousand who still adhered belonged

18

almost altogether to the slaveholding States, and had peculiar reasons for still adhering to the institution of Masonry. And, further, let it be distinctly observed that, as they adhered to Masonry, their testimony is null, because they still regarded themselves as under oath in no wise to reveal their secrets; consequently, they would, of course, deny that these books had truly revealed Masonry. I say again, it is mere madness to receive their testimony.

CHAPTER IV

CREDIBILITY OF THE BOOKS REVEALING FREEMASONRY

Further observe: (3.) The credibility of these books in which Masonry is revealed is evident from the following considerations:

(a.) The murder of Morgan by Freemasons was an emphatic acknowledgment that he had revealed their secrets. For, if he had not, he had not incurred the penalty of Masonic obligations. They murdered him because he had truly revealed their secrets; and they could have had no motive whatever for murdering him if he had not done so.

(b.) The credibility of these books is further sustained by the fact that adhering Masons did then, and have always, justified the murder of Morgan as that which their oaths obliged them to do. They have said that he deserved it; and that he had taken upon him the obligation consenting to suffer the penalty if he violated it. In the two small volumes published by Elder Stearns, letters will be found from the most respectable and reliable Christian men, that fully sustain this statement, that the adhering fraternity, with very few exceptions, at that time, justified the murder of Morgan. In thus justifying that murder they, of course, admit that he violated his oath, and had truly published Freemasonry. I would quote these testimonies; but, as they can be read from the books themselves, I will not cumber those pages by copying them.

(c.) The credibility of these books is sustained by the express testimony of the seceding Masons, who, after hearing them read, ordered them printed.

(d.) The testimony of these books is further sustained by the report of a committee appointed at that time by the legislature of Rhode Island. That body appointed a committee, and gave them authority to arrest and examine Freemasons to ascertain whether the oaths published in these books were truly the oaths of Freemasons. This committee succeeded in bringing before them men that had taken the first ten degrees of Freemasonry. They put them on oath under the pains and penalties of perjury. In these circumstances they did not dare to deny it; but owned to the committee that they were the oaths taken by Freemasons. I said that they did not dare to deny it, because they were well aware that of seceding Masons hundreds and thousands might be obtained who would confront them and prove them guilty of perjury if they denied it.

I should have said that these Masons that were arrested, and that testified before this committee, were not seceding, but adhering, Masons. So that here for the first ten degrees of Freemasonry we have the admission on oath of adhering Masons that these books truly published their oaths. These facts may be learned from the records of the legislature, or from John Quincy Adams' letters to Mr. Livingston, who was at the head of the Masonic institution in the State of New York at that time.

(e.) The credibility of these books is further sustained by the implied admission of the two thousand lodges that suspended because their secrets were revealed, and because they were ashamed any longer to be known as sustaining the institution. These lodges, as I have before said, contained some forty-five thousand members. Now it should be particularly noted that, of all the seceding Masons in the United States, not one of them has ever, to my knowledge, denied that these books had truly revealed Masonry; while it is true that the five thousand who did not secede would never acknowledge that these books were credible. A worthy minister, who used to reside in this place, who has himself taken a great many degrees in Masonry, wrote to one of our citizens, a few months since, denouncing the institution in strong terms. He is a man who has traveled much among Freemasons for many years in various parts of the United States; and in that letter he affirmed that he had never known but one adhering Mason who would not deny, to those who did not know better, that those books had truly revealed Masonry. This is what might be expected.

(f.) The credibility of these books is further sustained by the published individual testimony of a great many men of unquestionable veracity — men standing high in the Christian ministry, and in church and state.

The books to which I have alluded contain very much of this kind of testimony.

But to all this testimony adhering Masons have objected. First, that the movement against Freemasonry was a political one. Answer: I have already said that by its having seized upon all the civil offices, and totally obstructing the course of justice, it was forced into politics by Masons themselves.

It was found that there was no other way than for the people to rise up and take the offices out of their hands by political action. At first there was no thought on the part of any one, so far as I could learn, that it would ever become a political question. But it was soon found that there was no other alternative.

But, again, it is said, Why should we receive the testimony of those men who have passed away, rather than the testimony of the living, thousands of whom now affirm that those books did not truly reveal Masonry?

To this I answer that these men are every one of them sworn to lie about it expressly, or virtually. Observe, they must conceal as well as never reveal these secrets; therefore, as refusing to deny would be regarded as a virtual admission, they are sworn to make an impression amounting, morally, to a denial. At a recent conference of ministers and delegates from churches, a report was read by a committee previously appointed for that purpose, representing the true character of Freemasonry. I was not present, but am informed, by unquestionable authority, that after the report was read, a minister who was a Freemason represented the report as setting up a "man of straw" thereby intending to make the impression that the report was not true. But it was replied that the report may have exhibited "a man of straw," for such Freemasonry may be, but he was asked, is not the report true? To this question he refused to answer. Was this Chris-tian honesty? At recess another minister, also a Freemason, in conversation spoke of the report as trash, but on being pressed with the question, "Is it not true?" he refused to answer. These cases illustrate their manner of disposing of this question. Many of them dare not expressly deny the truthfulness of those revelations, but they will so express themselves as to amount to a denial. They have numerous methods of doing this. They intend to deceive, manifestly for selfish reasons, and are therefore guilty of lying, and so they will find it held at the solemn judgment. If they adhere to their oaths, they are sworn to deny that these books truly reveal Masonry; and, therefore, their testimony is not to be received at all. But thousands of the seceding Masons still survive, and universally adhere to their testimony that those books did truly reveal Masonry.

But it is said that Masonry is reformed, and is not now what it was at that time.

Answer: First, this, then, is a virtual acknowledgment that at that time it was truly revealed. This is contradicting themselves. As long as they can, they deny that these books truly reveal it. But when forty-five thousand witnesses are summoned, among whom are a great many of the most valuable citizens of the United States, insomuch that they can have no face to deny that Masonry was revealed, as it then was, then we are told, "Oh! it is reformed; it is not what it was."

But, again, if they have reformed, the burden of proof is upon them. It is for them to show whether they have reformed out of it those things that rendered it so odious in a moral point of view, and so dangerous in a political point of view, as those books revealed it to be.

Again, their authorities do not pretend that it has been reformed. Their most recently published books take exactly the opposite ground, claiming that it is one and identical with what it was in the beginning; and that it neither has been nor can be changed in any of its essential principles or usages. They expressly require of their candidates to conform to all the ancient principles and usages of the institution. In another number I shall endeavor to set this question of reform at rest. It were premature to do so before we have examined the books in which it is revealed.

I might sustain these assertions by copious extracts from their works, if it would not too much encumber this article. Let those who wish to know, get their books, and read them for themselves. If anything can be established by human testimony, it is forever beyond a doubt that Mr. Morgan, Elder Bernard, Mr. Richardson, and others that published Masonry, have published it substantially as it was and is.

I have already said that their secrets are never written by themselves. All their secrets are communicated orally. They take a great deal of pains to secure entire uniformity in regard to every work and sentiment which they teach. Each State has its lecturers, who go from lodge to lodge to teach and secure a uniformity as nearly perfect as possible.

And then there is a United States lecturer, who goes from State to State, to see that the grand lodges are all consistent with each other.

In spite, however, of all this painstaking and expense, slight verbal differences will exist among them. But these differences are only in words. The ideas are retained; but in some few instances they are expressed by different words, as we shall see when we come to examine the books themselves.

The fact is, that the great mass of young men who have joined them have been grossly deceived. Having been imposed upon, as I was imposed upon, they have been made to believe that the institution is a very different matter from what it really is.

We shall see hereafter how this imposition could be practiced upon them, and how it has been practiced upon them.

FREEMASONRY

I would not be understood as denouncing the individuals composing the whole fraternity; for I am perfectly well persuaded that the great mass of young men who belong to the institution are laboring under a great delusion in regard to its real object, character, and tendency.

Lastly, it is inquired why we go to the enemies of Freemasonry for a knowledge of what it is, instead of getting our information from its friends. "Why not," they say, "allow us to speak for ourselves! We know what it is, and we can inform the public what it is; and why should you go to our enemies?" But what do Freemasons mean by asking such questions? Do they consider us idiots? Do they want to insult our intelligence by asking us why we don't get their secrets from themselves? Of course, as they well know, we cannot learn what the secrets of Masonry are from its friends and adherents, because they are under oath to give us no information about them. We are, therefore, under the necessity, if we would know what it is, of taking the testimony of those who know what it is by having taken its degrees, and have, from conscientious motives, renounced the institution. If they are its enemies, it is only in the sense that they regard the institution as not only unworthy of patronage, but as so wicked in a moral point of view, and so dangerous in a political point of view, that they feel constrained to reveal its secrets, and publicly to renounce it. These are the only men from whom we can possibly get any information of what Freemasonry is. It is absurd for adhering Masons to ask us why we do not allow them to teach us what it is; for we know, and they know, that they can do no such thing without violating their oaths and these oaths they still acknowledge to be binding upon them. Under this head I take the liberty to subjoin—

1. The testimony of the *Albany Evening Journal Extra*, of October 27, 1831. This article, as its date demonstrates, was written at the time of the investigation of the Morgan murder, and refers to facts too notorious to be denied:

Since the public attention in this quarter has been roused by recent events to the practical evils of Freemasonry, numerous inquiries are made for the means of information respecting the ridiculous ceremonies, the unlawful oaths, the dangerous obligations, and the blasphemous mockeries of this order. Although these have been from year to year, for the last five years, spread before the public, yet as our citizens here were indifferent to the subject, they avoided reading what was so profusely laid before them; and the consequence is, that now, when they begin to feel and think on this momentous matter, they find themselves in want of the information necessary to enable them to understand it. It shall be my purpose to supply the deficiency to some extent by pointing out the sources of full and extensive knowledge, and by presenting as briefly as possible, the prominent features in the character of Freemasonry. It has become a question of such engrossing interest, that every man should desire to be informed, and every citizen who is called upon to act in reference to it in his capacity as AN ELECTOR, is bound by the highest duties of patriotism to act understandingly.

The first revelation of Masonry in this country was made by William Morgan. In 1826, he published a pamphlet, entitled "Illustrations in Masonry," in which the ceremonies of initiation and the obligations of the three first degrees were disclosed. For this publication he was kidnapped and forcibly carried away from a wife and two children, and was murdered by being drowned in the Niagara River. This was done by Freemasons. Thus he has sealed the truth of his revelations by sacrificing his own life, and the Freemasons established their accuracy incontrovertibly by the punishment they inflicted on him. For according to their own

27

bloody code, he could not have incurred the penalty of death, if he had not revealed their secrets. In February, 1828, a convention of seceding masons was held at Le Roy, in the County of Genesee, composed of some thirty or forty of the most respectable citizens. They published a declaration to the world under their signatures, in which they declared the revelations of William Morgan to be strictly true and perfectly accurate. Under the same responsibility they also published the oaths and obligations of the higher orders. In the course of the same year, Elder Bernard, a Baptist clergyman of good character, and who was a distinguished Mason, published a work, entitled "Light on Masonry," in which the ceremonies, oaths and mummeries of the order are given at full length. In 1829, on the trial of Elihu Mather, in Orleans County, the obligations of the three first degrees and of a Royal Arch Mason, were proved, at a Circuit Court held by Judge Gardiner, by the testimony of three seceding Masons and one adhering Mason. In obedience to a resolution of the Senate of New York, Judge Gardiner reported this evidence, and it was printed by order of the Senate. In 1830, on a trial in Rhode Island, the same obligations were proved in open court, and the trial was published at large in the newspapers. In 1831, on the trial of H. C. Witherell, at New Berlin, in Chenango County, the same obligations were proved by the oaths of three adhering Masons, among whom was General Welch, the sheriff of the county. In the year 1830 Avery Allyn, a regular Knight Templar, published a book, called the "Ritual of Freemasonry," in which the ceremonies of initiation, the lectures, oaths and mummeries of thirty-one degrees are fully exhibited. Thousands of Masons individually have, under their names in the public papers, declared these publications of Bernard and Allyn to be strictly accurate. These books may be found in our bookstores.

2. I next subjoin a tract, made up of "The Petition to the Legislature of Connecticut" against extra-judicial oaths, with an abstract of the evidence, and the report of the Committee to whom the subject was referred. Published in 1834:

> *To the Honorable General Assembly of the State of Connecticut, to be holden at Hartford, on the first Wednesday of May,* A.D. *1833:*
> The Petitioners, inhabitants of said State, respectfully request the attention of your Honorable body to the expediency of some legal provision to prevent the administration of oaths in all cases not authorized by law. It may justly be required of the Petitioners, before a compliance can be expected with this request, that a case should be made out requiring such Legislative provision; and your Petitioners confidently trust that satisfactory grounds for this application will be found to exist in the oaths which are administered in Masonic Lodges.
> The disclosures which have been recently made by the seceding Masons of the secret proceedings of those Lodges fully prove that the Institution of Freemasonry consists of numerous degrees which may be increased to an unlimited extent, and that an oath of an extraordinary character is administered at the entrance of every degree. Your Petitioners would not trespass upon the principles of decorum by an unnecessary recital of all these horrid imprecations, but justice to the cause they have espoused compels them to exhibit the following specimens, which are selected from the oaths administered in the different degrees: The Entered Apprentice Mason swears, "I will always

hail, ever conceal, and never reveal any part or parts, art or arts, point or points of the secrets, arts, and mysteries of Ancient Freemasonry which I have received, am about to receive, or may hereafter be instructed in;" "without the least equivocation, mental reservation, or self-evasion of mind in me whatever, binding myself under no less penalty than to have my throat cut across, my tongue torn out by the roots, and my body buried in the rough sands of the sea." The Master Mason swears, "I will obey all regular signs, summonses, or tokens, given, handed, sent, or thrown to me from the hand of a brother Master Mason;" "a Master Mason's secrets, given to me in charge as such, and I knowing them to be such, shall remain as secure and inviolable in my breast as in his own, when communicated to me, murder and treason excepted, and they left to my own election." The Royal Arch Mason swears, "I will aid and assist a companion Royal Arch Mason when engaged in any difficulty; and espouse his cause so far as to extricate him from the same, if in my power, whether he be right or wrong." "A Companion Royal Arch Mason's secrets, given me in charge as such, and I knowing them to be such, shall remain as secure and inviolable in my breast as in his own, without exception." The following obligations are contained in the oath of the Holy Thrice Illustrious order of the Cross, Knights, or Kadosh, etc.: "I swear to put confidence unlimited in every illustrious brother of the Cross as a true and worthy follower of the blessed Jesus;" "I swear to look on his enemies as my enemies, his friends as my friends, and to stand forth to mete out tender kindness or vengeance accordingly." "I solemnly swear, in the presence of Almighty God, that I will revenge the assassination of our worthy Master Hiram Abiff, not only on his murderers, but also on all who may betray the secrets of this degree." "I swear to take revenge on the traitors of Masonry."

It can not be necessary for your Petitioners to enter upon a formal argument in order to satisfy this enlightened Assembly that oaths like the foregoing ought not to be administered. The guarded and redundant language in which they are expressed, and the barbarous and abhorrent penalties annexed to them, were evidently designed to impose upon the mind of the candidate the necessity of entire and universal obedience to their requirements. They purport to be the injunctions of supreme power, and claim supremacy over every obligation, human or divine. In this light they were regarded and acted upon by Masons of high standing and character who were concerned in the last Masonic murder committed in the State of New York, or connected with the trials which sprang from it, and in this construction these Masons were justified and upheld by the Grand Chapter and Grand Lodge of that State. Such obligations are obviously inconsistent with our allegiance to the State, and the obedience which is required by our Maker, and with those fundamental principles which constitute the basis and the cement of civil and of religious communities. The Masonic oaths lead directly to the sacrifice of duties and the commission of crimes; they cherish a feeling of selfishness and of savage revenge, instead of the spirit of the Gospel, and are the ground-work of an insidious attempt to effect the entire overthrow of our holy religion.

It is for these reasons that your Petitioners respectfully request your Honors, by a suitable legal provision, to prohibit the administration of oaths not authorized by law; and they, as in duty bound, will ever pray.

FREEMASONRY

The foregoing was the petition of about fourteen hundred citizens of the State of Connecticut, and was presented to the Legislature at their session in May, 1833. By the House of Representatives it was referred to a select committee, who, having given notice of the time and place of their meeting, entered into an investigation of the subject. The sittings of the committee were open to the public, and every person who wished to hear the proceedings could attend, if he chose. Three witnesses were presented by the Petitioners, viz.: Mr. Hanks, of New York, and Messrs. Welch and Hatch, of this State, by whom they expected to substantiate the facts as set forth in the petition. In giving his testimony, Mr. Hanks read the several oaths, etc., as published in Allyn's Ritual, beginning with that of the Entered Apprentice, and pointing out, as he proceeded, any discrepancies or variations which he had practiced or known. He had taken, administered, or seen administered, the oaths, etc., in four different States of the Union viz,: New York, Pennsylvania, Virginia, and Ohio — had taken, himself, many degrees and testified from personal knowledge. The testimony of Mr. Hanks was full, explicit, and particular on the first seven degrees of Masonry, and his statements were supported by those of Messrs. Welch and Hatch, as far as their experience extended.

Among the facts proved by the testimony were the following, viz.: that Freemasonry, with its oaths and penalties, is substantially the same everywhere — that the variations are slight, and, in most instances, merely verbal, and such as have resulted from unwritten or traditionary communication — that the oaths and penalties of the first seven degrees are revealed to the world and correctly published by Mr. Allyn in his Ritual, and by others — that they are so administered in the lodges, and are to be understood according to the plain, literal import of the terms in which they are expressed, and as they have been explained by seceding Masons generally — that the declaration of the Massachusetts and Connecticut adhering

Masons can not be made, or signed understandingly, in consistence with truth — that in the Royal Arch oath the terms "murder and treason not excepted" are sometimes used; sometimes the expression "in all cases whatsoever," or "in all cases without exception." Some other verbal alterations were noticed, which need not be detailed here. It appeared, also, from the statements of the witnesses, that the proportion of funds disposed of for charitable purposes is extremely small, while the lodges are scenes of extravagant mirth and bacchanalian revelry, and the admission, passing, and raising of candidates occasions of much indecent spout and ridiculous merriment, accompanied with mock murders, feigned discoveries, and profane and blasphemous ceremonies and representations.

From the evidence before them the committee came to the conclusions expressed in the following.

REPORT
To the Honorable General Assembly of the State of Connecticut now in Session:

The committee to whom was referred the petition of Gaius Lyman and others beg leave respectfully to report that we have had the same under consideration, and inquired, by legal evidence, into the truth of the matters therein set forth, and are of the opinion that the same have been substantially proved, and are true. The committee, at the commencement of the investigation, adopted the rule, and made known the same to the petitioners, that we should attend to no evidence except such as, in our opinion, would be admissible in a court of law. The petitioners accordingly summoned before us sundry witnesses who, for aught we knew or could discover to the contrary, were men of respectability and intelligence, and upon their testimony, and upon *that alone*, have we come to our present result. It was proved by these witnesses that oaths similar in character (and some of them identical in phraseology) to those set forth in the petition had been, in their presence and within their hearing, repeatedly administered in this State. The committee believe the administration of such oaths to be highly improper, and that the same should be prohibited by legal enactment. Our reasons for this opinion are:

1. Because they are unauthorized by law.

2. Because they bind the person to whom they are administered to disregard and violate the law.

3. Because they are, in their natural tendency, subversive of public morals and blasphemous.

4. Because the penalties attached to the breach of them are such as are entirely unknown to our law, and are forbidden both by the Constitution of the United States and by the Constitution of this State.

First, then, these oaths are not authorized by law. In our code of statute law we have an act which points out the cases in which oaths shall or may be administered, and prescribes their several forms. In this act we find no such oaths. Indeed, we find, upon examination of this code, that although extra judicial oaths are nowhere expressly prohibited, their unlawfulness is throughout clearly implied. And the implication is no less clear, that no persons, except those expressly authorized by law, may rightfully administer oaths. The committee would barely refer to a number of those acts in which particular persons are, on particular occasions and for particular purposes, authorized to administer oaths. In the act relative to insolvency, the commissioners are expressly authorized to administer an oath to the insolvent debtor. In the act relative to surveyors, the surveyors are authorized to administer an oath to the chairmen. In the act relating to oaths, passed in 1822, Clerks of the Senate and House of

Representatives, and the Chairmen of Committees are, during the session of the Legislature, authorized to administer oaths. There are other acts of the same nature, to which it can not be necessary particularly to refer. The inference, as we think plainly deducible from these acts, is, that *all* persons have not the right to administer oaths and that those oaths only which the law prescribes may be lawfully administered. And we need only ask this Honorable Body whether the public sense of propriety would not be socked at witnessing in open daylight, the administration of an oath by a person not by law authorized, and in a case not by law provided for. For instance, suppose a clergyman, upon the admission of a member into his church, should require him to kneel down, place his hand upon the Bible, and then solemnly swear that he would observe all the rules and regulations of that church, upon no less penalty than to have his throat cut across, his tongue torn out by the roots, and his body buried in the rough sands of the sea; would not an involuntary shudder pervade the whole community at such a horrid exhibition; and would not our first impression be that this clergyman had violated the law, and that he ought forthwith to be prosecuted? And yet we may search our statue book in vain for any penal enactment that would reach this case. Again, suppose that any one of the charitable and benevolent societies of the present day should, on the admission of a member, compel him to swear by the ever-living God that he would obey all the laws of the society "upon no less penalty than to have his left breast torn open, his heart and vitals taken therefrom, thrown over his left shoulder, and carried into the valley of Jehoshaphat, there to become a prey to the wild beasts of the field and the vultures of the air." And, moreover, suppose

35

this oath to be administered by some one not by law authorized to administer *any* oath. We need scarcely ask whether an insulted community would not, under a sense that their laws had been wantonly trampled upon, call aloud, and with earnestness, upon the ministers of justice to punish such awful and disgusting profanity. And yet the ministers of justice could afford them no aid, inasmuch as the law has not, on this subject, clothed them with any authority.

Secondly. We object to the administration of oaths like those set forth in the petition, because they bind the person receiving them to disregard and violate the law. In one of the oaths, for instance, the person receiving it swears that he will assist a companion of a certain degree, so far as to extricate him from difficulty, whether he be right or wrong. He also swears that he will keep the secrets of a companion of a certain degree *without exception,* or as the witnesses testified they had heard it administered, "murder and treason not excepted." Now, the committee believe it to be morally wrong, as well as inconsistent with our allegiance to the government under which we live, and a direct violation of the law, to keep secret the commission of any great and flagrant offense against the government. He who conceals treason is himself guilty of misprision of treason. He who conceals murder is himself (in some cases at least) a murderer.

Thirdly. We consider the administration of extra-judicial oaths, especially such as are set forth in said petition, improper, because in their tendency they are opposed to sound morals and are blasphemous. The obligation to assist another so far as to extricate him from difficulty, whether he be right or wrong, and to conceal another's secrets, even though those secrets should involve the highest and most enormous crimes, is most assuredly opposed to the spirit of the Gospel, and to the pure system of morality therein inculcated. And to call upon the great and awful name of Jehovah to give sanction to such obligations is, in our opinion, the height of blasphemy.

Fourthly. We believe such oaths to be improper, because the penalties attached to them are such as are unknown to our law, and are opposed both to the Constitution of the United States and to the Constitution of this State. If the breach of those oaths constitute the crime of perjury, then, in our opinion, such breach should be punished as perjury in other cases is punished. By our law every person who shall commit perjury, and shall be thereof duly convicted, shall suffer imprisonment in the Connecticut State Prison not less than two nor more than five years; and this is the extent of the pains and penalties which the humanity of our law will suffer to be inflicted upon him. But to the violation of the oaths above referred to is annexed a great variety of most cruel and inhuman punishments, such are not known in the criminal codes of any civilized nation on the earth. Among them are the tearing out of the tongue, or splitting it from tip to roots — the cutting of the throat across from ear to ear — the tearing out of the heart and vitals, and exposing them to be destroyed by wild beasts and birds of prey, etc. These penalties we believe to be forbidden by the tenth article of the amendments of the Constitution of the United States, which prohibits the infliction of all cruel and unusual punishments; and by the tenth section of the first article of the Constitution of this State, which declares that "No person shall be arrested, detained, or punished, except in cases clearly warranted by law." For these and for various other reasons which must be obvious to the good sense of this Honorable Body, we are of the opinion that the prayer of the petition ought to be granted, and we would, therefore, recommend the passage of the accompanying Bill for a public Act. All of which is respectfully submitted. Signed per order,

THOMAS BACKUS, *Chairman*

3. I introduce the published renunciation of Freemasonry by Jarvis F. Hanks, of New York, 1829, and of Calvin Hatch, published 1831. Also, the published renunciation of Henry Fish, Edwin Chapman, and Bliss Welch, 1830. These are found on the cover of the tract, and are only specimens of a multitude of similar renunciations published in various books and journals.

RENUNCIATION.
To the Editor of the Anti-Masonic Beacon.

SIR: The time has come when I feel constrained, from a sense of duty to God, my neighbor, and myself, to make void my allegiance to the Masonic Institution. In thus taking leave of Freemasonry, I am not sensible of the least hostility to Masons; but act under a solemn conviction that Masonry is a wicked imposture, a refuge of lies, a substitute for the Gospel of Christ; that it is contrary to the laws of God and our country, and superior to either, in the estimation of its disciples; and lastly, that it is the most powerful and successful engine ever employed by the devil to destroy the souls of men.

I was initiated into Masonry in 1821, and have taken eighteen degrees. My motives were curiosity and the expectation of personal advantage, while, at the same time, I was dishonest enough to profess that disinterested benevolence to my fellow-men was my object. I have been intrusted with the highest offices in the gift of a Lodge and Chapter, viz.: Worshipful Master and Most Excellent High Priest, which I acknowledge, at that time, I considered very flattering distinctions. I approved of the abduction of William Morgan as a just act of Masonry, and had I been called upon to assist, should, under the opinions I then held, have felt bound to attend the summons and obey it. I remained in favor of the Institution several months after the abduction of Morgan.

I was convinced of the evil and folly of Masonry from an inquiry instituted in my own mind, which I was determined should be conducted privately, candidly, impartially, and, if possible, without prejudice. Under the scrutiny of the investigation I brought the Law of God contained in the Old and New Testaments, the laws of our country, the Masonic oaths (so many as I have taken), Masonic professions, and Masonic practice. I then resolved not to be influenced by the fear or favor of man, who can only "kill the body, and after that has no more that he can do," but by the fear of God, "who, after he hath killed, hath power to cast into hell." (Luke xii. 4,5.) I feel assured that any Mason, or any man, taking the same course, must arrive at the same conclusion.

Yours, JARVIS F. HANKS
NEW YORK, *February* 13, 1829

CALVIN HATCH'S RENUNCIATION OF FREEMASONRY
To the Church of Christ in Farmington:

BRETHREN: Impressed with a sense of duty, I would solicit your attention, while I make the following statement of facts. Soon after I arrived at the age of twenty-one years I was induced (principally from curiosity) to become a Freemason; and before I was twenty-two, I advanced to the third, and soon after to the fourth degree of the then *hidden mysteries* of that Institution, and remained a tolerably regular attendant upon its stated meetings, until February, 1819; since which I have never attended any of its meetings, though often requested.

Hoodwinked to the principles of the Institution, I felt that, as a professed follower of the Lord Jesus Christ, it was not profitable to spend my time in the lodge-room.

Another fact I wish to notice; that for three years I was accustomed to hear prayers offered at the lodge by a man who was considered an infidel; which, to my mind, was utterly revolting.

Within about a year my attention has been particularly called to this subject. At first, I felt that the Institution could not be bad, except by being in the hands of bad men. I satisfied myself that my withdrawment from the lodge, while Masonry was in good repute, spoke a language which could not be misunderstood; and still, I confess I felt some veneration for the Institution, on account of its beneficence in relieving its afflicted members.

Early last spring I became satisfied that one of our citizens had fallen a sacrifice to Masonic vengeance; yet, whether the Institution could be charged with it, was with me a question. I found that it was thus charged by those opposed to the Institution, and I hastily and rashly resolved to read no more upon the subject, because I considered the charge unjust. In the course of the last summer I had many misgivings for this decision, which closed every avenue to information. Knowing that many of my Christian brethren were grieved that any professor of the religion of Christ should remain even a nominal member of a society, the principles of which they believed were anti-Christian, and opposed to the best interests of our country.

Feeling that some deference was due to their judgment, I, early in the fall, with prayerfulness, divesting myself of all prejudice, took up the subject for investigating the principles, and sought information through the press, and soon became satisfied that I had a duty to perform which I had long neglected; and in December last, without consulting anyone, came to the conclusion that nothing short of absolving myself from all connection with the Masonic Fraternity, and from all its obligations, would be answerable to my duty as a citizen and a member of the church of Christ. Since that time I have read the proceedings of the United States Anti-Masonic Convention, disclosing facts before unknown to me, and am of the opinion that it is the bounden duty of every professor of religion who feels bound in the least by Masonic obligations to read the doings of that convention, with prayerfulness and without prejudice, before he decides upon the path of duty.

I feel that some acknowledgments are due from me to those brethren who have been grieved by my dilatoriness upon a subject to plain and a duty so clear. And if I have thus offended any of my brethren, I pray them to forgive; and however great my sin has been, I trust I have forgiveness of my God.

I can not dismiss the subject without beseeching my Christian brethren who remain as I have done, to examine and decide, as in the presence of God, without delay; for what we do must be done quickly.

CALVIN HATCH
FARMINGTON, *February* 3, 1831

———

COPY OF MY RENUNCIATION SENT BY MAIL
TO NEW MILFORD, FEBRUARY 3, 1831
To the Officers of St. Peter's Lodge,
New Milford, State of Connecticut:
Gentlemen: For more than twenty years I have been a member of your lodge; and now, from a conviction that it is my duty as a citizen and a professed follower of our blessed Savior no longer to remain, even as I

41

have been for the last twelve years, a nominal member of a society whose principles are opposed to the best interests of our country, and whose rites are, many of them, not only immoral, but a profanation of Scripture, and, consequently opposed to the religion of the Gospel, I do therefore, absolve myself from all its obligations whatever.

CALVIN HATCH
FARMINGTON, *December* 25, 1830

––––––

RENUNCIATION

Having been initiated some years since in the mysteries of Freemasonry, but without finding any of those advantages which were so bountifully promised by the Fraternity, and now being fully convinced that the Institution is corrupt to the very core, and used to promote ends tending to subvert our free institutions, we deem it our duty publicly to renounce all obligations to the "Craft,' believing ourselves to be freed from its oaths, inasmuch as no man can bind himself to do anything contrary to the allegiance he owes to his country, or the duties he owes to his Maker.

HENRY FISH, Salisbury, Master Mason
EDWIN CHAPMAN, Windsor, M. Mason
BLISS WELCH, Chatham, Royal Arch
Dated at HARTFORD, *Feb.* 4, 1830

CHAPTER V

EXAMINATION OF THE BOOKS
REVEALING FREEMASONRY

Having established the fact that Bernard in his "Light on Masonry," William Morgan, Allyn, Richardson, and others, all of whom substantially agree, have truly revealed Freemasonry as it was at that time, I will now enter upon an examination of some of these books, assuming as I must, or abandon all idea that any thing can ever be proved by human testimony, that they contain a veritable revelation of Freemasonry.

After I have examined these books, and learned and shown what Freemasonry was at their date, I shall consider the question of its having undergone any material change since that date, and also whether it can be so changed as to be an innocent institution and still retain the distinguishing characteristics of Freemasonry.

That I may do no injustice to any one, I shall not hold Masons responsible for oaths and degrees which are above and beyond them and which they have not taken and of which they have no knowledge. The question of their moral and responsible relation to the institution, *as a whole,* will receive notice in another place. At present I shall hold Masons responsible for those oaths, principles, teachings and degrees of which they have knowledge.

In these numbers I need only to notice a few points in the oaths of Masons, and I recommend all persons to obtain the books in which their oaths, ceremonies, and secrets are fully revealed. The first of their oaths is that of an Entered Apprentice. These oaths are administered in the following manner: The candidate stands on his knees, with his hands on the Holy Bible. The Worshipful Master pronounces the oath in short sentences, and the candidate repeats after him. The oath of the Entered Apprentice is as follows: "I, A.B., of my own free will and accord, in presence of Almighty God and this worshipful lodge of Free and Accepted Masons, dedicated to God and held forth to the holy order to St. John, do hereby and hereon most sincerely promise and swear, that I will always hail, ever conceal, and never reveal any part or parts, art or arts, point or points of the secrets, arts, and mysteries of ancient Freemasonry, which I have received, am about to receive, or may hereafter be instructed in, to any person or persons in the known world, except it be a true and lawful brother Mason, or within the body of a just and lawfully constituted lodge of such; and not unto him or unto them whom I shall hear so to be, but unto him and them only whom I shall find so to be after strict trial and due examination, or lawful information.

"Furthermore, do I promise and swear, that I will not write, print, stamp, stain, hew, cut, carve, indent, paint, or engrave it on anything movable or immovable under the whole canopy of Heaven, whereby or whereon the least letter, figure, character, mark, stain, shadow, or resemblance may become legible or intelligible to myself or to any other person in the known world, whereby the secrets of Masonry may be unlawfully obtained through my unworthiness. To all of which I do most solemnly and sincerely promise and swear, without the least equivocation, mental reservation, or self-evasion of mind in me whatever; binding myself under no less penalty than to have my throat cut across, my tongue torn out by the roots, and my body buried in the rough sands of the sea at low-water mark, where the tide ebbs and flows twice in twenty-four hours. So help me God, and keep me steadfast in the due performance of the same."—*Light on Masonry, 8th edition, page 27.*

Upon this oath I remark:

1. That the administration and taking of it are in direct violation of both the law and gospel of God. Jesus prohibits the taking of oaths. Mat. V. 34. "But I say unto you swear not at all." It is generally conceded that He intended only to forbid

the taking of extra judicial oaths. That He did formally and positively forbid the taking, and of course the administering of all oaths not regularly administered for judicial and governmental purposes, is, I believe, universally admitted. Here then we find that in the first step in Freemasonry the express command of Christ is set at naught.

2. The administration and taking of this oath is a taking of the name of God in vain and is therefore an awful profanity. Exod. xx:7: "Thou shalt not take the name of the Lord thy God in vain: for the Lord will not hold him guiltless that taketh his name in vain." Professing Christian Freemasons, do you hear and remember this, and are you aware that in taking or administering this oath you take the name of God in vain and that He will not hold you guiltless? Do you also remember that whenever you are present aiding, abetting, and consenting to the administering, and taking of this or any other Masonic oath you are guilty of violating the express command of Christ above quoted, and also the express prohibition of the lawgiver at Sinai? And yet you can see nothing unchristian in Freemasonry.

3. This oath pledges the candidate to keep whatever secrets they may communicate to him. But, for aught he knows, it may be unlawful to keep them. This oath is a snare to his soul. It must be wicked to thus commit himself on oath. The spirit of God's word forbids it.

4. The administrator of this oath had just assured the candidate that there was nothing in it inconsistent with his duty to God or to man. How is it, professed Christian, that you did not remember that you had no right to take an oath at all under such circumstances and for such reasons. Why did you not inquire of the Master by what authority he was about to administer an oath, and by what authority he expected and required you to take it? Why did you not ask him if God would hold him guiltless if he administered an oath in His name, and you guiltless if you took the oath. And when you have

seen this or any other Masonic oath administered why have you not rebuked the violation of God's law and left the lodge?

5. Why did the Master assure the candidate that there was nothing in the oath contrary to his obligations to God or man, and then instantly proceed to violate the laws of both God and man and to require of the candidate the same violation of law, human and divine?

6. The penalty for violating this oath is monstrous, barbarous, savage, and is utterly repugnant to all laws of morality, religion or decency. Binding myself "under no less a penalty than to have my throat cut across, my tongue torn out by the roots, and my body buried in the sands of the sea at low-water mark, etc." Now, has any man a right to incur such a penalty as this?

I say again: such a penalty is savage, barbarous, unchristian, inhuman, abominable. It should be here remarked that in this oath is really found the virus of all that follows in Freemasonry. The candidate is sworn to keep secret everything that is to be revealed to him in Freemasonry of which as yet he knows absolutely nothing. This is frequently repeated in the obligations that follow.

It will be observed that the candidate says, "to all of which I do solemnly and sincerely promise and swear, without the least equivocation, mental reservation, or self-evasion of mind in me, whatever." Richardson, who published the Freemason's Monitor in 1860, on the 4th page of his preface, says of Masonry: "The oaths and obligations were then undoubtedly binding (that is when Freemasonry was first established), not only for the protection of the members but for the preservation of the very imperfect arts and sciences of that period. To suppose the oaths mean anything now is simply absurd." What! How is this compatible with what is said in this first oath of Masonry, and hence binding through every degree of Masonry. "ALL THIS, I MOST SOLEMNLY AND SINCERELY PROMISE AND SWEAR, WITHOUT THE LEAST EQUIVOCATION, MENTAL RESERVATION, OR SELF-EVASION OF MIND IN ME

WHATEVER." Any now we are told by one of the highest Masonic authorities, that, to suppose that Masonic oaths mean anything in these days, is simply absurd. THEN, SURELY THEY ARE BLASPHEMY.

CR80

CHAPTER VI

MASTER'S DEGREE

I pass over the second degree of Masonry, the oath of which, in substance is similar to that in the first, and in this number will consider the oath, or obligation of a Master Mason. I do not notice the ridiculous manner in which the candidate for the different degrees, is dressed and conducted into the lodge. The scenes through which they pass, are most humiliating and ridiculous, and cannot fail to be so regarded by all who will read the books in which they are described. I quote from the eighth edition of "Light on Masonry," by Elder David Bernard, published by W.J. Shuey, Dayton, Ohio. The obligation of the Master's degree will be found on the seventy-third and seventy-fourth pages of this work, and is as follows: "I, A.B., of my own free will and accord, in the presence of Almighty God, and this worshipful Lodge of Master Masons, erected to God, and dedicated to the holy order of St. John, do hereby and hereon, most solemnly and sincerely promise and swear, in addition to my former obligations, that I will not give the degree of Master Mason to any one of an inferior degree, nor to any one in the known world, except it be to a true and lawful brother or brethren Master Mason, or within the body of a just and lawfully constituted lodge of such; and not unto him nor unto them whom I shall hear so to be, but unto him and them only whom I shall find so to be, after strict trial and due examination, or lawful information received. Furthermore, do I promise and swear, that I will not give the Master's word which I shall hereafter receive neither in the lodge nor out of it, except it be on the five points of fellowship, and then not above my breath. Furthermore, do I promise and swear, that I will not give the grand hailing sign of distress, except I am in real distress, or for the benefit of the craft when at work; or should I ever see that sign given, or hear the word accompany-

49

ing it and the person who gave it, appearing to be in distress, I will fly to his relief at the risk of my life, should there be a greater probability of saving his life than of losing my own. Furthermore, do I promise and swear that I will not wrong this lodge, nor a brother of this degree, to the value of one cent knowingly, myself, nor suffer it to be done by others, if in my power to prevent. Furthermore, do I promise and swear, that I will not be at the initiating, passing, and raising, a candidate at one communication, without a regular dispensation from the Grand Lodge for the same. Furthermore, do I promise and swear, that I will not be at the initiating, passing, or raising a candidate in a clandestine lodge, I knowing it to be such. Furthermore, do I promise and swear, that I will not be at the initiating of an old man in dotage, a young man in nonage, an atheist, irreligious libertine, idiot, madman, hermaphrodite, nor woman. Furthermore, do I promise and swear, that I will not speak evil of a brother Master Mason, neither behind his back, nor before his face, but will apprise him of all approaching danger if in my power. Furthermore, do I promise and swear, that I will not violate the chastity of a Master Mason's wife, mother, sister, or daughter, I knowing them to be such, nor suffer it to be done by others, if in my power to prevent it. Furthermore, do I promise and swear, that I will support the constitution of the Grand Lodge of the State of _____, under which this lodge is held, and conform to all the by-laws, rules and regulations of this, or any other lodge, of which I may at any time hereafter become a member. Furthermore, do I promise and swear, that I will obey all regular signs, summons, or tokens, given, handed, sent, or thrown to me, from the hand of another brother Master Mason, or from the body of a just and lawfully constituted lodge of such, provided it be within the length of my cable tow. Furthermore, do I promise and swear, that a Master Mason's secrets, given to me in charge as such, and I knowing them to be such, shall remain as secure and inviolable in my breast as in his own, murder and treason excepted, and they left to my own election. Furthermore, do I promise and swear, that I will go on a Master Mason's errand whenever required, even should I have to go barefoot and bareheaded, if within the length of my cable tow. Furthermore, do I promise and swear, that I will always remember a brother Master Mason when on my knees, offering up my devotions to Almighty God. Furthermore, do I promise and swear, that I will be aiding and assisting all poor, indigent Master Masons, their wives and orphans, wheresoever disposed around the globe, as far as in my power without injuring myself or family materially. Furthermore, do I promise and swear, that if any part of this solemn oath or obligation be omitted at this time that I will hold myself amenable thereto, whenever informed. To all which I do most solemnly promise and swear, with a fixed and steady purpose of mind in me, to keep and perform the same, binding myself under no less penalty than to have my body severed in two in the midst, and divided to the north and south, my bowels burnt to ashes in the center and the ashes scattered before the four winds of heaven, that there might not the least track or trace of remembrance remain among men and Masons of so vile and perjured a wretch as I should be, were I ever to prove willfully guilty of violating any part of this my solemn oath or obligation on a Master Mason. So help me God, and keep me steadfast in the due performance of the same."

1. The first sentence is both profane and false. The Master instructs the kneeling candidate with his hand on God's Holy Word to affirm, and the candidate does affirm that the lodge in which he is kneeling is erected to God and dedicated to the holy order of St. John. Remember this is said in and of every Master Masons' lodge. But is this true? No, indeed it is mere mockery. The words are a mere profane form. Does not every Freemason know this?

2. This, and all the following oaths of Masonry, are administered and taken as additions to all the previous oaths

51

which the candidate has taken. (See the oath.) All that is wicked and profane in the former oaths is indorsed (sic) and reaffirmed in this and in every succeeding oath. Thus Freemasons proceed to pile oath upon oath in a manner most shocking and revolting. And is this a Christian institution? Is this obedience to Him who as said "swear not at all?"

3. The grand hailing sign of distress mentioned in this oath, consists in raising both hands to heaven in the attitude of supplication. The words accompanying this sign are, *"O Lord, my God, is there no help for the widow's son?"* The candidate is told by the Master that this attitude was taken and these words were used by Solomon when he was informed of the murder of Hiram Abiff. Of this, "Light on Masonry" will give the reader full information. This whole story of the murder of Hiram Abiff is a profane falsehood, as I shall more fully show in another place. Hiram Abiff was never murdered. Solomon never gave any such sign, or uttered any such words. The whole story is false; both the grand hailing sign of distress, and the accompanying words, are a profane mockery, and an insult to God. But what is the thing promised in this part of a Master Mason's oath? Observe, the candidate swears, "should I ever see that sign given, or hear the word accompanying it, and the person who gave it, appearing to be in distress, I will fly to his relief at the risk of my life, should there be a greater probability of saving his life than of losing my own." Observe, it matters not what is the cause of the distress in which a Master Mason may be — if he has committed a crime, and is likely to be arrested, or has been arrested; if he is imprisoned, or likely to be imprisoned; if he is on trial in a court of justice and likely to be convicted, and a Master Mason is on the bench as a judge, or on the jury or called as a witness; or is a Master Mason a sheriff and has the prisoner in custody; or is he a constable, having charge of the jury to whom the case is to be submitted; or is he a prosecuting attorney, appointed by the government to prosecute him for his crime, and secure his conviction — in

any of these cases, the prisoner giving the grand hailing sign of distress, binds, by a most solemn oath, the judge, jurymen, sheriff, constable, witness, attorney, if a Master Mason, to seek to release him, at the hazard of his life. All who are acquainted with the practical results of this section of the Master's oath, as they appeared in the investigations connected with the murder of William Morgan, are aware that the Master Masons kept this oath inviolate, when efforts were made to convict the kidnappers and murderers, insomuch that it was found impossible to execute the laws. Cases are reported as having repeatedly occurred in the administration of justice, where this hailing sign of distress has prevailed to rescue the guilty from the hand of justice. In another part of this oath, you will observe, the candidate swears, that he will apprise a brother Master Mason of approaching danger, if within his power. This binds a Master Mason to give a criminal notice, if he understands that he is about to be arrested. If the sheriff has a writ for the arrest of a brother Master Mason, this oath lays him under an obligation not to arrest him, but to give him notice, that if he does not keep out of the way, he shall be obliged to arrest him. If the magistrate who issued the writ is a Master Mason, his oath obliges him to give the criminal Master Mason warning, so that he may evade the execution of the writ. Reader, get and read the pamphlet published by Judge Whitney, of Belvidere, Illinois. It can be had, I believe, at the bookstores in this town. This pamphlet will give you an account of the trial of Judge Whitney, who was Master of a lodge, before the Grand Lodge of Illinois. It will show you how completely this oath may prevail to obstruct the whole course of justice, and render the execution of the law impossible. If a Master Mason is suspected of a crime, and his case comes before a justice of the peace who is a Master Mason, or before a grand jury upon which there is a Master Mason, or before a court or petit jury in which are Master Masons, if they keep inviolate their oath, it is impossible to reach the execution of the law. Furthermore, if there be

FREEMASONRY

Master Masons in the community, who hear of the guilt and danger of a brother Master Mason, they are sworn to give him warning. It is no doubt for this reason, that masons try to secure amongst themselves all the offices connected with the administration of justice. At the time of the murder of Morgan, it was found that to such an extent were these offices in the hands of Freemasons that the courts were entirely impotent. I quote the following from "Stearns' Letters on Freemasonry," page 127: "In speaking of the murder of William Morgan, of the justice of it, and of the impossibility of punishing his murderers, a justice of the peace in Middlebury, a sober, respectable man, and a Mason, said, 'that a man had a right to pledge his life,' and then observed: 'What can you do? What can a rat do with a lion? Why are you judged? who are your sheriffs? and who will be your jurymen?'" It is perfectly plain that if Freemasons mean anything by this oath, as they have given frequent evidence that they do, this obligation must be an effectual bar to the administration of justice wherever Freemasons are numerous. No wonder, therefore, that dishonest men among them are very anxious greatly to multiply their numbers. In the days of William Morgan, they had so multiplied their numbers that it was found impossible, and in these days Freemasons have become so numerous, that in many places it will be found impossible to execute the criminal laws. Even in commercial transactions where Freemasons are parties to a suit, it will be found impossible to secure the ends of justice. Let not Freemasons complain of this assertion.

4. You will observe that in this oath the candidate also swears, that "a Master Mason's secrets, given to me in charge as such...shall remain as secure and inviolate in my breast as in his own, murder and treason excepted, and they left to my own election." Now, this section of the oath is very broad, and may be understood to cover secrets of every description. But to put it beyond all doubt whether crimes are to be kept secret, murder and treason are excepted, showing that the oath has

54

respect particularly to concealing the crimes of a Master Mason. He may commit Theft, Robbery, Arson, Adultery, Rape, or any crime whatever, Murder and Treason excepted, and however well the commission of these crimes may be known to a Master Mason, if a Master Mason has committed them, he is under oath to conceal them. Now, is this right? Is this consistent with duty, either to God or man? Must not this often prove a fatal bar to the detection of crime, and the administration of justice? Certainly it must, or Freemasons must very frequently violate their solemn oath. If Freemasons deny this, in the denial they maintain that Masons care nothing for their oaths. It is self-evident that this Master's oath is either a conspiracy against the execution of law, or Master Masons care nothing for the solemnity of an oath. Gentlemen, take which horn of the dilemma you please! If these oaths are kept inviolate the course of justice must be effectually obstructed. If they are not kept, Master Masons are guilty of false swearing, and that continually. Which shall we believe to be true? Do Master Masons continually treat this solemn oath with contempt, or, do they respect their oaths, conceal the crimes of Master Masons, and fly to their rescue if they are detected and likely to be punished? Let not Master Masons, or any body else, exclaim: "Oh! these oaths are very innocent things! Crimes will be detected, criminals will be punished, for Masons care nothing for their oaths." Indeed! And does this excuse them? It is only by being guilty of false swearing that they can fail to thoroughly obstruct the course of justice. They are certainly under the most solemn oath to do that, in case of crime committed by a Master Mason, which will effectually defeat the execution of law. Let it be then particularly observed, that in every community where there are Master Masons, they either compose a class of conspirators against the administration of criminal law, and the execution of justice; or, they are a class of false swearers who care nothing for the solemnity of an oath. Let this not be regarded as a light thing. It is a most serious and important matter, and that which I have stated is neither false nor extravagant. It is a literal and solemn truth. Let it be well pondered. There is the oath; read it for yourself, mark its different points and promises, and you will see there is no escape from these conclusions.

5. The candidate in this oath swears, "I will not wrong this lodge, nor a brother of this degree to the value of one cent, knowingly myself nor suffer it to be done by others, if in my power to prevent." Now observe, he makes this promise "under no less penalty, than to have my body severed in two in the midst, and divided to the north and south, my bowels burnt to ashes in the center, and scattered before the four winds of heaven, that there might not the least track or trace of remembrance remain among men or Masons of so vile or perjured a wretch as I should be, were I ever to prove wilfully guilty of violating any part of this my solemn oath or obligation as Master Mason. So help me God, and keep me steadfast in the due performance of the same." Now, observe, one part of this Master's obligation is that which I have just quoted, that he will not wrong the lodge, nor a brother of this degree to the value of one cent. For doing this, he solemnly agrees to incur the awful penalty just above written. Is this just, as between man and man? Has any man a right to take such an oath under such penalties? Christian Freemason, can you see nothing wrong is this? Is not this profane, abominable, monstrous?

6. Observe, upon the same penalty, the candidate proceeds: "Furthermore do I promise and swear, that I will not be at the initiating, passing, and raising a candidate at one communication without a regular dispensation from the Grand Lodge for the same." Observe, then, to do this is so great a crime among Masons as to incur this awful penalty. The candidate proceeds: "Furthermore do I promise and swear, that I will not be at the initiating of an old man in his dotage, a young man in his nonage, an atheist, irreligious libertine, idiot,

madman, hermaphrodite, nor woman." To do this, observe, is so great a crime among Masons as to incur the awful penalty attached to this oath. And this is Masonic benevolence! It professes to be a saving institution, and excludes the greater part of mankind from its benefits! The candidate proceeds: "Furthermore do I promise and swear, that I will not speak evil of a brother Master Mason, neither behind his back, nor before his face." Now, observe again, to do this is to incur this awful penalty, for this is *one part* of the oath. But who does not know that Freemasons violate this part of the oath, as well as that which relates to wronging each other, almost continually? The candidate proceeds: "Furthermore do I promise and swear, that I will not violate the chastity of a Master Mason's wife, sister, or daughter, I knowing them to be such, nor suffer it to be done by others, if in my power to prevent." But why not promise this in respect to all women? If this oath had included all women, it would have the appearance of justice and benevolence, but as it is, it is only an odious partiality, and does not imply even the semblance of virtue. The candidate proceeds: "Furthermore do I promise and swear, that I will support the constitution of the Grand Lodge of the State of _____, under which this lodge is held, and conform to all the bylaws, rules and regulations of this or any other lodge of which I may, at any time hereafter, become a member." Observe that to violate this part of the obligation is to incur the awful penalty attached to this oath. The candidate proceeds: "Furthermore do I promise and swear, that I will obey all regular signs, summonses, or tokens given, handed, sent, or thrown to me from the hand of a brother Master Mason, or from the body of a just and lawfully constituted lodge of such, provided it be within the length of my cable tow." This, indeed, puts a rope around the neck of every offending brother. He is under oath to answer any sign or summons given him from a brother Master Mason, or from a lodge. If he refuses or neglects to respond to the summons, he incurs the penalty, and is liable to have it executed upon him. The cable tow is literally a rope of several yards in length, but in a Master's Lodge is understood to represent three miles. In the degrees of Knighthood the distance is reckoned to be forty miles. This is fearful, and the responding to such summonses has, doubtless, cost many a man his life, by placing him in the hands of an exasperated lodge. The candidate proceeds: "Furthermore do I promise and swear, that I will go on a Master Mason's errand, whenever required, even should I have to go barefoot and bareheaded, if within the length of my cable tow." Now, failure to do this incurs the awful penalty of this obligation. A Master Mason's errand! What errand? From the words it would seem any errand, however trivial it may be; every errand, however frequently, a Master Mason might wish to send another on an errand. If it does not mean this, what does it mean? But whatever it means a failure incurs the whole penalty. The candidate proceeds: "Furthermore do I promise and swear, that I will always remember a brother Master Mason when on my knees offering up my devotions to Almighty God." But do Masons do this? In secret, family, public, social prayer, do they do this? Professed Christian Mason, do you do it? If not, you are guilty of false swearing every time you omit it. What! on your knees offering up your devotions to Almighty God, and guilty at that very moment, of violating a solemn oath, by neglecting to pray for Master Masons! Remember, to fail in this respect incurs the awful penalty attached to this obligation. Now comes that part of the obligation upon which they lay so much stress as proving Masonry to be a benevolent institution: "Furthermore do I promise and swear, that I will be aiding and assisting all poor, indigent Master Masons, their wives and orphans, wherever disposed round the globe, as far as in my power, without injuring myself or family materially." In another place I shall show that there is no benevolence whatever in doing this, as every candidate pays into the public treasure money to compose a fund for the supply of the wants of the families of indigent Freemasons, simply upon the principle of a mutual insurance company. At present I simply remark that a failure to do this incurs the whole terrible penalty of this obligation. The candidate concludes his promises by saying: "Furthermore do I promise and swear, that if any part of this solemn oath and obligation be omitted at this time, I will hold myself amenable thereto, whenever informed."

Some months since I received a letter from a Master Mason who was manifestly a conscientious man. He informed me that he had been reading my letters in the *Independent*, on Freemasonry — that his mind was so distressed, in view of his Masonic obligations and relations, that he was wholly unable to attend to business, and that he should become deranged, if he could not escape from these entanglements — that he must and would renounce Freemasonry at all hazards. When he took the oath of the Master's degree the clause pledging him to keep a Master Mason's secrets, murder and treason excepted, was omitted, so that he was not aware of that clause until afterward. This clause, however, that I last quoted, bound him fast. No wonder that this conscientious man was frightened when he came to understand his true position. In administering this long oath to any conscientious man, any part of it that would shock a tender conscience may be omitted, and yet the candidate is pledged to hold himself amenable to that part, or those parts, that have been omitted, whenever informed of the same. This is a trap and a snare into which many a tender conscience has been betrayed. And is this an oath which a Christian man may take, or any other man, without sin? Can any man administer this oath, or take it, or be voluntarily present, aiding and abetting, and be guiltless of awful profanity and blasphemy? I have dwelt the longer upon this oath, because probably two-thirds of the Masons in the United States have gone no further than this degree. Now, is it not perfectly plain that a man who has taken this oath ought not to be intrusted with the office of a magis-trate, a sheriff, marshal or constable? That he is not to be credited as a witness where a Master Mason is a party? That he ought not to be allowed a place on a jury where a Master Mason is a party? And, in short, that he can not safely be intrusted with any office of honor or profit, either in Church or State? Is it not plain that a Master's Lodge, in any community, is a dangerous institution, and that the whole country is interested in the utter suppression of such an institution?

Let not this opinion be regarded as too severe. The fact is that Freemasons intend to fulfill their vows, or they do not. If Master Masons intend to do what they swear to do, is it right to intrust them with the execution of the laws? If they do *not* intend to fulfill their vows, of what avail will their oath of office be, since they have no regard for the solemnity of an oath? In every view of the subject it is plain that such men ought not to be trusted. Take either horn of the dilemma, it amounts to the same thing. I shall have more to say on this subject hereafter.

CHAPTER VII

ROYAL ARCH DEGREE

The fourth degree of Masonry is that of "Mark Master." The fifth is that of "Past Master." The sixth is that of "Most Excellent Master." In these the same points, in substance, are sworn to as in the Master's degree. In each succeeding oath the candidate recognizes and reaffirms all of his past obligations. In nearly every obligation the candidates swear implicit allegiance to the Grand Lodge of the United States and to the Grand Lodge of the State under which his lodge holds its charter. The candidate swears, also, that he will never be present at the raising of any person to a higher degree who has not regularly taken each and all of the previous or lower degrees. In the first degree secrecy alone is enjoined. After this, additional clauses are introduced at every step, until the oaths of some of the higher degrees spread over several pages. They nearly all pledge pecuniary help to poor, indigent, worthy Masons, and their families, as far as they can *without material injury to themselves and families* They never promise to *deny themselves* or *families* any comfort or luxury for the purpose of helping indigent, worthy Masons or their families. They never promise in their oaths to give pecuniary aid to any but Masons and their families. These families, by their head, have paid into the Masonic fund the amount that entitles them to aid, in case of pecuniary want, on the principle of mutual insurance against want.

All Masons above the third, or master's degree, are sworn to keep inviolate the secrets of a brother, murder and treason excepted, up to the seventh, or Royal Arch degree. In the oath of this degree the candidate, as we shall see, swears to keep all the secrets of a companion of this degree, murder and treason not excepted. All Masons of and above this degree are solemnly bound to do this. The same is true of all the points sworn to in this obligation which we proceed to examine.

61

FREEMASONRY

In reviewing this and the degrees above it, I shall not need to give them in full, as they are substantially and almost verbatim alike, except as new points are added as the candidate goes on from one degree to another. The Royal Arch degree is taken in a lodge called a chapter. A Mason of this degree is called a companion, while in the lower degrees Masons address each other as brothers. After swearing to the same points contained in previously taken oaths, the kneeling candidate, with hands on the Holy Bible, proceeds: "I further more promise and swear, that I will aid and assist a companion Royal Arch Mason when engaged in any difficulty, and espouse his cause so far as to extricate him from the same, if within my power, whether he be right or wrong.

Here, then, we have a class of men sworn, under most frightful penalties, to espouse the cause of a companion so far as to extricate him from any difficulty, to the extent of their power, whether he is *right* or *wrong*. How can such a man be safely intrusted with any office connected with the administration of the law? He means to abide by and perform this solemn oath, or he does not. If he does, will he not inevitably defeat the due execution of law, if intrusted with the office connected with it? Suppose he is a magistrate, a sheriff, marshal, or constable, will he not be able to prevent the execution of justice, if he does all within his power, as he is solemnly sworn to do? If on a jury, if sworn as a witness, how can he be trusted, if he fulfills his Masonic vows?

But suppose he does not intend to abide by and fulfill his vows, but still adheres, and does not renounce them; suppose he still recognizes their obligation, but fails to fulfill them, is he a man to be trusted with an office? If he does not respect and fulfill his Masonic oaths, the validity of which he acknowledges by continued adherence, of what avail will be his oath of office? Of what use will it be for him to swear that he will faithfully execute the laws, if he has taken the oath of this degree, and either fulfills or fails to fulfill it? If he fulfills it,

62

he surely will not execute the law upon a companion Royal Arch Mason. If he still adheres to, but fails to fulfill his oath, he does not respect the solemnity of an oath, and ought not to be intrusted with an office. If he publicly, sincerely, and penitently renounces his Masonic oath as unlawful, profane, and not binding, he may be trusted with office, but while he adheres he must violate either his oath of office, or his Masonic oath, whenever the accused is a Royal Arch Mason, and, indeed, whenever such an one is involved in any legal difficulty.

I beseech the public not to think this severe. There is, in fact, no third way. Take either horn of the dilemma and it amounts to the same thing. To treat this lightly, as some are disposed to do, or to get over it under cover of the plea of charity, is worse than nonsense; it is wicked to ignore the truth, and proceed as if there were no great wrong in this case. There is great wrong, great sin, and great danger in this case — danger to both Church and State, danger to the souls of men thus situated. I beseech this class of men to consider this matter, and renounce this position. If they will not, I see neither justice nor safety in allowing such men to hold an office in Church or State.

But what is the moral character of a man who espouses the cause, and does all he can to rescue a criminal from the hands of justice? I answer, he is a partaker of his guilt. He is truly an accessory after the fact. This oath does not contemplate the professional services of an advocate employed to defend an accused person in a court of justice. But even in this case an advocate has no right to defeat the due administration of justice, and turn the criminal loose to prey upon society. When he does this he sins both against God and society. It is his business to see that no injustice is done the accused; to secure for him a fair and impartial trial, but not to rescue him, if guilty. An advocate who would "espouse the cause" of a criminal "so far as to extricate him from his difficulty, whether right or wrong," would deserve the execration of both God and man.

FREEMASONRY

The candidate in this degree proceeds, as follows: "Also, that I will promote a companion Royal Arch Mason's political preferment in preference to another of equal qualifications." Bernard, who has taken this and many other Masonic oaths, says, in his "Light on Masonry," in a footnote, that this clause of the oath is, in some chapters, made a distinct point in the obligation, thus: "I furthermore promise and swear, that I will vote for a companion Royal Arch Mason before any other of equal qualifications," and in some chapters both are left out of the obligation. Upon this clause I remark:

1. Freemasons deny that Freemasonry has anything to do with any man's political opinions, or actions, provided he be not the enemy of his country. From this obligation, or oath, he can judge of the truth or falsehood of this profession. Again, who does not know that thousands of the Southern rebels were and are accepted Freemasons. How does this fact comport with the pretense that a Freemason must be loyal to the government under which he lives. In the higher degrees they swear to be loyal and true to their government, but are the Southern Masons so?

2. We see why such efforts are made to increase the number of Royal Arch Masons, and the reasons held out to induce political aspirants to become Royal Arch Masons. It is said, I suppose truly, that Royal Arch Masons are multiplying by scores of thousands in this country. It is, beyond doubt, the design of their leaders to control the elections and secure the offices throughout the country. From letters received from reliable parties I learn that in some localities Masons avow this design. But whether they avow or deny it, this oath unmistakably reveals their design. Why is this clause found in this oath? It is presumption and foolhardiness to ignore this plain revelation of their design to control the government, secure the offices, and have everything their own way. If the public can not be aroused to look this conspiracy in the face, and rise up and put it down in time, they will surely find, too

late, that their hands are tied, and that virtual slavery or a bloody revolution awaits us. Our children and grandchildren will reap the bitter fruits of our own folly and credulity. What do Freemasons mean by this oath? They either intend to keep it, or not to keep it. If they mean to do as they have promised under the most solemn oath to do, then Freemasonry, at least Freemasonry of this and all the higher degrees, is a political conspiracy to secure the offices and the control of the government. I say Freemasonry of this and of all the higher degrees, for be it remembered that all Masons of and above this degree have taken the oath of this degree. I quote the following from an able editorial in the *Albany Evening Journal Extra*, October 27, 1831: "An addition was made to the Master's oath, in the northern part of this State, a few years since, by Gov. Pitcher, who introduced it from Vermont. It was to the effect that, in voting for officers, a preference should be given to a Mason over another candidate of equal qualifications. Very respectable testimony of the fact was published very generally in the newspapers, about two years since, and has never, to the knowledge of the writer, been contradicted or questioned. It is admitted that this obligation, in terms, has not generally been administered (that is, in a Master's Lodge), but it is insisted that if the principle be once admitted that men in our country may band together in secret conclave, for any purpose not known to the laws, and may bind themselves under obligations involving the penalty of death for their transgressions, they may as well pledge themselves to any new object, or purpose, as to those for which they have already associated. There is no limit to the extent of such associations, if they are allowed at all. The principle itself is radically wrong. But independent of any positive obligation, the very creation of such artificial ties of brotherhood, the strength which they acquire by frequent repetition and by the associations of the fraternity, necessarily produce a clannish attachment which will ordinarily exhibit itself in the most important concerns of life in bestowing business and patronage on a brother, and in elevating him to office and rank which will reflect back honor upon the order to which he belongs. The inevitable result, therefore, of such institutions is to give one class of citizens unequal and unjust advantages over those who are not of the favored order. And when we find this natural result hastened and strengthened by obligations, under the most awful penalties, to fly to the relief of a brother, to espouse his cause, whether right or wrong, and to conceal his crimes, have not the rest of the community a right to say to these exclusives, these privileged orders, "we will not submit to your usurpations, and until you restore your fellow citizens to equal rights and privileges with you, we will not give you our votes or trust you with public office." To these remarks I fully subscribe. But I return to another clause of this oath. The candidate proceeds: "Furthermore do I promise and swear, that a companion Royal Arch Mason's secrets, given me in charge as such, and I knowing them to be such, shall remain as secure and inviolable in my breast as in his own, *murder and treason not excepted.*" Bernard says, in a footnote, "In some chapters this is administered, 'All the secrets of a companion, without exception.'" Upon this clause I remark:

1. That Freemasonry waxes worse and worse as you ascend from the lower to the higher degrees. It will be remembered that in the Master's oath murder and treason were excepted in the oath of secrecy. In this degree murder and treason are *not* excepted. Now, as all Masons who take the degrees above this have also taken this oath, it follows that all that army of Freemasons, composed of Royal Arch Masons, and all who have taken the degrees above this, are under the most solemn oath to conceal each other's crimes, without exception. And what an institution is this to be allowed existence under any government, especially under a republican form of government? Is it safe to have such a set of men scattered broadcast over all the United States? Let us look this thing squarely in the face. It can not be honestly denied that Royal

Arch Masons take this oath. But a short time since a minister of the Gospel of my acquaintance was confronted with this oath, and he did not deny having taken it. Now, if all that vast army of Masons who have taken this oath intend to do as they swear to do, what must be the result? Scores and hundreds of thousands of men, scattered broadcast over the whole land, are pledged by the most solemn oath, and under the penalty of death, to conceal each other's crimes, without exception. Are such men to be safely intrusted with office, either in Church or State? And must not a government be on the verge of ruin when such a conspiracy is allowed to multiply its numbers at such a frightful rate as it is doing, at this time, in this country? Will the people of the United States have the foolhardiness to ignore the crime and danger of this conspiracy against their liberty? Or will they good-naturedly assume that Freemasons mean no such thing? Why, then, is this oath? Will they, under the cover of mock charity, assume that these men will not cover up each other's crimes? What kind of charity is this? Is it charity to believe that a set of men will lie under oath, as all Freemasons above the degree of Fellow Craft must do, if they do not conceal each other's crimes? Again, what right have Freemasons, themselves, to complain of a want of charity in those who regard them as conspirators against good government? Why, what shall we do? If they do not repent of, and renounce, these oaths, we must either regard them as conspirators against government, or as men who will *lie*, under the solemnity of a most awful oath. The gentlemen must choose which horn of the dilemma they will take. On the one hand, they are sworn conspirators against the execution of the criminal laws; on the other, they are a class of men that do not regard the solemnity of an oath. This is the exact truth, and it is folly and madness to ignore it. Freemasons, therefore, have no right to complain of us, if we take them at their word, and believe that they mean to do what they have sworn they will do. They demand charity of us. Is it not charitable to believe

CHAPTER VIII

SWORN TO PERSECUTE

Masons are sworn to persecute until death anyone who violates Masonic obligation. In the oath of the THRICE ILLUSTRIOUS ORDER of the CROSS the candidate swears, as follows, "Light on Masonry," eighth edition, p. 199: "You further swear, that should you know another to violate any essential point of this obligation, you will use your most decided endeavors, by the blessing of God, to bring such person to the strictest and most condign punishment, agreeably to the rules and usages of our ancient fraternity; and this, by pointing him out to the world as an unworthy vagabond, by opposing his interest, by deranging his business, by transferring his character after him wherever he may go, and by exposing him to the contempt of the whole fraternity and of the world, during his whole natural life." The penalty of this obligation is as follows: "To all and every part thereof we then bind you, and by ancient usage you bind yourself, under the no less infamous penalty than dying the death of a traitor, by having a spear, or other sharp instrument, like our Divine Master, thrust into your left side, bearing testimony, even in death, to the power and justice of the mark of the Holy Cross." Upon this obligation I remark:

1. Here we have an explanation of the notorious fact that Freemasons try, in every way, to ruin the reputation of all who renounce Masonry. The air has almost been darkened by the immense number of falsehoods that have been circulated, by Freemasons, to destroy the reputation of every man who has renounced Freemasonry, and published it to the world, or has written against it. No pains have been spared to destroy all confidence in the testimony of such men. Does not this oath render it impossible for us to believe what Freemasons

say of the character of those who violate their obligations? Who of us that lived forty years ago does not remember how Freemasons endeavored to destroy the reputation of William Morgan, of Elder Bernard, of Elder Stearns, and also of Mr. Allyn, and who that is at all acquainted with facts does not know that the utmost pains are taken to destroy the reputation of every man that dares to take his pen and expose their institution. When I had occasion to quote Elder Bernard's book, in preaching on the subject of Freemasonry a few months ago, I was told in the streets, before I got home, that he was a man of bad character. I knew better, and knew well how to understand such representations, for this is the way in which the testimony of all such men is sought to be disposed of by Freemasons. Will this be denied? What, then, is the meaning of this oath? Are not Masons under oath to do this? Indeed they are. A few months since I received the following letter. For reasons which will be appreciated, I omit name and date. The writer says: "About a week since, a man calling himself Professor W. E. Moore, the great South American explorer, came to this place, lecturing on Freemasonry. He is a Mason, and has given private lectures to the lodges here, and has lectured once before the public. He claims to have been at Oberlin, recently, and that while there he had an interview with you, and that he tested you sufficiently to satisfy himself that you had never been a Mason; and further, he says that the conversation he had with you resulted to his great satisfaction, and to your great discomfiture." At nearly the same date of this letter, I received, from the same place, a letter from a Freemason of my acquaintance, giving substantially the same account of this Professor Moore. In this letter, however, it is added that his conversation with me compelled me to confess that I never had been a Mason, and to say I would publish no more against Masonry. This last letter I have mislaid, so that I can not lay my hand upon it. From the first I quote *verbatim et literatim* I replied to these letters, as I now assert, that every word of what this man says of me is false. That I never saw or heard of this man, to my knowledge, until I received those letters. But this is nothing new or strange. Such false representations are just what we are to expect, if Freemasons of this and the higher degrees fulfill their vows. Why should they be believed, and how can they complain of us for not believing what they say of men who have renounced Masonry and oppose it? It is mere folly and madness to believe them. It is not difficult, if Freemasons desire it, to produce almost any amount of testimony to prove that every manner and degree of falsehood is resorted to destroy the testimony of men who witness against them. Any man who will renounce these horrid oaths, and expose their profanity to the public, should make up his mind beforehand to endure any amount of slander and persecution which the ingenuity of Freemasons can invent.

In the degree of Knights Adepts of the Eagle or Sun, "Light on Masonry," eighth edition, page 269, we have the following: "*The man peeping.* Be the man you saw peeping, and who was discovered, and seized, and conducted to death, *is an emblem of those who come to be initiated into our sacred mysteries through a motive of curiosity; and if so indiscreet as to divulge their obligations,* WE ARE BOUND TO CAUSE THEIR DEATH, AND TAKE VENGEANCE ON THE TREASON BY THE DESTRUCTION OF THE TRAITORS!!!" Here we find that Freemasons of this and the higher degrees are solemnly pledged to destroy the lives of those who violate their obligations. Deacon William A. Bartlett, of Pella, Iowa, in his public renunciation of Freemasonry, says — "Letters on Masonry," by Elder John G. Stearns, page 169 — "During the winter or spring following my initiation, a resolution was offered in the lodge for adoption, and to be published outside the lodge, condemning the abduction of Morgan. After much discussion, the Worshipful Master called another to the chair, and said, 'Brethren, what do you mean by offering such a resolution as this? Had we been at Batavia, we would have done just what those brethren have done, and taken the life of Morgan, because

CHAPTER IX

AWFUL PROFANITY OF MASONIC OATHS

In the degree of Templar and Knight of Malta, as found in the seventh edition of "Light on Masonry," page 182, in a lecture in which the candidate is giving an account of what he had passed through, he says, "I then took the cup (the upper part of the human skull) in my hand, and repeated, after the Grand Commander, the following obligation: 'This pure wine I now take in testimony of my belief in the mortality of the body and the immortality of the soul — and may this libation appear as a witness against me both here and here-after — and as the sins of the world were laid upon the head of the Savior, so may all the sins committed by the person whose skull this was be heaped upon my head, in addition to my own, should I ever; knowingly or willfully, violate or transgress any obligation that I have heretofore taken, take at this time, or shall at any future period take, in relation to any degree of Masonry or order of Knighthood. So help me God?'" Now, observe what a horrid imprecation is here. These Knights Templar and Knights of Malta take their oaths sustained by such a horrid penalty as this. They say that they will incur this penalty, not merely if they violate the peculiar obligation of this degree, but "any obligation that I have heretofore taken, take at this time, or shall at any future period take in relation to any degree of Masonry or order of Knighthood." This is called "the sealed obligation." Here, in the most solemn manner, the candidate, drinking wine out of a human skull, takes upon himself this obligation, under the penalty of a double damnation. What can exceed the profanity and wickedness of this?

On the 185th page of the same book, we find a note quoted from the work of Brother Allyn, who renounced Masonry and published on the subject. I will quote the note entire. Mr. Allyn says of the fifth libation, or *sealed obligation*, it "is referred to

73

FREEMASONRY

by Templars in confidential communications, relative to matters of great importance, when other Masonic obligations seem insufficient to secure *secrecy, silence, and safety.* Such, for instance, was the murder of William Morgan, which was communicated from one Templar to another, under the pledge, and upon this sealed obligation." He also remarks, in another place: "When I received this degree I objected to drink from the human skull, and to take the profane oath required by the rules of the order. I observed to the Most Eminent that I supposed that that part of the ceremonies would be dispensed with. The Sir Knights charged upon me, and the Most Eminent said: 'Pilgrim, you here see the swords of your companions drawn to defend you in the discharge of every duty we require of you. They are also drawn to *avenge any violation of the rules of our order.* We expect you to proceed.' A clergyman, an acquaintance of mine, came forward, and said: 'Companion Allyn, this part of the ceremonies is never dispensed with. I, and all the Sir Knights, have drank from the cup and taken the fifth libation. It is perfectly proper, and will be qualified to your satisfaction.' I then drank of the cup of double damnation."

Now, can any profanity be more horrible than this? And yet there is nothing in Masonry, we are told, that is at all inconsistent with the Christian religion! On the 187th page of the same volume, the "Knight of the Christian Mark," at the conclusion of his obligation says: "All this I promise in the name of the Father, of the Son, and of the Holy Ghost: and if I perform it not, let me be ANATHEMA MARANATHA! ANATHEMA MARANATHA!!" Anathema Maranatha is understood to mean accursed at the Lord's coming. Again, the "Knights of the Red Cross" take their obligations upon the following penalty, page 164: "To all of which I do most solemnly promise and swear, binding myself under no less penalty than that of having my house torn down, the timbers thereof set up, and I hanged thereon; and when the last trump shall blow, that I be forever excluded from the society of all true and courteous Knights, should I ever, willfully

74

or knowingly, violate any part of this solemn obligation of Knight of the Red Cross. So help me, God, and keep me steadfast to keep and perform the same."

The "Knights of the Eagle, and Sovereign Prince of Rose Croix de Heroden," in receiving this degree, pass through the following, page 253, of Bernard's eighth edition of "Light on Masonry:" "During this time the brethren in the second department take off their black decorations, and put on the red, and, also, uncover the jewels. The candidate knocks on the door, and the Warden, for answer, shuts the door in his face. The Master of Ceremonies says: 'These marks of indignity are not sufficiently humiliating; you must pass through more rigorous proofs, before you can find it.' He then takes off the candidate the chasuble and black apron, and puts over him a black cloth, covered with ashes and dust, and says to him: 'I am going to conduct you into the darkest and most dismal place, from whence the word shall triumphantly come to the glory and advantage of Masonry.' He then takes from him his covering, and makes him go three times around (showing him the representation of the torments of the damned), when he is led to the door of the chapter, and the Master of Ceremonies says to him: *The horrors which you have just now seen are but a faint representation of those you shall suffer, if you break through our laws, or infringe the obligation you have taken.'"In a footnote, the editor says: "This certainly caps the climax, and renders the institution of Masonry complete. The torments of the damned, the awful punishment which the Almighty inflicts on the violators of his righteous law is but a faint emblem of the punishment which Masonry here declares *shall be inflicted on the violators of Masonic law,* or those who are guilty of an infraction of Masonic obligations!" But I get sick of pursuing these loathsome and blasphemous details; and I fear I shall so shock my readers that they will be as wearied as I am myself. In reading over these oaths, it would seem as if a Masonic lodge was a place where men had assembled to commit the utmost blasphemy of which they were capable, to mock and scoff at all that is sacred, and to beget among themselves the utmost contempt for every form of moral obligation. These oaths sound as if the men who were taking and administering them were determined to annihilate their moral sense, and to render themselves incapable of making any moral discrimina-tions, and certainly, if they can see no sin in taking and admin-istering such oaths under such penalties, they have succeeded, whether intentionally or not, in rendering themselves utterly blind, as regards the moral character of their conduct. By repeating their blasphemy they have put out their own eyes. Now these oaths mean something, or they do not. Masons, when they take them, mean to abide by them, or they do not. If they do not, to take them is blasphemy. If they do mean to abide by them, they are sworn to perform deeds, not only the most injurious to society, to government, and the church of God of any that can well be named, but they swear, in case of the violation of any point of these obligations, to seek to have the penalties inflicted on the violator. In other words, in such a case, they swear to commit murder; and every man who ad-heres to such obligations is under oath to seek to accomplish the violent death, not only of every man who shall betray the secrets, but, also, of everyone who shall violate *any point* or *part* of these obligations. Now, the solemn question arises, are these oaths a mere farce, a mere taking of the name of God in vain, in the most trifling manner, and under the most solemn circumstances? or, are we to understand that the Masonic in-stitution is a *conspiracy*, its members taking, in all seriousness and good faith, such horrid oaths to do such horrid deeds, upon such horrid penalties? Which are we to understand to be true? If either is true, I ask the church of God, I ask the world, what more abominable institution ever existed than this? Any yet we are told that in all this trifling with oaths, or, if not trifling, this horrid conspiracy, there is nothing incon-sistent with the Christian religion! And even ministers of the

Gospel are found who can justify it and eulogize it in a manner most profane, and even blasphemous. Now, in charity, I suppose it to be true that the great mass of Masons, who are nominally so, and who have, in a hurry and under great excitement, taken more or less of the degrees, have only a very confused conception of what Masonry really is. Surely, if Masons really understood what Masonry is, as it is delineated in these books, no Christian Mason would think himself at liberty to remain another day a member of the fraternity. The fact is, a great many *nominal* Masons are not so in *reality*. It is as plain as possible that a man, knowing what it is, and embracing it in his heart, can not be a Christian man. To say he can is to belie the very nature of Christianity.

But here let me ask, in concluding this article, *what is there in Masonry to justify the taking of such oaths, under such penalties?* If there is any *good* in Masonry, why should it be concealed? and why should such oaths be taken to conceal it? If Masonry is an evil thing, and its secrets are evil, of course, to take any oath to conceal the wickedness is utterly unjustifiable. Does Masonry exact these oaths for the sake of concealing from outsiders the miserable falsehoods that they palm off upon their candidates, which everywhere abound in Masonry? But what is there in these stories, if true, that should be concealed? If Hiram Abiff was murdered as Masons pretend; if the Ark of the Covenant, with its sacred contents, was really found in the vault under ground, as Masons pretend, is there any justifiable reason for concealing from the whole world these facts. I have sought in vain for a reason to justify the taking of any oaths at all in Masonry. And it is passing strange that such oaths under such penalties, should ever have been so much as dreamed of by Masons as being justified by their secrets. The fact is, their stringent secrecy must be designed, in part, to excite the curiosity of men, and draw candidates into the snare. The highest Masonic authority has affirmed that their secrecy is essential to their existence; and that, if their secrets were exposed, the institution could not live. Now, this is no doubt true, and is the great reason, as I conceive, for guarding their secrets with such horrid oaths. But I said, in an early number, that Masonry is a swindle. Where are the important secrets which they promise to their candidates? For what do the candidates pay their money but really to be imposed upon? But it may be well asked, why do Masons, once embarked in Masonry, go on, from one degree to another multiplying their oaths, obligations, and imprecations? When they are once within a lodge to take a degree, they dare not do otherwise than to go forward. I could quote numerous instances from the writings of seceding Masons showing how they have been urged from step to step, and assured, if they would proceed, that everything would be explained to their satisfaction. They have been told, as in the case of Mr. Allyn just noticed, that everything would be qualified and explained to their satisfactions. Upon Mr. Allyn, as we have seen, the Sir Knights drew their swords when he hesitated to go forward; and the Most Eminent informed him that he must go forward, or their swords would avenge his disobedience.

The fact is when once within the lodge, they dare not stop short of taking the obligation belonging to the degree; and they are persuaded by those who have taken higher degrees, to go forward from one degree to another.

And the great Masonic argument to keep them steadfast in concealing the imposition that has been practiced upon them, and to persuade them not to renounce and expose what they have passed through, is, that of having their throats cut, their tongues torn out by the roots, their heart and vitals torn out and thrown to the vultures of the air, drowning and murder.

Masons profess not to invite or persuade any to join the lodges; and the candidates, when they come forward for their degrees, are asked if they come forward of their own free will and accord. To this, of course, they answer, yes.

But what has made them willing? They have been persuaded to it. They have been invited to join; — they have been urged to join; motives of self-interest have been set before them in such a light as to gain their consent. They are thus made willing; and, therefore, truthfully say, that they do it of their own free will and accord.

But it is almost, if not quite, the universal testimony of renouncing Masons, that they were persuaded to it. They were made willing to join by such representations as over-persuaded them. I do not believe that one in five hundred of those who join the Masonic lodge, join without being persuaded to do so. But let me say also, that the great mass of Freemasons have never taken more than the first three degrees. They may know nothing about the higher degrees. Now in what sense are they responsible for the wickedness of the institution as revealed in the higher degrees? I answer, they would not be responsible at all, if they neither knew anything of those degrees, nor had any opportunity to know anything of them.

But as these books have been widely circulated, and are secretly kept by Masons, and are better known to Freemasons at present by far then they are to the outward world, — those who have taken the lower degrees, if they continue to sustain the institution, which is in reality a unit, become morally responsible for the wickedness of the higher degrees. But the obligations in the first three degrees are by no means innocent. They are such obligations as no man has any right to take or to administer. To adhere to the institution is to indorse (sic) it. But again, why do not Freemasons now, who have these books, and who know, or ought to know thoroughly the nature, designs, and tendency of the institution, publicly renounce the whole thing, confess their sin, and proclaim their independence of the order? I answer, first — They have seared their consciences by what they have done, and have, therefore, very little sense of the great sinfulness of remaining a member of such an abominable institution. I must say that I am utterly amazed at the want of conscientiousness among Masons on this subject. As I have said, they have put out the eyes of their moral sense, and do not at all appreciate the awful guilt of their position. And, secondly — They *dare* not. And if by their oaths they mean anything, it is not to be wondered at that they are afraid to renounce Freemasonry. Why the fraternity are under oath to persecute them, to represent them as perjured vagabonds, to destroy their characters, their business, and their influence, and to follow them from place to place, transferring their character after them during their whole natural life. This surely is enough to deter common men from renouncing their allegiance to the institution. To be sure, this danger does not excuse them; but weak as human nature is, it is not wonderful that it has its influence.

But again, Masons are under oath, if they renounce the order, to seek the destruction of their lives. And they have given terrible proof that their oaths are not a dead letter in this respect, not only in the murder of William Morgan, but of many others who have renounced their allegiance to the brotherhood. In a sermon which lies before me, delivered by Rev. Moses Thacher, a man well known in the Christian world, and who has himself taken many degrees of Masonry, he says: "The institution is dangerous to civil and religious rights. It is stained with blood. I have reliable historical evidence of not less than seven individuals, including Morgan, murdered under Masonic law." Since this sermon was preached other cases have come to light, and are constantly coming to light, in which persons have been murdered for disclosing Masonic secrets. And if the truth shall ever be known in this world, I believe it will be found that scores of persons, in this and other countries, have been murdered for unfaithfulness to Masonic obligations. Freemasons understand quite well the malignity of the spirit of Freemasonry. They understand that it will not argue, that it will not discuss the reasonableness or unreasonableness, the virtue or the sin of the institution; but that its argument is *assassination.* I am now daily in the receipt of letters from various parts of the country, expressing the highest satisfaction that anybody can be found who dares write against the institution at this day. The fact is, there are a great many men belonging to the institution, who are heartily sick of it, and would fain be rid of it; but who dare not open their mouths or whisper to any individual in the world their secret abhorrence of the institution. But it is time to speak out. And I do beg my brethren in the ministry, and the whole Christian Church, to examine it for themselves, and not turn away from looking the evil in the face until it is too late.

CHAPTER X

PERVERSE AND PROFANE USE
OF THE HOLY BIBLE

In this number I wish to call the attention of my readers to some of the cases in which Freemasons misapply and misrepresent, and most profanely, if not blasphemously, use the Holy Scriptures. I will not go far into the sickening details; but far enough, I trust, to lead serious persons to reflect upon the nature of a society that can trifle with such solemn things.

The "Knights of the East and West" take the following oath, and then pass through the following ceremonies: — See pp. 214-220 of the first edition, or eighth edition, 230-240, of Bernard's "Light on Masonry" — "I_____, do promise and solemnly swear and declare, in the awful presence of the only One Most Holy Puissant, Almighty, and Most Merciful Grand Architect of Heaven and Earth, who created the universe and myself through His infinite goodness, and conducts it with wisdom and justice, and in the presence of the Most Excellent and Upright Princes and Knights of the East and West, here present in convocation and grand council, on my sacred word of honor, and under every tie both moral and religious, that I never will reveal to any person whomsoever below me, or to whom the same may not belong by being legally and lawfully initiated, the secrets of this degree which are now about to be communicated to me, under the penalty of not only being dishonored, but to consider my life as the immediate forfeiture, and that to be taken from me with all the tortures and pains to be inflicted in manner as I have consented to in my preceding degrees. I further solemnly swear and sincerely promise upon my sacred word of honor, under the penalty of the severe wrath of the Almighty Creator of Heaven and Earth; and may He have mercy on my soul in the great and awful day of judgment agreeably to my conformity thereto. Amen. Amen. Amen. The All Puissant then takes the ewer filled with perfumed ointment, and anoints his head, eyes, mouth, heart, the tip of his right ear, hand, and foot and says, "You are now my dear brother, received a member of our society. You will recollect to live up to the precepts of it; and also, remember that those parts of your body which have the greatest power of assisting you in good or evil, have this day been made holy." The master of Ceremonies then places the candidate between the two Wardens, with the draft before him. The Senior Warden says to him, "Examine with deliberation and attention everything which the All Puissant is going to show you." After a short pause, he, the S. W., says, "Is there mortal here worthy to open the book with the seven seals?" All the brethren cast their eyes down and sigh. The Senior Warden hearing their signs, says to them, "Venerable and respectable brethren, be not afflicted here is a victim (pointing to the candidate) whose courage will give you content."

S. W. to the candidate, "Do you know the reason why the ancients have a long beard?"

CAN. "I do not, but I presume you do."

S. W. "They are those who came here after passing through great tribulation, and having washed their robes in their own blood: will you purchase your robes at so great a price?"

CAN. "Yes; I am willing."

The Wardens then conduct him to the basin, and bare both his arms; they place a ligature on each, the same as in performing the operation of blood-letting. Each Warden being armed with a lancet, makes an incision in each of his arms just deep enough to draw a drop of blood, which is wiped on a napkin, and then shown to the brethren. The Senior Warden then says, "See, my brethren, a man who has spilled his blood to acquire a knowledge of your mysteries, and shrunk not from the trial."

Then the All Puissant opens the FIRST SEAL of the great book, and takes from thence a bone quiver filled with arrows, and a crown, and gives them to one of the Ancients, and says to him, "Depart and continue the conquest." He opens the SECOND SEAL, and takes out a sword, and gives it to the next aged, and says, "Go and destroy peace among the profane and wicked brethren, that they may never appear in our Council." He opens the THIRD SEAL, and takes a balance, and gives it to the next aged, and says, "Dispense rigid justice to the profane and wicked brethren." He opens the FOURTH SEAL, and takes out a skull, and gives it to the next aged, and says, "Go and endeavor to convince the wicked that death is the reward of their guilt." He opens the FIFTH SEAL, and takes out a cloth stained with blood, and gives it to the next aged, and says, "When is the time (or the time will arrive) that we shall revenge and punish the profane and wicked, who have destroyed so many of their brethren by false accusations." He opens the SIXTH SEAL, and that moment the sun is darkened and the moon stained with blood! He opens the SEVENTH SEAL, and takes out incense, which he gives to a brother, and also a vase, with seven trumpets, and gives one to each of the seven aged brethren. After this the four old man [sic] in the four corners show their inflated bladders (beeves bladders filled with wind, under their arms), representing the four winds, when the All Puissant says: "Here is seen the fulfillment of a prophecy (Rev. vii. 3); strike not nor punish the profane and wicked of our order until I have selected the true and worthy Masons." Then the four winds raise their bladders, and one of the trumpets sounds, when the two Wardens cover the candidate's arms, and take from him his apron and jewels of the last degree. The second trumpet sounds, when the Junior Warden gives the candidate the apron and jewel of this degree. The third trumpet sounds, when the Senior Warden gives him a long beard. The fourth trumpet sounds, and the Junior Warden gives him a crown of gold. The fifth trumpet sounds, and the Senior Warden gives him a girdle of gold. The sixth trumpet sounds, and the Junior Warden gives him the sign, token, and words. The seventh trumpet sounds, on which they all sound together, when the Senior Warden conducts the candidate to the vacant canopy.

[This canopy, it will be recollected, is at the right side of the All Puissant, who represents Jehovah. The sounding of the seventh trumpet, and the conducting of the candidate to the canopy, is a representation of the end of the world, and the glorification of true Masons at the right hand of God, having "passed through the trials of Freemasonry," and "washed their robes in their own blood!" If this is not Antichrist, what is?"— Compiler.]

The editor also adds the following footnote in explanation of the foregoing: — "Compare the foregoing with the fifth, sixth and seventh chapters of Revelation, and the reader will discover that the All Puissant represents Jehovah seated on the throne of heaven; also, the Lamb of God, opening the seven seals. The Senior Warden represents the strong angel proclaiming: "Who is worthy to open the book," &c. The aged brethren, and the four old men with bladders, the angels of God with power; and Masonry claiming its faithful servants as the servants of God, the 144,000 who were sealed in their foreheads, and of whom it is said, "These are they who were not defiled with women; for they are virgins. These are they which follow the Lamb," &c. See Rev. 14th chapter.

The following ceremonies are performed in the "Knights of the Christian Mark," found in the same book as the preceding, pp. 168-170; or eighth edition, 188-190:

"The Knights come to order; the Senior Knight takes his seat; the candidate continues standing; the conductor brings a white robe, the Senior Knight says; 'Thus saith the Lord, he that believeth and endureth to the end shall overcome, and I will cause his iniquities to pass from him, and he shall dwell in my presence for ever and ever. Take away his filthy garments from him, and clothe him with a change of raiment. For he that overcometh, the same shall be clothed in white raiment, and his name shall be written in the book of life, and I will confess his name before my Father and His holy angels. He that hath an ear let him hear what the Spirit saith unto the true believer. Set ye a fair miter upon his head, place a palm in his hand, for he shall go in and out, and minister before me, saith the Lord of hosts; and he shall be a disciple of that rod taken from the branch of the stem of Jesse. For a branch has grown out of his root, and the Spirit of the Lord hath rested upon it the Spirit of his wisdom and might, and righteousness is the girdle of his loins, and faithfulness the girdle of his reins; and he stands as an insignia to the people, and him shall the Gentiles seek, and his rest shall be glorious. Cause them that have charge over the city to draw near, everyone with the destroying weapon in his hand.' The six grand ministers come from the north with swords and shields. The first is clothed in white, and has an ink-horn by his side, and stands before the Invincible Knight, who says: 'Go through the city; run in the midst thereof, and smite; let not thine eye spare, neither have pity; for they have not executed my judgements with clean hands, saith the Lord of hosts.' The candidate is instructed to exclaim: 'Woe is me, for I am a man of unclean lips, and my dwelling has been in the tents of Kedar, and among the children of Meshec.' Then he that has the ink-horn by his side, takes a live coal with the tongs from the altar, and touches the lips of the candidate, and says: 'If ye believe, thine iniquities shall be taken away, they sins shall be purged. I will that these be clean with the branch that is given up before me. All thy sins are removed, and thine iniquities blotted out. For I have trodden the wine-press alone, and with me was none of my people for behold I come with dyed garments from Bozrah, mighty to save. Refuse not, therefore, to hearken; draw not away thy shoulders; shut not thine ear that thou shouldst not hear.' The six ministers now proceed as though they were about to commence the slaughter, when the Senior Knight says to him with the ink-horn: 'Stay thine hand; proceed no further until thou hast set a mark on those that are faithful in the house of the Lord, and trust in the power of his might. Take ye the signet, and set a mark on the forehead of my people that have passed through great tribulation, and have washed their robes, and have made them white in the blood of the Lamb, which was slain from the foundation of the world.' The minister takes the signet and presses it on the candidate's forehead. He leaves the mark in red letters, 'King of kings, and Lord of lords.' [Footnote: — 'The reader is requested to turn to the following passages: — Isa. vi. 5-7. Ps. cxx 5. Isa. xliii. 15, and lxiii. 1-3. Rev. viii. 2-14, and xix. 16, and xv. 3. Zech. iii. 7. Song of Solomon viii. 6,7. The impious perversion of these passages is incapable of defense or excuse.] The Minister opens the scroll, and says: 'Sir Invincible Knight, the number of the sealed is one hundred and forty-four thousand.' The Invincible Knight strikes four, and all the knights stand before him. He says, 'Salvation belongeth to our God which sitteth upon the throne, and to the Lamb.' All the members fall on their faces, and say: 'Amen. Blessing, honor, glory, wisdom, thanksgiving and power, might, majesty, and dominion, be unto our God for ever and ever. Amen.' They all cast down crowns and palm branches, and rise up and say: 'Great and numberless are thy works, thou King of saints. Behold, the star which I laid before Joshua, on which is engraved seven eyes as the engraving of a signet, shall be set as a seal on thine arm, as a seal on thine heart; for love is stronger than death, many waters cannot quench it. If a man would give all the treasures of his house for love, he cannot obtain it; it is the gift of God through Jesus Christ our Lord.'"

The following is found in the Royal Arch degree, pp. 126, first edition, 137, eighth edition:

"Question. — 'Are you a Royal Arch Mason' Answer. — '*I am that I am.*'" [Note. "I am that I am," is one of the peculiar names of the Deity; and to use it as above, is, to say the least, taking the name of God in vain. How must the humble disciple of

Jesus feel when constrained thus to answer the question, "Are you a Royal Arch Mason?"] L. on Masonry, seventh edition. On pp. 154, 155. we have a description of a ceremony in the same degree, as follows: "The candidates next receive the obligation, travel the room, attend the prayer, travel again, and are shown a representation of the Lord appearing to Moses from the burning bush. This last is done in various ways. Sometimes an earthen pot is filled with earth, and green bushes set around the edge of it, and a candle in the center; and sometimes a stool is provided with holes about the edge, in which bushes are placed, and a bundle of rags or tow, saturated with oil of turpentine, placed in the center, to which fire is communicated. Sometimes a large bush is suspended from the ceiling, around the stem of which tow is wound wet with the oil of turpentine. In whatever way the bush is prepared, when the words are read, 'He looked and behold the bush burned with fire,' etc., the bandage is removed from the eyes of the candidate, and they see the fire in the bush; and at the words, 'Draw not nigh hither, put off thy shoes' etc., the shoes of the candidate are taken off, and they remain in the same situation while the rest of the passage to the words, 'And Moses hid his face; for he was afraid to look upon God,' is read. The bandage is then replaced, and the candidates again travel about the room while the next passage of Scripture is read."

[Note. "This is frequently represented in this manner: When the person reading comes to that part where it says, 'God called to him out of the midst of the bush, and said,' etc., he stops reading, and a person behind the bush calls out, 'Moses, Moses.' The conductor answers, 'Here am I.' The person behind the bush then says: 'Draw not nigh hither; put off thy shoes from off thy feet, for the place whereon thou standest is holy ground.' His shoes are then slipped off. 'Moreover, I am the God of Abraham, and the God of Isaac, and the God of Jacob.' The person first reading then says: 'And Moses hid his face, for he was afraid to look upon God.' At these words the bandage is placed over the candidate's eyes."] And, if any persons will examine, and read the books through for themselves, in which these revelations are made, they will find that the higher degrees are replete with the same shocking and monstrous perversion of the Scriptures. Many of the most solemn passages in the Bible are selected, read in their lodges, repeated by their candidates, and applied in a manner to shocking to read.

Here you observe the candidate taking the Royal Arch degree, when asked if he is a Royal Arch Mason, replies: "I am that I am;" which is represented in the Bible as being said by Jehovah himself. This answer was given by God to Moses when he inquired after the Divine name. God answered, "I am that I am." Just think! a Christian, when inquired of if he is a Royal Arch Mason, affirms of himself, *"I am that I am,"* taking to himself the name of the God of Israel.

Again, in this representation of the burning bush, the candidate is told to take off his shoes from off his feet, for the place on which he stands is holy ground; and then the Master of the lodge claims to be the God of Abraham, of Isaac, and of Jacob. Now how awfully profane and blasphemous is this!

Again, observe that that most solemn scene, depicted in the ninth chapter of Ezekiel, is misapplied in the most profane manner. Reader, the chapter is short; will you not take your Bible and read it?

So again, in those chapters in Revelation, the opening of the seals by the Son of God is misapplied, and profanely misrepresented. Just think! four aged men, with bladders filled with wind, are made to represent the four angels that hold the four winds from desolating the earth till the servants of God were sealed in their foreheads. What a shocking misapplication and misrepresentation do we find here. And the cases are numerous in which, as I have said, the most solemn passages in the Word of God are used in their mummeries and childish ceremonies, in so shocking a manner that we can hardly endure to read them. I beg my Christian readers to examine these books for themselves, and then see what they think of the assertions of so many professors of religion and even of professed Christian ministers, that "there is nothing in Freemasonry inconsistent with the religion of Jesus Christ!" I cannot imagine anything more directly calculated to bring the Word of God into contempt, than such a use of it in Masonic lodges. It is enough to make one's blood curdle in his veins to think that a Christian minister, or any Christian whatever, should allow himself to pass through such an abominable scene as is frequently represented in the degrees of Masonry: — multiplying their horrid oaths, heaping one imprecation upon another, gathering up from every part of the Divine oracles the most solemn and awful sayings of Jehovah, and applying them in a manner so revolting, that the scene must make a Christian's heart tremble, and his whole soul to loathe such proceedings.

In some of my numerous letters I am requested to quote the oaths entire. But this would be to rewrite a great part of the books in which Masonry is revealed. Some of these degrees have several different oaths to sustain them, filling several pages of the work, I can only give parts of these oaths, and must leave the readers to consult the books for themselves which I beseech them to do.

CRSO

CHAPTER XI

FREEMASONRY IMPOSES ON THE IGNORANT

In what is called the "Sublime Degree of Master Masons" there are the following gross misrepresentations worthy of notice:

First, Hiram Abiff is represented as going daily into the Most Holy place for secret prayer; whereas the Bible representation is that no one was allowed to enter the Most Holy place, except the high priest. Neither Solomon nor Hiram were allowed to enter it. And the high priest was allowed to enter it only once a year, and that on the great day of atonement, "not without blood, which he offered first for himself and then for the errors of the people."

Again, this Hiram is represented in Masonry as having been murdered by three ruffians, who demanded of him the master's word.

As he refused to give it, they murdered him, and buried him at a distance from Jerusalem, in a grave "six feet deep perpendicular," where he remained fourteen days.

Then, after a great deal of twaddle and misrepresentation in regard to the supposed circumstances of his murder and burial, Solomon is represented as raising him from this depth in the earth by the Master's grip, and that "upon the five points of fellowship," which are, "foot to foot, knee to knee, breast to breast, hand to back, and mouth to ear."

It is no wonder that infidel Masons should ridicule the credulity of professed Christian Masons in crediting such a ridiculous story as this.

Again, Masonry goes on to represent that, after Hiram was thus raised from this grave, six feet deep — "foot to foot, knee to knee, breast to breast, hand to back, and mouth to ear" — he was brought up to Jerusalem, and buried under the Most Holy place in King Solomon's Temple. I will quote from the lecture of this degree, as found in the seventh edition of Bernard, p. 81: "Question [speaking of the body]. — What did they do with the body? Answer. — Raised it in a Masonic form, and carried it up to the temple for more decent interment. Q. — Where was it buried? A. — Under the Sanctum Sanctorum, or Holy of Holies, over which they erected a marble monument, with this inscription delineated thereon, A virgin weeping over a broken column, with a book open before her; in her right hand a sprig of cassia; in her left, an urn; Time standing behind her, with his hands infolded in the ringlets of her hair."

Now, observe, this burial was under the Most Holy place in King Solomon's Temple; and the marble monument was erected over it, and consequently must have been in the Most Holy place itself. Does not every careful reader of the Bible know that this is false? We have a minute description in the Bible of everything relating to the Most Holy place — its form, size, embellishments, and of every article of furniture there was in it. No such statue was ever there, and the whole story is a gross falsehood.

But let me quote a little further from this lecture, continuing on page 81: "Q. — What does a Master's lodge represent? A. — The Sanctum Sanctorum, or Holy of Holies of King Solomon's Temple. Q. — How long was the temple building? A. — Seven years; during which it rained not in the daytime, that the workmen might not be obstructed in their labor." This is a likely story! Is there anything of this kind in the Bible? And does anyone believe that a miracle of this kind could have been wrought without having been recorded in the Bible? But again: "Q. — What supported the temple? A. — Fourteen hundred and fifty-three columns, and two thousand one hundred and six pilasters, all hewn from the finest Parian marble." Where did they get this? Again: "Q. — What further supported it? A. — Three grand columns or pillars. Q. — What were they called? A. — Wisdom, Strength, and Beauty. Q. — What did they represent? A. — The pillar of Wisdom represented Solomon, King of Israel, whose wisdom contrived the mighty fabric." But the Bible represents Solomon as having received the whole plan of the temple from David, who received it directly from God. Solomon never contrived the building at all. — 1 Chron., xxviii. 11, 12, 20.

Again, on page 82, we have the following: "Q. — How many constitute a Master's lodge? A. — Three Master Masons. Q.— Where did they usually meet? A. — In the sanctum sanctorum, or Holy of holies of King Solomon's Temple." Now, this misrepresentation is kept up; and in the work of making a Master Mason they make the lodge represent the Most Holy place in King Solomon's Temple. A Masonic lodge in the Most Holy place of King Solomon's Temple! What an absurd, unscriptural, and ridiculous representation is this! And yet this is seriously taught to the candidate whenever a Master Mason is made.

But, again, this whole representation in regard to Hiram Abiff is utterly false. If anyone will examine the fourth chapter of 2 Chron. he will see that Hiram Abiff finished the work for which he was employed; and, so far as we can get any light from the Bible, he must have lived till after the temple was finished. Where and when he died we know not, as he, no doubt, returned to Hiram, King of Tyre, who sent him to assist Solomon. But that he died in the manner represented by Freemasons, that he was buried in a grave six feet deep, and raised upon the five points of fellowship, that he was then buried again under the Most Holy place of King Solomon's Temple, and a marble monument erected in the Most Holy place to his memory, is a glaring falsehood.

Again, Masonry teaches that the Master's word could only be given by three persons standing in a peculiar attitude, and each one repeating one of its syllables. That this word was known at the time by only three persons, Solomon, Hiram, King of Tyre, and Hiram Abiff; and that, consequently, when Hiram was killed, the word was lost, as they were under oath never to give it except in that particular manner.

Now, in the Royal Arch degree, Masonry professes to give an account of the manner in which that word was recovered.

Some men, it is said, were employed in digging about the temple, and discovered a stone, which proved to be the keystone of an arch covering a vault deep under ground, constructed, as it is said, by Hiram Abiff, in which they found the Ark of the Covenant.

On pp. 78, 89, of Richardson's "Monitor of Freemasonry," we have their explanation of this pretended discovery as follows. On p. 78: "*Principal Sojourner.*— Most Excellent, in pursuance of your orders, we repaired to the secret vault and let down one of our companions. The sun at this time was at its meridian height, the rays of which enabled him to discover a small box or chest standing on a pedestal, curiously wrought and overlaid with gold.... We have brought this chest up for the examination of the Grand Council. *High Priest* [looking with surprise at the Ark]. — Companion King this is the Ark of the Covenant of God. *King* [looking at it.] — It is undoubtedly the true Ark of the Covenant, Most Excellent. *High Priest* [taking the Ark]. — Let us open it, and see what valuable treasure it may contain. [Opens the Ark, and takes out a book.] *High Priest to the King.* — Companion, here is a very ancient looking book. What can it be? Let us read it. [Reads the first three verses of the first chapter of Genesis.]"

After reading several other passages, the High Priest says: "This is a book of the law — long lost, but now found. Holiness to the Lord! [He repeats this twice]. *King.* — A book of the law — long lost, but now found. Holiness to the Lord! Scribe repeats the same. *High Priest to Candidates* — You now see that the world is indebted to Masonry for the preservation of this sacred volume. Had it not been for the wisdom and precaution of our ancient brethren, this, the only remaining copy of the law, would have been destroyed at the destruction of Jerusalem." After several further misrepresentation, on p. 79, we have the following: "Looking again into the Ark, the High Priest takes out four pieces of paper, which he examines closely, consults with the king and scribe, and then puts them together so as to show a key to the ineffable characters of this degree. After examining the key, he proceeds to read by the aid of it the characters on the four sides of the Ark. High Priest reading first side: Deposited in the year three thousand. Second side: By Solomon, King of Israel. Third side: Hiram, King of Tyre, and Hiram Abiff. South side; For the good of Masonry generally, but the Jewish nation in particular." If any one will consult the ceremonies just as they occur, and as they are recorded by Richardson, he will see to what an extent the candidate is misinformed and deceived in this degree. And the same in substance may be learned from "Light on Masonry." Now, observe, Masonry teaches in this most solemn manner that in Solomon's time the Ark of the Covenant, with its sacred contents, was buried in a vault by Solomon and the two Hirams.

Solomon was only the third king of Israel. And when did he have this Ark buried? Did it not stand in the Most Holy place during his own reign? Was not the Ark of the Covenant, with its sacred contents, in the Most Holy place in the temple after Solomon's day? What reader of the Bible does not know that this representation of Masonry is false? Again, the candidate is also falsely taught that the world is indebted to Masonry for preserving the book of the law; that, but for this discovery of the Ark with its contents in that vault, no book of the law would have been preserved, as this was the only copy in existence. But this, again, is utterly false. Masonry teaches that, but for the discovery of this volume, the Bible would have been lost at the destruction of Jerusalem. But there is no truth in this for copies had been multiplied before the first, and still further multiplied before the last, destruction of Jerusalem.

The following examples I extract from Professor Morgan's report: "It is alleged that, in consequence of the murder of Hiram Abiff, a particular keystone failed of its designation;

but that Solomon caused search to be made for it, when it was found by means of certain initial letters which Hiram had employed as a mark. These letters were the initials of the English words, *Hiram, Tyrian, widow's son sent to King Solomon*. These initial letters are now employed as the *mark* of the Mark Master's degree. Masons sometimes wear a seal or trinket with these letters on it. I have seen them exhibited in a picture of a seal or badge in a widely circulated Masonic manual. Here we have Hiram, who never could have known one word of English — the English language not existing till thousands of years after his time — employing the initials of eight English words as his mark. And, in honor of his employing them, Mark Masters display them as their mark, and thus display the ignorance or imposture of their craft."

Another alleged historic fact is given in Richardson's "Monitor of Freemasonry," p.155 — the Gold Plate story. "In the ceremonies connected with the degree of 'Grand Elect, Perfect, and Sublime Mason,' the master says: 'I will now give you the true pronunciation of the name of the Deity as revealed to Enoch; and he engraved the letters composing it on a triangular plate of gold, which was hidden for many ages in the bowels of the earth, and lost to mankind. The mysterious words which you received in the preceding degrees are all so many corruptions of the true name of God which was engraved on the triangle of Enoch. In this engraving the *vowel points are so arranged as to give the pronunciation thus,* YOWHO. This word, when thus pronounced, is called the Ineffable word, which cannot be altered as other words are; and the degrees are called, on this account, Ineffable degrees. This word, you will recollect, was not found until after the death of Hiram Abiff; consequently, the word engraved by him on the ark is not the true name of God.'

"Here we have a most ridiculous piece of imposture, more than parallel with the gold plate imposture of Mormonism. Every Hebrew scholar of the most moderate attainments knows that the *vowel points*, here alleged to have been used by Enoch before the flood, did not even exist till six or eight centuries after the birth of Christ. Besides, the merest smatterer in Hebrew, with very little thought, would know that the name of God could not, by any proper arrangement of vowels, be pronounced in this way.

"The story could impose only on the grossest ignorance, or most careless inconsiderateness."

To quote all that is scandalously false in its teachings and pretensions would be to quote these books almost entire. We hear professed Christians, and even ministers, claiming that Freemasonry enables them to better understand the Bible. Can it be that they are so ignorant as to believe this? But this is often urged as an inducement to join the lodge. Indeed Masonry claims that, to this day, none but Freemasons know even the true name of God. After Enoch's day, the Divine name was unknown until recovered by Freemasons in the days of Solomon, and that this true name of God is preserved by them as a Masonic secret. Of course, all others are worshiping they know not what. So this is Masonic benevolence and piety, to conceal from all but their craft the name of the true God. How wise and benevolent Freemasonry is! I wonder how many ministers of the Gospel are engaged in keeping this secret! They only of all ministers know the true name of God, and have joined a conspiracy to conceal it from all but Masons!

Before I close this number, I wish to ask Freemasons who have taken the degrees above the Fellow craft, or second degree, have you believed the teaching of these degrees, as you have taken them one after another? Have you believed that the lodges, chapters, commanderies, etc., were really erected to God, and consecrated to the holy order of Zerubbabel and St. John? Have you believed what you are taught in the Master's degree, respecting King Solomon, Hiram, king of Tyre, and Hiram Abiff? Have you believed the teachings of the Royal Arch degree, and of all those degrees in which King Solomon figures so largely?

FREEMASONRY

Have you believed that to Masonry the church owes the preservation of the only remaining copy of the law of God? Have you believed the Gold Plate story, that Enoch lived in the place where the Temple of Solomon was afterward built, that he built, deep in the earth, nine arches, one above the other, in which, on the place where the temple was afterward built, he deposited a golden plate on which was written the true name of God, that this name was written with the Hebrew vowels attached, and that its true pronunciation is YOWHO, as Masonry teaches? Now you have believed these, and other outrageous falsehoods taught in Masonry, or you have not. If you have believed them, you have been greatly imposed upon, you have been grossly deceived. Will you allow yourselves to still give countenance to an institution that teaches such falsehoods as these? Had I space I could fill scores of pages with the palpable falsehoods which Masonry teaches its membership. How can you adhere to an institution so basely false and hypocritical as this? The secrets are all out. Both you and the world are now made aware of the base falsehoods that are palmed off upon its members by Freemasonry. Professed Christian Freemason, how can you hold up your head either in the church or before the world, if you still adhere to this most hypocritical institution? Just think of the Worshipful Masters, the Grand High Priests, in their mitres and priestly robes, the great and pompous dignitaries of Masonry arrayed in their sacerdotal robes, solemnly teaching their members such vile falsehoods as these, claiming that to Freemasons the church owes the preservation of the law of God, and that the true name of God is known only to Freemasons! Shame! But I said you have either been made to believe these things or you have not. If you have never believed them, pray, let me ask you how it is that you have ever given any countenance to this institution when you did not at all believe its teaching? How is it that you have not long since renounced and denounced an institution whose teaching is replete with falsehoods taught under the most solemn circumstances? These falsehoods are taught as Masonic secrets, under the sanction of the most awful and solemn oaths. What shall we say of an institution that binds its members by such oaths, to keep and preserve as truth and secrets, such a tissue of profane falsehood? You see nothing in it inconsistent with Christianity! Why, my dear brother, how amazing it is that you can be so blinded! Are you not afraid that you shall be given over to believe a lie, that you may be damned, because you believe not the truth, but have pleasure in unrighteousness?

CHAPTER XII

MASONRY SUSCEPTIBLE OF CHANGE ONLY BY ADDITIONS

In proof of this, I first appeal to the testimony of Masons themselves. Hear the testimony, given under oath, of Benjamin Russell, once Grand Master of the Grand Lodge of Massachusetts. His and other depositions were given in Boston, before a justice of the peace, by request of Masons themselves. Observe, he was an ex-Grand Master of one of the most important lodges in the world. This surely is conclusive Masonic authority. He says: *"The Masonic institution has been, and now is, the same in every place. No deviation has been made, or can be made at any time, from its usages, rules and regulations."* Observe, he does not say that no *additions* can be made, but no *deviations.* He proceeds: "Such is its nature, that no innovations on its customs can be introduced, or sanctioned, by any person or persons. DeWitt Clinton, the former Governor of New York and Grand Master of the Grand Lodge of New York and of the United States, also made an affidavit on the same occasion. He says: *"The principles of Masonry are essentially the same and uniform in every place"* (Powell, p.40, as quoted by Stearns). In Hardy's Monitor, a standard Masonic work, we have the following, p. 96: *"Masonry stands in no need of improvement; any attempt, therefore, to introduce the least innovation will be reprobated, not by one, but by the whole fraternity."* The Grand Lodge of Connecticut asserts: "It is not in the power of man, nor in any body of men, to remove the ancient landmarks of Masonry" (Allyn's Ritual, p. 14). These are the highest Masonic authorities, and to the same effect might be quoted from all their standard works.

Second. — From the nature of the institution it cannot be changed, except by addition. In proof of this I observe:

FREEMASONRY

I. That Masonry is extended over the civilized world, at least Masons themselves boast that it includes men of every language, and of every clime. They claim for Masonry that it is a universal language; that men of every country and language can reveal themselves to each other as Freemasons; that by their signs and grips and pass words, etc., they can not only know each other as Masons, but as having taken such and such degrees of the order; that as soon as they reveal themselves to each other as having taken certain degrees of Masonry, they know their obligations, each to the other — what they may demand or expect of each other, and what each is under oath to do for the other. Now this must be true, or of what avail would Masonry be to those who are traveling through different countries, where there are different languages. Unless their methods of knowing each other were uniform, universal, and unchangable [sic.], it is plain that they could not know each other as Masons. It is true in some particular localities there may be an additional pass word or sign, to indicate that they belong to that locality, but in all that is essentially Masonic, it must be universal and unchangable [sic].

II. The same is true with respect to their oaths. They must all, in every place, be under the same obligations to each other, or it would introduce endless confusion and uncertainty. Every Mason, of every place, must know that every other Mason, having taken the same degrees, has taken the same oaths that he himself has taken; that he owes the same duties and can claim the same privileges of any other Mason of the same degree. If this were not so, Masonry would be of no value among strangers. Furthermore, if their obligations were not exactly alike, they would necessarily be betrayed into violating them. If they found that they claimed duties of each other which were not necessarily imposed by the obligations of both, or claimed privileges of each other not conferred by the obligations of both, they would in this way make each other acquainted with their respective obligations which were not in fact alike.

104

Thus each would reveal to the other, secrets which he was sworn to keep.

III. The oaths of every degree, from the lowest to the highest, must be uniform, everywhere the same, and unchangable. If they were not the same in every country, in every language, and at every time, Masonry would be a perfect babel. New degrees may be added *ad infinitum,* but a Mason of any degree must know that Masons of the same degree in every place, have taken the same oath that he has taken, and have taken all the oaths of the previous degrees, just as he has himself. If this were not true, Masons could not everywhere know with what they might entrust each other. Suppose, for example, that the obligation to conceal each other's crimes, and to keep each other's secrets, was not universal and unchangeable, how would they know with what they might trust each other in different places? Suppose the obligation to assist each other in getting out of any difficulty, whether right or wrong, was not uniform and universal, how would they know what they might demand of, or were under obligation to perform for, each other? But can not its objectionable points, it may be asked, be dropped out, and what is valuable preserved? Drop from the obligation, for instance, in any place, the clause that binds them to keep each other's secrets, murder and treason excepted, or without exception, — to deliver each other from difficultly, whether right or wrong, to give each other precedence in business or politics, to give each other warning of any approaching danger and the like. Now if you drop out any one of these, at any time or place, you introduce confusion, and Masons could not understand each other. Furthermore, drop out the most objectionable features of Masonry, and you have robbed it of its principle value to the membership, you have annihilated the principal reasons for becoming and for remaining a Mason. But the changes are manifestly impossible. There is nowhere any authority for such change; and, as has been stated, the whole fraternity would rebuke any attempt at such innovation.

FREEMASONRY

We may rest assured, therefore, that Freemasonry is not, and can not be, essentially changed, except by addition. To this point all their highest authorities bear the fullest testimony. Its very nature forbids essential innovations at any time or in any place. But should Masons affirm that the institution is changed, how are we to know what changes have been made? They are under oath to keep this a profound secret. Suppose they were to affirm that, since the revelations made by Morgan, Bernard, and others, the institution has been greatly improved, this is a virtual admission that those books are true, which they have so often denied. But since they have first denied that those books were true, and now virtually admit their truth, by claiming that Masonry has been improved since those books were written, what reason have we to believe them? I have, in a previous number, shown that it is irrational to believe what Masons themselves say in respect to their secrets. I do not know that any intelligent and respectable Freemason pretends that Masonry has been improved. But suppose they should, how shall we know in what respects it has been improved, that we may judge for ourselves whether the changes *are* improvements. If any number of them were now to affirm that Masonry, as it now exists, is divested of all the objectionable features that formerly belonged to it, how shall we know whether this is true? They have always denied that it had any objectionable features; they have always claimed that it needed no improvement, and their highest authorities have many times affirmed that all improvement and innovation were impossible. In view of all the testimony in the case, we have no right to believe that Masonry is at all improved from what it was forty years ago. As late as 1860, Richardson revealed sixty-two degrees of Masonry as it then existed. It was then the same in every essential feature as when Bernard made his revelation in 1829, and when Avery Allyn made his revelation in 1831. We are all, therefore, under the most solemn obligations to believe that Masonry is, in all important particulars, just what is has been since its various degrees have been adopted and promulgated. We certainly do greatly err and sin, if, in view of all the facts, we assume, and act upon the assumption, that Freemasonry is divested of its immoral and obnoxious features. Such an assumption is utterly unwarranted, because, on the one hand, there is no evidence of the fact, and, on the other, there is positive and abundant proof that no such change has been made. We are all, therefore, responsible to God and to humanity for the course we shall take respecting the institution. We are bound to judge of it, and to treat it, according to the evidence in the case, which is, that *Freemasonry is necessarily a wicked institution, and incapable of thorough moral reformation.*

I have spoken frequently of its having the character, in certain respects, of a mutual aid, or mutual insurance, company. It is inquired, are all these necessarily wicked? I answer, no. The benefits of these institutions may be real and great. For example, an insurance company that insures persons against loss by shipwreck, by fire, or by what we call accident of any kind, may be very beneficial to society. When they help each other in cases of calamity that involve no crime, they are not necessarily wicked, but may be very useful. The benefits of these companies are open to all upon reasonable conditions; and if any do not reap the fruits of them, it is not the fault of the society, but of those who neglect to avail themselves of its benefits. But Freemasonry is by no means a mere insurance or mutual aid society. The moral character of any institution must depend on the end at which it aims; — that is, the moral character of any society is found in the end it is intended to secure. Mutual aid and insurance companies, as they exist for business purposes, do not necessarily deprive any one of his rights, and are often highly useful. The members of such societies or companies do not know each other, nor exert over each other any personal influence whatever. They are not bound by any oath to render each other any unlawful assistance, to conceal each other's crimes, nor "to espouse each other's cause, whether right or wrong." There is no clannish spirit engendered by their frequent meeting together, nor by mutual pledges under the most awful oaths and penalties, to treat each other with any favoriteism [sic.] under any circumstances. But Freemasonry, on the contrary, does pledge its members by the most solemn oaths, to aid each other in a manner that sets aside the rights of others. For example, they are sworn first, in the Master's degree, to conceal each other's crimes, "murder and treason only excepted;" second, in the Royal Arch degree, "murder and treason not excepted;" in this same degree they swear to endeavor to extricate each other, if involved in any difficulty, whether they are right or wrong; third, they also swear to promote each other's political elevation in preference to any one of equal qualifications who is not a Freemason; fourth, to give each other the preference in business transactions. — See Richardson's Monitor of Freemasonry, p.92. Degree of Secret Monitor: "I furthermore promise and swear that I will caution a brother Secret Monitor by signs, word or token, whenever I see him doing, or about to do, any thing contrary to his interest in buying or selling. I furthermore promise and swear, that I will assist a brother Secret Monitor in preference to any other person by introducing him to business, by sending him custom, or in *any other manner* in which I can throw a penny in his way." They swear "to represent all who violate their Masonic oaths as worthless vagabonds, and to send this character after them to ruin their business and their reputation wherever they may go and be to the end of their lives.' They also swear to seek the condign punishment of all such in the infliction of the penalties of their oaths upon them. They swear to seek their death. They swear to a stringent exclusiveness, excluding from their society all that would most naturally need aid and sympathy, and receiving none who are not "physically perfect." Old men in dotage, young men in nonage, all women, idiots and other needy classes, are all excluded. Freemasonry has a vast fund of money at its disposal. The fraternity are very numerous. They boast of numbering in this country at the present time six hundred thousand, and that they are multiplying faster than ever. They permeate every community, and their influence is almost omnipresent. Of course, such an aid society as this will everywhere and in every thing ignore and trample on the rights of others to secure advantages for each other. As an illustration of the workings of this society, I make an extract of two from "The American Freemason," published in Louisville, Kentucky, dated April 8, 5854, that is 1854, and edited by Robert Morris, an eminent Masonic author. From the eighty-fifth page I quote as follows: "Lynn, Indiana. — In hauling a load of pork to the depot a year or two since, I found the rush of wagons so great that the delivery was fully three days behind. This was a serious matter to me, for I would not lose so much time from my business, and was seriously weighing the propriety of going on to Cincinnati with my load, when the freight agent, learning from a casual remark of mine, that I was a Freemason, was kind enough at once to order my errand attended to, and in three hours I was unloaded, and ready, with a light heart, to set my face homeward. Is it not an admirable thing, this Masonic spirit of brotherly love?" To this the editor adds: "Verily, it is. We have seen it in many varieties of form, but our kindhearted brother's is but an every-day experience of Masonic practice, but to the world how inexplicable do such things appear." Here we have a specimen of Masonic brotherly love. But was this right, to give this preference to this man, and wrong all who were there before him, and had a right to have their business done before him! He gained three days's time, and saved the expense of waiting for his turn, whilst others were obliged to lose both the time and expense. And this we are coolly told, by high Masonic authority, is the "constant practice of Freemasons." What an exquisite brotherly love is this. It is delicious! But this is in entire accordance with the spirit of their oaths. But is it not a trampling on the rights of others! In this same paper we have, in an illustration of the nature of Freemasonry, a tale, the substance of which is, that a criminal, under sentence of death, was set free by Freemasons under the pretense that he was not guilty of the murder for which he was condemned. So they took the case into their own hands, and set aside the judgment of the court and jury. Observe, this is given as an illustration of the manner in which Freemasons aid each other. These cases are given as their own boast of specimens of their brotherly love. But is this consistent with right and good government? The fact is, that it is impossible to engage in any business, to travel, to do any thing, to go anywhere without feeling the influence of this and other secret societies. Wrongs are constantly inflicted upon individuals and upon society, of which the wronged are unaware. We can be wronged any day by a favoritism practiced by these societies, without being aware how or by whom we are wronged. I was informed of late, that in a large manufacturing establishment, poor men, dependent for their daily bread upon their labors in the factory, were turned out to give place to Freemasons who were no better workmen than themselves. Indeed it is inevitable that such a society should act upon such a principle. But it may be asked, can not Masonry be essentially reformed, so that it shall involve no wrong? I answer, no, unless its very fundamental principle and aim be reversed, and then it would cease to be Freemasonry. In its workings it is a constant wrong inflicted upon society. It is an incessant and wide-spread conspiracy for the concealment of crime, to obstruct the course of justice, and, in many instances, to persecute the innocent and let the wicked go free. To reform it, its ends and its means must both be reformed. It must cease to be exclusive and selfish. It must cease to promise aid in many forms in which it does promise it. I have said that it was more than an innocent mutual aid society. Its members are pledged to aid each other in concealing iniquity, and in many ways that trample upon the rights of others.

And it is because this society promises aid in so many ways, and under so many circumstances, that men unite themselves to it. I have never heard any better reason assigned for belonging to it, than that, in many respects, one might reap a personal advantage from it. Now reform it, and make it a truly benevolent society; reform out of it all unrighteous favoritism, and all those forms of aid which are inconsistent with the universal good, and the highest well-being of society in general, and you have altered its essential nature; it is no longer Freemasonry, or any thing like Freemasonry. To *reform* it is to destroy it. In this view of Freemasonry, it is easy to see how difficult, if not impossible, it is for a man to be a consistent Freemason and yet a Christian. Just conceive of a Christian constantly receiving the preference over others as good as himself, in traveling, in railroad cars, on steamboats, at hotels, and everywhere, an in business transactions, and in almost all the relations of life, allowing himself to be preferred to others who have equal rights with himself. To be sure, in traveling, he may bless himself because he is so comfortable, and that so much pains are taken to give him the preference in every thing. If at a hotel, he may have the best seat at the table, and the best room in the house, and may find himself everywhere more favored than others.

But can he honestly accept this? Has he any right to accept it? No, indeed, he has not! He is constantly favored at the expense of others. He constantly has more than his right, while others are deprived of their rights. In other words, he is selfish, and that continually. He finds a personal benefit in it. Yes, and that is why he adheres to it. But again, if true to his oath, he is not only thus constantly receiving benefits unjustly, or to the injury of others, but also conferring them.

Whenever he sees a Masonic sign and recognizes a Masonic brother, he, of course, must do by him as a Freemason, as he himself is done by.

How can a man who is a Christian allow himself to be influenced by such motives as are presented in Freemasonry?

FREEMASONRY

Now let it be understood that all action is to be judged by its motive. No man has a right to receive or confer favors that interfere with the rights of others. And a man who can travel about the country and make himself known as a Freemason for the purpose of being indulged, and finding the best place in a hotel, or the best seat in a railroad car, or the best state-room in a steamboat, must be a selfish man, and can not be a Christian, — for a selfish man is not a Christian. Let it then be understood that Masonry in its fundamental principle, in which its moral character is found, is not reformed, and can not be reformed without destroying its very nature.

It can not be a part of general benevolence but stands unalterable opposed to the highest well-being of society in general. The same, let me say, is true to a greater or less extent of all secret societies, whose members are bound by oath or pledge to treat each other with a favoritism that ignores the rights of others. Now, it has been said, and I think truly, that in the late war if a man wished preferment and high rank, he must be a high Mason. Such things were managed so much by high Masons that it was difficult for a man to rise in rank unless he could make himself known as a high Mason. And let the facts become known — and, I hope that measures will be taken to make them known — and I believe it will be found that the great mass of the lucrative offices in the United States are in the hands of the Freemasons.

It is evident that they are aiming to seize upon the government, and to wield it in their own interest. They are fast doing this, and unless the nation awake soon it will be too late. And let the church of God also awake to the fact that many of her ministers and members are uniting with a society so selfish and wicked as this, and are defending it, and are ready to persecute all who will not unite with them in this thing. What Mr. Morris said of the nature of Freemasonry, that is, that it was the constant practice of Freemasons to give each other the preference, as in the case of the man delivering his load, is

112

really what every observant man, especially if he has ever been himself a Mason, knows to be true.

When Freemasons say that it is "a good thing," they mean by this that men reap personal advantage from it. But I am bound to say, that I should feel utterly ashamed to have any one offer to give me a right that belonged to others because I was a Mason.

It has been frequently said, by persons: "If I was going to travel, I would become a Freemason." A physician in the United States Army in the late war, said to a relative of his: "If I were going into the army again, I would be sure to become a Freemason. There is such a constant favoritism shown by Freemasons to each other, on every occasion, that were I going to take the field again, I would be sure to avail myself of the benefits of that institution." Now, in opposition to this, I would say, that were I going to travel, or were I going to enlist in the army, I should be ashamed to avail myself of any such benefits at all. It is not right that any such favoritism should exist, and any man ought to reject with indignation the proposal of such favoritism. Any man should blush, if he has entertained the thought of allowing himself to be placed in such a selfish position. But it is asserted, no doubt with truth, that often times the lives of brother Masons have been spared, simply because of this relation. But shall a man save his life by wrongdoing? He had better remember, that if he attempts this, he ruins his own soul. He that would thus "save his life, shall lose it." A man can gain nothing in the end by wrong-doing; let him do right, and if, by so doing, he loses his life, he will be sure to save it. With my present knowledge of Freemasonry I would not become a Freemason to save my life a thousand times.

CHAPTER XIII

THE CLAIM OF FREEMASONRY TO GREAT ANTIQUITY IS FALSE

We have seen that Freemasonry has been truly revealed. We have examined its *oaths, principles, claims,* and *teaching,* so far as to prepare the way for an examination of its moral character and tendencies, and also its relations to both Church and State. This I now proceed to do. And

1. *Its claims to great antiquity are false* Every one at all acquainted with the claims of Freemasonry knows that it professes to have existed in the days of Solomon; and it is claimed that Solomon himself was a Freemason, and that John the Baptist and John the Evangelist were Freemasons. Indeed, the writers frequently trace it back as coeval with the creation itself. Masons have claimed for their institution an antiquity antecedent to human government; and from this they have argued that they have a right to execute the penalties of their oaths, because Masonry is older than government. Now an examination will show that this claim is utterly false. Their own highest authorities now pronounce it to be false; and still these claims are kept up, and their oaths and ceremonies, and the whole structure of the institution profess the greatest antiquity.

Solomon, for instance, figures as a Freemason everywhere in their ceremonies.

Their lodges are dedicated to St. John; and in the third degree there is a scene professed to have been enacted in the temple and at the building of the Temple of Solomon.

Now, all this is utterly fallacious, a false pretense, and a swindle; because it is the obtaining of money from those who join them under false pretenses.

FREEMASONRY

Steinbrenner, a great Masonic historian, after much research, with manifest candor, says that Speculative Freemasonry — which is the only form of Freemasonry now existing — dates no further back than 1717. The article of Freemasonry in the new "American Encyclopedia" agrees with this statement of Steinbrenner. Indeed, all modern research on this subject has resulted in dating the commencement of Freemasonry, as it now exists, not far from the middle of the eighteenth century.

Dr. Dalcho, the compiler of the book of constitutions for South Carolina, says: *"Neither Adam, nor Noah, nor Nimrod, nor Moses, nor Joshua, nor David, nor Solomon, nor Hiram, nor St. John the Baptist, nor St. John the Evangelist, were Freemasons. Hypothesis in history is absurd. There is no record, sacred or profane, to induce us to believe that those holy men were Freemasons; and our traditions do not go back to those days. To assert that they were Freemasons may make the vulgar stare, but will rather excite the contempt than the admiration of the wise."*

Now, observe, this is a high authority, and should be conclusive with Masons, because it is one of their own leaders who affirms this. But, if this is true, what shall we think of the claims of Freemasonry itself? For every one who reads these revelations of Freemasonry will see that Solomon, and Hiram, and those ancient worthies everywhere figure in these rites and ceremonies; so that, if these men were indeed not Masons, then Freemasonry is a sham, an imposture, and a swindle. What! has it come to this, that this boasted claim of antiquity, which everywhere lies at the foundation of Masonic rites, ceremonies, and pretensions, is now discovered to be false?

Through all the Masonic degrees the pretense is kept up that Masonry has always been one and the same; and that its degrees are ancient, and all its principles and usages of great antiquity. Let any one examine the books in which it is revealed, and he can not help being struck with this. Furthermore, in the orations, sermons, and puffs that are so common with

116

Masons on all occasions on which they show themselves off, they flaunt their very ancient date, their very ancient principles and usages, and they pledge their candidates, from one degree to another, to conform to all the ancient rites, principles, and usages of the order.

But what shall we at the present day say of these pretensions? I have before me the *Masonic Monthly* for October, 1867, printed in Boston. It will not be denied, I suppose, that this is one of their standard authorities. At any rate, whatever may be said of the editor of this paper, it will not be denied that the authorities quoted in the discussions in this number are high, if not the very highest authorities in the Masonic fraternity. If I had space to quote nearly this entire number, I should be very happy to do so, for it is occupied almost entirely, from beginning to end, with exposing these pretensions to which I have alluded. It appeals to their own standard authorities; and insists that Speculative Freemasonry, in all its higher degrees, is an imposture and a swindle. It quotes their great historian — Steinbrenner of New York — to show that Speculative Freemasonry was first established in London, in 1717; and that at that time Masonry consisted, probably, of but *one* degree. That about 1725 a Mr. Anderson added two degrees; and, as the writer in this number states, began the *Christianizing* of Freemasonry. There is at this day a great division among Freemasons themselves, the point of disagreement being this: One party maintains that the Christian religion is of no more authority with Masons than any other form of religion; that Masonry proper does not recognize the Bible as of any higher authority than the sacred books of heathen nations, or than the Koran of Mohammed; that Freemasonry proper recognizes all religions as equally valid, and that so far as Masonry is concerned it matters not at all what the religion of its adherents is, provided they be not Atheists. The other party maintains that Masonry is founded upon the Bible, and that it is substantially a Christian institution.

117

FREEMASONRY

This controversy is assuming extensive proportions, and it is very interesting for outsiders to look into it. I say *outsiders* — and I might say it is important, and would be very creditable, for the members of the fraternity to understand this matter better than they do; for I doubt if one in twenty of them is posted in regard to the real state of this question among the fraternity themselves. Mr. Evans, who is the editor of this *Masonic Monthly*, takes the ground, and I think sustains it fully from their own authorities, that all the upper degrees of Masonry are an imposture.

He goes on to show where and by whom, in several important cases, these upper degrees were manufactured and palmed off on the brotherhood as ancient Freemasonry.

For example, he shows that Mr. Oliver, one of their most prolific authors, asserts that one of the grand lodges in London gave charters, about the middle of the eighteenth century, to the Masonic lodges in France; and that in France they immediately betook themselves to manufacturing degrees and palming them off on the public as of very ancient origin. They proceeded to manufacture a thousand of these degrees in France. Many of them they asserted they had received from Scotland; but the Grand Lodge of Scotland denied ever having known of those degrees.

It is also asserted in this number that the Royal Arch degree was at first but an appendage to a master's lodge, and had no separate charter, and for a long time was not recognized at all as any part of Freemasonry. And it informs us when and by whom the Royal Arch degree was manufactured. This number also shows that many of the Masonic degrees have originated in Charleston, South Carolina; and that a man by the name of Webb, in Massachusetts, manufactured the Templars' degrees. In short, we find here their own standard authorities showing up all the higher degrees of Masonry as having been gotten up and palmed off on the fraternity in order to make money out of them; and is not this a swindle? I

118

wish to call the attention especially of the fraternity to these statements in this number of the *Masonic Monthly*.

Indeed, it is now common for the highest and best informed Masons to ridicule the pretense that Speculative Freemasonry is an ancient institution, as a humbug and a lie, having no foundation in correct history at all. Now will Freemasons examine this subject for themselves? — for they have been imposed upon.

I am particularly anxious to have professed Christians who are Freemasons thoroughly understand this matter. They have regarded Freemasonry as entirely consistent with the Christian religion, and have professed to see in it nothing with which a Christian can not have fellowship. In the third, or Master's degree we find the story of Hiram Abiff introduced into Masonry.

Now this number of the *Monthly* charges, that this class of Freemasons went on to construct all the subsequent degrees of Freemasonry from the Bible, by ransacking the whole Old and New Testaments for striking passages from which they could construct new degrees, thus leaving the impression that Masonry was a divine institution, and founded upon the Bible.

If professed Christians who are Freemasons will really examine this subject, they will see that a Masonic lodge is no place for a Christian.

But suppose it should be asked, may we not innocently take those degrees that are founded upon the Bible, and that recognize the Christian religion as of divine authority? I answer, Christians cannot be hypocrites. Let it be distinctly understood, that all these higher degrees are shown to be an imposture; and that this Christianizing of Freemasonry has consisted in heaping up a vast mass of falsehood, and of palming it off upon the fraternity as truth and as ancient Freemasonry.

Can Masonic orators be honest in still claiming for Speculative Masonry great antiquity, divine authority, and that it is a saving institution? Masons are themselves now showing that the whole fabric of Speculative Freemasonry is an enormous falsehood. Stone Masonry, doubtless, had its simple degree, and its pass words and signs by which they knew each other. It also had its obligations. But upon that little stem have been engrafted a great number of spurious and hypocritical degrees.

This does seem to be undeniable. Now will Freemasons be frank enough to acknowledge this, and to say frankly that they have been imposed upon? Will they come out from all fellowship with such an imposture and such a swindle?

It has then come at last to this, that the highest authority among Freemasons has taken the ground that the Freemasonry which has been so eulogized throughout the length and breadth of the land, and which has drawn in so many professed Christians and ministers, is nothing less than an enormous cheat. That those behind the curtain, who have manufactured and sold these degrees — those Grand Chapters and Encampments and Commanderies, and all those pompous assemblies — have been engaged in enticing the brotherhood who had taken the lower degrees, to come up into their ranks and pay their money, that they may line their pockets. Now remember that these positions are fully sustained by Masons themselves, as their views are set forth in this number of the *Masonic Monthly.*

I do most earnestly entreat Freemasons to inform themselves on this subject; and not turn around and tell us that they, being Freemasons, know more about it than we do ourselves. The fact is, my friends, many of you do not. You do not read. I have myself recently conversed with a Freemason who admitted to me that he was entirely ignorant of what was being said in Masonic periodicals on this subject. I do not believe that one in twenty of the Masonic fraternity in this country is aware of the intense hypocrisy with which all the higher degrees of Masonry have been palmed off upon them, and upon the whole fraternity. Can men of honor and of principle allow their names and influence to be used to sustain such an enormous mass of false pretension?

But again, no one can read Bernard on Masonry through, or any of these authors, without perceiving the most unmistakable evidence that most of the degrees in Masonry are of modern date. I do not know why so much stress should be laid upon the antiquity of Masonry by those who embrace and adhere to it. It surely does not prove that it is of any value, or that it is true. Sin is of very ancient date, heathenism is of very ancient date, and most of the abominations that are in the world are of very ancient date; but this is no reason for embracing them, or regarding them as of any great importance.

But to certain minds there is a charm in the appearance and profession of antiquity; and young Masons are universally deceived in this respect, and led to believe that it is one of the most ancient of existing institutions, if not the very most so. Now I would not object to Masonry because it is of modern origin; for this would not prove it to be false, if it did not profess to be of ancient origin. I notice this false pretense not because I think its being of recent date would prove it unworthy of notice, or of immoral character or tendency. But observe that its pretensions from first to last are that it is of very ancient date; and it is traced back to the days of inspiration, and is claimed to have been founded and patronized by inspired men.

What would Masonry be if all its claims to antiquity were stricken out, and if those degrees in Masonry, and those ceremonies and usages, were abolished that rest upon the claim that Solomon, that Hiram Abiff, and John the Evangelist, were Freemasons? What would remain of Freemasonry if all those claims found in the very body of the institution were stricken out? Why, their very lodges are dedicated to the holy order of St. John and Zerubbabel, etc. But what had St. John to do with Freemasonry? Manifestly nothing. He never heard or thought of it. Nor did Solomon or Zerubbabel.

And here let me say a word to young men who have been urged to unite with this fraternity, and who have been made

121

to believe that the institution is so very ancient that it was established and patronized by those holy men. My dear young men, you have been deceived. You have been imposed upon as I was imposed upon. You have been made to believe a lie. They have drawn your money from you under false pretenses that some very ancient mysteries were to be revealed to you; and that the institution was one established as far back, at least, as the days of Solomon, and that St. John was the patron of the institution. Now this, relay upon it is but a pretense, a sham, and imposture, and a swindle. I beg you to believe me; and if you will examine the subject for yourselves, you will find it to be true.

Your own best historian, Steinbrenner, will teach you that Freemasonry, as you know it, and as it is now universally known, dates no further back than the eighteenth century. And Dr. Dalcho, who is good authority with the brotherhood, as we have seen, repudiates the idea of its antiquity as that which "may make the vulgar stare, but will rather excite the contempt than the admiration of the wise." I know that Masons affirm that the institution in its present form is the descendant of a brotherhood of stone masons, whose history may be traced back for some seven hundred years. But remember that Freemasonry, as you know it, and as it now exists, is not at all what it was among those simple artisans. The name is preserved, and some of its symbols, for the purpose of claiming for it great antiquity. But do not be deceived. If you will examine the subject for yourselves, you will find that modern Freemasonry is entirely another thing from that from which it claims to be descended. And when you hear ministers, or orators, on any occasion, claiming for Speculative Freemasonry — which is the only form in which it now exists — a great antiquity, let it be settled, I pray you, in your minds, that such claims are utterly false; and that those who make them are either grossly ignorant or intensely dishonest. *King Solomon a stone mason! Hiram a Grand Master of a Grand Lodge of stone masons! Those* *men uniting in a lodge with a company of stone masons!*Does any one really believe the silly tale?

How long shall the intelligent of this generation be insulted by having this pretended antiquity of Freemasonry paraded before the public? Do not intelligent Freemasons blush to hear their orators on public occasions, and even ministers of the Gospel in their Masonic sermons, flaunt the silly falsehoods of the great antiquity of Freemasonry before the public, and claim that Enoch, Zerubbabel, Solomon, the St. Johns, and all the ancient worthies were Freemasons!

CHAPTER XIV

THE BOASTED BENEVOLENCE OF FREEMASONS A SHAM

The law of God requires universal benevolence, supreme love to God, and equal love to our neighbor — that is, to all mankind.

This the Gospel also requires, and this is undeniable. But does Masonry inculcate this morality? and is this Masonic benevolence?

By no means. Masonic oaths require partial benevolence; or strictly, they require no benevolence at all. For real benevolence is universal in its own nature. It is good-willing; that is, it consists in willing the well-being or good of universal being — and that for its own sake, and not because the good belongs to this or that particular individual.

In other words, true benevolence is necessarily impartial. But Masonic oaths not only do not require impartial and universal benevolence, but they require the exact opposite of this. The law and Gospel of God allow and require us to discriminate in our doing good between the holy and the wicked.

They require us to do good, as we have opportunity, to all men, but especially to the household of faith. But the Masonic oaths make no such discriminations as this, nor do they allow it. These oaths require Masons to discriminate between Masons and those that are not Masons; giving the preference to Masons, even if they are not Christians, rather than to Christians if they are not Masons.

Now this is directly opposite to both the law and the Gospel. But this is the benevolence and morality of Freemasonry, undeniably.

The law and the Gospel require our discriminations in our treatment of men to be conditional upon their holiness and likeness to God and their faith in Jesus Christ.

FREEMASONRY

But the oaths of Freemasons require their discriminations to be founded upon the mere relation of a brother Mason, whatever his Christian or moral character may be.

It is not pretended that a man may not be a good and worthy Mason who is not a Christian. It is admitted and claimed by Freemasonry that a man's religion, or religious character has nothing to do with his being a Mason. If he admits the being of a God this is enough.

Now this, I say again, is not only not in accordance with Christian morality, and with the law and Gospel of God; but it is directly opposed to both law and Gospel.

But, again, the utter want of true benevolence in the Masonic institution will further appear if we consider the exclusiveness of the institution. A minister in Cleveland, recently defending the institution of Masonry, declared that the glory of Masonry consists in its exclusiveness. But is this in accordance with the benevolence required in the Gospel?

Masonry, observe, professes to be a benevolent institution. But, first, it excludes all women from a participation in its rights, ceremonies, privileges, and blessings, whatever they may be. Secondly, it excludes all old men in their dotage. Thirdly, it excludes all young men in their nonage; that is, under twenty-one years of age. Several other classes are excluded; but these that I have named comprise a vast majority, probably not less than two-thirds of all mankind. Again, they admit no deformed person, and none but those who are physically perfect. In short, they admit none who are likely to become chargeable to the institution.

Some time since the Grand Lodge of the State of New York adopted a series of articles defining certain landmarks and principles of Freemasonry. These articles have been accepted and eulogized by the Masonic press. The first is as follows. I quote it from the American Freemasons, edited by "Robert Morris, Knight Templar, and author of various Masonic works," with his preface and strictures. These articles Mr. Morris regards as high Masonic authority. The number from which I

126

quote is dated at Louisville, Kentucky, 8th of April, 5854, Masonic date, in other words, in 1854, fourteen years ago.

"Our New York brethren are eminent for the matchless ability with which their Grand Lodge documents are prepared. In this department they have set the example for others, and there are yet a few that would do well to look to the East for more light. We copy their 'Thirty-four Articles' with some condensation and a few comments of our own, and present them to our readers as a well-digested system of Masonic law and practice.

"'ARTICLE I. It is not proper to initiate into our lodges persons of the Negro race; and their exclusion is in accordance with Masonic law, and the ancient charges and regulations. Because of their depressed social condition; their general want of intelligence, which unfits them as a body to work in or adorn the craft; the impropriety of making them our equals in one place, when from their social condition and the circumstances which almost everywhere attach to them, we can not do so in others; their not being, as a general think, *free-born*; the impossibility, or at least the difficulty, of ascertaining, if we once commence, their free birth, and where the line of intelligence and social elevation commences and ends, or divides portions of their race; and finally, their not being as a race "persons of good report," or who can be "well recommended" as subjects for initiation, their very seldom being persons who have any "trade, estate, office, occupation or visible way of acquiring an honest livelihood and working in the craft, as becomes members of this ancient and most honorable fraternity, who ought not only to earn what is sufficient for themselves and families, but likewise something to spare for works of charity and for supporting the ancient grandeur and dignity of the royal craft, eating no man's bread for naught;" and their general positive deficiency of natural endowments. All which would render it impossible, as a general thing, to conciliate and continue between them and us good will and private affection or brotherly love, which cements into one united body the members of this ancient fraternity.'

127

"COMMENT. These arguments can not be successfully controverted. We, in the Southern or slave-holding States, whose experience with the colored race is greater than that of others, affirm the New York doctrine in every particular. However occasional instances may be offered to the contrary, they are but the exceptions to prove the general rule, that the race ought not to amalgamate socially or physically.

"'ARTICLE II. No person of the Negro race shall be examined or admitted as a visitor of any lodge of Masons under this jurisdiction, if made in an African lodge in North America. Because all such lodges are clandestine and without legal authority.'"

Here we have their benevolence unmasked. A depressed social condition is a bar to admission to this benevolent society. What if the Christian church should adopt such an article? Is this Christian benevolence? Is it consistent with Christian morality? Christian ministers, is this the morality you teach and practice? You profess to teach and practice the precepts of Christ, and join and hold fast to a society whose law is to exclude men for being in a depressed social position, whatever their wants, their moral and religious character may be. You boast of your benevolence and exclude the very class who have most need of sympathy and benevolence, and are *you* a professed disciple, and perhaps a professed minister of Jesus. SHAME!

But is this real benevolence, or Gospel morality? No, indeed! It is the very opposite of Gospel morality or true benevolence. In a recent number of the *National Freemason* — I think its date is the 18th of January — it is admitted by the editor of that great national organ that benevolent institutions have been so much multiplied that there is now seldom any call upon Masons for charitable donations. Yes, but who has multiplied these benevolent societies? Surely Masons have not done this. Christians have done it. And Masonry now seems forced to admit that Christian benevolence has covered the whole field, and left them nothing to do. So far as I have had experience in Freemasonry, I can say that I do not recollect a single instance in which the lodge to which I belonged ever gave any money to any charitable object whatever.

As a Freemason, I never was called upon, and to my recollection I never gave a cent as a Freemason, either to an individual as a matter of charity or to any object whatever. My dues and fees to the lodges, of course, I paid regularly; but that the money thus collected was given to any charitable object whatever I do not believe.

Again, Freemasonry, at the best, is but a mutual insurance company. Their oaths pledge them to assist each other, if in distress or in necessitous circumstances; and each other's families, if left in want. This they can well afford to do, on the principle of mutual insurance: for they have vast sums, almost incalculable in amount, taking the whole fraternity together; and they can layout almost any amount of money in fitting up their sumptuous lodges of the higher degrees, in building Masonic temples, in seeking each other's promotion to office, and in defending each other in case any one of them commits a crime and is liable to suffer for it.

The following estimate, taken from a note in the revised edition of Bernard's "Light on Masonry," p.96, will give some idea how large are the sums held by Masons. "Supposing that in the United States there are 500,000 Entered Apprentices, 400,000 Masters, and 200,000 Royal Arch Masons, also 10,000 Knights, and that they all paid the usual fees for the degrees, the amount would be the enormous sum of $11,250,000; the yearly interest of which, at seven per cent, is $787,500, which sum (allowing $100 to each individual) would support 7,875 persons.

Now, I ask: Do Masons, by their charities, support this number of poor in the United States? Do they support one-tenth part of this number? Supposing they do, is it necessary to give $10, or $50 for the privilege of contributing $1, $5, or $50 masonically? Must the privilege of being a charitable man be bought with gold? How many there are who have rendered themselves incompent (sic) to bestow charities, by their payment for and attendance on Masonic secrets and ceremonies! If all the money paid for the degrees of Masonry was applied to charitable purposes, the subject would appear differently; but it is principally devoted to the erection of Masonic temples, support of the Grand Lodges, and for refreshment for the craft, and I think I may add, for their support in kid-napping and murder."

It is no doubt true that but a very small part of their funds is ever used for the support of even their own poor. If it is, it behooves them to show it, and let the public know. They boast much of their benevolence; and the charities of Freemasons are frequently compared with those of the church — and that, too, boastfully; they maintaining that they are more benevolent and charitable, and do more for the poor and destitute than even the church has done.

But let us look at this. Is there any truth in all this boasting? What has Freemasonry done for general education in any part of the world? Let them tell us. Again, what has Freemasonry done for the general poor? Nothing. What have they done for their own poor, as a matter of charity and benevolence? Absolutely nothing. They have not even disbursed the funds which have been paid in for that purpose. Let them show, if they can, that on the principle of a mutual insurance society they have faithfully paid out to their own poor that fund which has been paid in by Masons for the purpose of securing to themselves and families, in case they should be reduced to poverty, what would meet their absolute necessities. We challenge them to show any such thing. We challenge them to show that, on the principle of benevolence and charity, they have really done anything for either the general poor or their own poor. They compare themselves with the Church of Christ in this respect! What have they done for the Southern poor during our great struggle, and during the long period of starvation and distress that has reigned in the South? What have Freemasons, as such, done for the freedmen? And what are they now doing? What have they done in any age of the world, as Freemasons, for Christian missions, for the conversion of the world, for the salvation of the souls of men? What! compare themselves boastfully with the Church of God, as being more benevolent than Christians?

The fact is, the Church of Christ has done ten thousand times as much for humanity as they have ever done. And she has not done it on the principle of a mutual insurance company, but as a matter of true benevolence, including in her charities the poor, the lowly, the halt and the blind, the old and the young, the black and the white.

The Church of Christ has done more for the bodies of men, ten thousand times more, than Freemasonry has ever done or ever will do.

Besides, the Church of Christ has poured out its treasure like a flood to enlighten mankind generally, to save their souls, and to do them good both for time and eternity. But what has Freemasonry done in this respect? Their boasted benevolence is a sham. I admit that they do sometimes afford relief to an indigent brother Mason, and to the families of such. I admit that they have often done this. But I maintain that this is not done as an act of Christian charity, but only as an act of Masonic charity; and that Masonic charity is only the part payment of a debt. Masons pay in their money to the Masonic fund; and this fund is that out of which their poor are helped, when they are helped at all.

What individuals do for individuals, on rare occasions, is but a trifle. Indeed, it is seldom that they are called on as individuals. The help granted to the poor is almost always taken from the funds of the lodges. And I seriously doubt whether there is a lodge in the United States that has ever paid as much for the support of their own poor as has been paid in to their funds by those who have joined the lodge. Let it be understood, then, that their boast of benevolence and of Christian morality is utterly false. Their oaths do not pledge them at all to the performance of any truly Christian morality;

but to a Masonic benevolence, which is the opposite of true Christian morality.

Instead, therefore, of Masonry's inculcating really sound morality, instead of its being almost or quite true religion, the very perfection of that morality which their oaths oblige them to practice is anti-Christian, and opposed to both the law and gospel of God. It is partial. And here let me again appeal to the dear young men who have been persuaded to join the Masonic fraternity under the impression that it is a benevolent institution. Do not, my dear young men, suffer yourselves to be deceived in this respect. If you have well considered what the law and Gospel require, you will soon perceive that the benevolence and morality required by your Masonic oaths is not Gospel morality or true benevolence at all; but that it is altogether a spurious and selfish morality. Indeed, you yourselves are aware that you joined the lodge from selfish motives; and that the morality inculcated by Masons is an exclusive, one-sided, and selfish affair altogether. In some of the lectures, you are aware that occasionally the duty of universal good-will is in few words, inculcated. But you also know that your oaths, which lay down the rule of your duty in this respect, require no such thing as universal and impartial benevolence; but that they require the opposite of this. That is, they require you to prefer a Mason because he is a Mason to a Christian because he is a Christian; and, instead of requiring you to do good especially to the household of faith, your oaths require you to do good especially to those who are Freemasons, whether they belong to the household of faith or not. But this you know to be anti-Christian, and not according to the Gospel. But you know alas that Christians devote themselves to doing good to Masons and to those who are not Masons, to all classes and descriptions of men. And this they do, not on the principle, as I have said, of a mutual insurance society, but as a mere matter of benevolence. They deny themselves for the sake of doing good to the most lowly and even to the most wicked men.

Do not allow yourselves, therefore, to suppose that there is any good in Masonry. We often hear it said, and sometimes by professed Christians and Christian ministers, that "Masonry is a good thing."

But be not deceived. If by good is intended morally good, the assertion is false. *There is nothing morally good in Freemasonry.* If there are any good men who are Freemasons, Freemasonry has not made them so; but Christianity has made them so. They are good not by virtue of their Freemasonry, but by virtue of their Christianity. They have not been made good by anything they have found in Freemasonry; but, if they are good, they have been made good by Christianity, in spite of Freemasonry. I must say that I have always been ashamed of Freemasons whenever I have read, in their orations, or in the sermons of ministers who have eulogized it, or in their eulogistic books, the pretense that Freemasonry is a benevolent institution. Many have claimed it to be religion, and true religion. This question I shall examine in another place. But the thing I wish to fix your especial attention upon in the conclusion of this article, is, that Freemasonry has not just claims to Christian morality or benevolence; but that in its best estate it is only partiality, and the doing in a very slovenly manner the work of a mutual insurance company. I do not claim that as a mutual insurance company it is necessarily wicked but I do insist that, being at best a mutual insurance company, it is wicked and shameful to flaunt their hypocritical professions of benevolence before the public as they constantly do. How long shall an intelligent people be nauseated with this pretense? How can they expect us to have the least respect for such claims to benevolence? We must regard the putting forth of such claims as an insult to our common sense.

CHAPTER XV

FREEMASONRY IS A FALSE RELIGION

Some Freemasons claim that Freemasonry is a saving institution, and that it is true religion. Others hold a different opinion, claiming that it is the *handmaid of religion,* a system of *refined morality.* Others still are free to admit that it is only a mutual aid or mutual insurance society. This discrepancy of views among them is very striking, as every one knows who has been in the habit of reading sermons, lectures, and orations on Masonry published by themselves. In this article I propose to inquire, first, Do their standard authorities claim that Masonry is identical with true religion? secondly, Does Freemasonry itself claim to be true religion? and, thirdly, Are these claims valid?

1. Do their standard authorities claim that Masonry is true religion?

I quote Salem Town. I read his work some forty years ago. The book professes on its title-page to be "A System of Speculative Masonry, exhibited in a course of lectures before the Grand Chapter of the State of New York, at their annual meetings in the City of Albany." It was reduced to a regular system by their special request, and recommended to the public by them as a system of Freemasonry. It is also recommended by nine grand officers, in whose presence the lectures were delivered; by another who had examined them; and by "the Hon. DeWitt Clinton, General Grand High Priest of the General Grand Chapter of the United States of America, Grand Master of the Grand Lodge of the State of New York, etc., etc."

The book was extensively patronized and subscribed for by Freemasons throughout the country, and has always been considered by the fraternity as a standard authority. From this author I quote as follows:

FREEMASONRY

"The principles of Freemasonry have the same coeternal and unshaken foundations, contain and inculcate the same truths in substance, and propose the same ultimate end, as the doctrines of Christianity." — P. 53. Again he says: "The same system of faith and the same practical duties taught by revelation are contained in and required by the Masonic institution." — P.174. "Speculative Masonry combines those great and fundamental principles which constitute the very essence of the Christian system." — P.37. "It is no secret that there is not a duty enjoined nor a virtue required in the volume of inspiration but what is found in and taught by Speculative Freemasonry." "The characteristic principles are such as embrace the whole subject-matter of divine economy." — P.31.

Again he says: "As the WORD in the first verse of St. John constitutes both the foundation, the subject-matter, and the great ultimate end of the Christian economy, so does the same WORD, in all its relations to man, time, and eternity, constitute the very spirit and essence of Speculative Freemasonry." — P. 155. Again, referring to the promise of the Messiah, he says: "The same precious promise is the great cornerstone in the edifice of Speculative Freemasonry." — P.171. Again he says: "The Jewish order of priesthood from Aaron to Zacharias, and even till the coming of Messias, was confirmation of the great event, which issued in the redemption of man. All pointed to the eternal priesthood of the Son of God, who by his own blood made atonement for sin, and consecrated the way to the Holy of holies. *This constitutes the great and ultimate point of Masonic research.*" — P.121.

"That a knowledge of the divine WORD., or Logos, should have been the object of so much religious research from time immemorial adds not a little to the honor of Speculative Freemasonry." — P.151.

Again he says: "It is a great truth, and weighty as eternity, that the present and ever lasting well-being of mankind is solely and ultimately intended." — P.170. This he says of

Freemasonry. But again he says: "Speculative Masonry, according to present acceptation, has an ultimate reference to that spiritual building erected by virtue in the heart, and summarily implies the arrangement and perfection of those holy and sublime principles by which the soul is fitted for a meet temple of God in a world of immortality" — P. 63. Does not Freemasonry profess to be a saving religion?

Again he says, "In advancing to the fourth degree, the good man is greatly encouraged to persevere in the ways of well-doing even to the end. He has a name which no man knoweth save him that receiveth it. If, therefore, he be rejected and cast forth among the rubbish of the world, he knows full well that the great Master-builder of the universe, having chosen and prepared him a lively stone in that spiritual building in the heavens, will bring him forth in triumph, while shouting grace, grace to the Divine Redeemer. Then the Freemason is assured of his election and final salvation. Hence, opens the fifth degree, where he discovers his election to, and his glorified station in, the kingdom of his Father." Then again he is assured of his "election and glorified station in the kingdom of his Father." If this is not claiming for Freemasonry a saving power what is? Salem Town is the great light in Freemasonry, as the title and history of his work imports. Does he not claim that Freemasonry is a saving religion? To be sure he does, or no words can assert such a claim. "With these views, the sixth degree is conferred, where the riches of divine grace are opened in boundless prospect." "Then he beholds in the eighth degree, that all the heavenly sojourners will be admitted within the veil of God's presence, where they will become kings and priests before the throne of his glory forever and ever.' — Pp. 79-81. By the "heavenly sojourners," he certainly means Freemasons. Observe what he asserts of them: "Then he (the Freemason) beholds in the eighth degree that all the heavenly sojourners will be admitted within the veil of God's presence, where they will become kings and priests before the throne of his glory forever and ever." This clenches the claim. "The maxims of wisdom are gradually unfolded till the whole duty of man is clearly and persuasively exhibited to the mind." — P. 184.

Again, "Principles and duties which lie at the foundation of the Masonic system, and are solemnly enjoined upon every brother; whoever, therefore, shall conscientiously discharge them in the fear of God fulfills the whole duty of man." — P. 48. Then he claims for Freemasonry all that is or can be claimed for the law or Gospel of God.

Again he says: "The Divine Being views no moral character in a man with greater complacency than his who in heart strictly conforms to Masonic requirements." "The more prominent features of a true Masonic character are literally marked with the highest beauties." Pp. 33, 185. Then again he represents Masonry as forming as holy a character in man as the Gospel does or can.

Again he says that "every good Mason is of necessity truly and emphatically a Christian." — P. 37. Then he represents Freemasonry as identical with Christianity. A true Mason must necessarily be a true Christian. That Masonry professes to conduct its disciples to heaven we find affirmed by Town, in the following language. Of the inducements to practice the precepts of Masonry he says: "They are found in that eternal weight of glory, that crown of joy and rejoicing laid up for the faithful in a future world." — P. 188.

By the faithful here he means faithful Freemasons. This same writer claims that Solomon organized the institution by inspiration from God. On page 187, he says: "So Masonry was transmitted from Enoch, through Noah, Abraham, Moses, and their successors, till Solomon, being inspired of God, established a regular form of administration."

This will suffice for the purpose of showing what is claimed for Masonry by their standard authorities. The same in substance might be quoted from various other standard writers. I have made these quotations from Elder Stearns' book, not finding in my library a copy of Town. In another place I shall find it convenient to quote sundry others of their standard writers, who, while they claim it to be a religion do not consider it the Christian religion.

This conducts us (2) to the second inquiry: What does Freemasonry claim for itself?

And here I might quote from almost any of the Masonic degrees to show that this claim is put forth in almost every part of the whole institution. As Town claims for it, so it claims for itself, a *power to conduct its disciples to heaven.* Any one who will take pains to read Bernard's "Light on Masonry" through, will be satisfied that Town claims for the institution no more than it claims for itself.

I beg of all who feel any interest in this subject to get and read Bernard on Masonry; to read it through, and see if Town has not rightly represented the claims of Freemasonry. I deny, observe, that he has rightly represented its principles, and that which it really requires of Masons. That he has misrepresented Masonic law I insist. But in respect to its promises of heaven as a reward for being good Freemasons he has not misrepresented it. It claims to be a saving institution. This certainly will appear to any person who will take the pains to examine its teachings and its claims as revealed in "Light on Masonry." Mr. Town has grossly misrepresented Masonic law and morality as we have seen in examining its claims to benevolence, and in scrutinizing their oaths and their profane use of Scripture. But that Mr. Town has not misrepresented the *claims* of Masonry to be a saving religion has been abundantly shown in these pages by quotations from "Light on Masonry." I might quote many pages from the body of Masonry where it teaches the candidates that the observance of Masonic law, principles and usages will secure his salvation. The Gospel professes no more than this, that those who obey it shall be saved. Surely Masonry claims to be a saving religion just as much as the Gospel of Christ does.

FREEMASONRY

Just take the following from the degree of "The Knights of the East and West." "Light on Masonry," first edition, p. 217, already quoted in another place.

In explaining the ceremony of sounding the seventh trumpet, and conducting the candidate to the vacant canopy, we find the following:

> This canopy it will be recollected is at the right side of the All Puissant who represents JEHOVAH. The sounding of the seventh trumpet, and the conducting of the candidate to the vacant canopy, is a representation of the end of the world, and the glorification of all true Masons at the right hand of God, having passed through the trials of Freemasonry and washed their robes in their own blood.

If Freemasonry does not claim to be a saving religion how can such a claim be made? The compiler adds: "If this is not Antichrist what is?" But I must beg of the reader to examine the books that reveal Masonry for themselves, since to quote the claims of Masonry on this head further than I have done, would not only be useless and tiresome, but would swell this work too much.

This brings me (3) to the third inquire: Are the claims that Masonry is a true and saving religion valid?

To this question I reply that it is utterly false; and in this respect Freemasonry is a *fatal delusion.* From the quotations that I have made from Town, it will be perceived that he represents Freemasonry as identical with Christianity.

Mr. Preston is another of their standard writers. I quote the following note from Stearns on Masonry, p. 28: "Mr. Preston's book, entitled 'Illustrations of Masonry,' has been extensively patronized by the fraternity as a standard work. The copy before me is the first American, from the tenth London edition." Mr. Preston says in his book, p. 30: "The universal

140

principles of the art unite in one indissoluble bond of affection men of the most opposite tenets, of the most distant countries, and of the most contradictory opinions." Again, p.125, he says: "Our celebrated annotator has taken no notice of Masons having the art of working miracles, and foresaying things to come. But this was certainly not the least important of their doctrines. Hence, astrology was admitted as one of the arts which they taught, and the study of it warmly recommended."

"This study became, in the course of time, a regular science." So here we learn that Masons formerly claimed the power of working miracles. I quote again from Bradley, p. 8. He says: "We leave every member to choose and support those principles of religion and those forms of government which appear consistent to his views." In the work of Preston, p. 51, we have the following: "As a Mason, you are to study the moral law as contained in the sacred code, the Bible; and *in countries where that book is not known, whatever is understood to contain the will or law of God.*" O, then, in every country Masons are to embrace the prevalent religion, whatever it may be, and accept whatever is claimed in any country where they may reside, *to be the law and will of God* But is this Christianity, or consistent with it? It is well known and admitted that Masonry claims to have descended from the earliest ages, and that the institution has existed in all countries and under all religions; and that the ancient philosophers of Greece and Rome, the astrologers and soothsayers, and the great men of all heathen nations have belonged to that fraternity.

It is also well known that at this time there are multitudes of Jews, Mohammedans, and skeptics of every grade belonging to the institution. I do not know that this is denied by any intelligent Mason. Now, if this is so, how can Freemasonry be the true religion, or at all consistent with it? Multitudes of Universalists and Unitarians, and of terrorists of every grade, are Freemasons; and yet Freemasonry itself claims to save its disciples, to conduct them to heaven!

FREEMASONRY

The third question proposed for discussion in my last number is: Are the claims of Masonry to be a true and saving institution valid? To this I answer, No. This will appear if we consider, first, that the morality which it inculcates is not the morality of the law and Gospel of God. The law and the Gospel, as I have shown in a former number, lay down the same rule of life. And Christ, in commenting upon the true meaning and spirit of the law, says: "If ye love them that love you, what thank have ye? Do not even the publicans the same?" He requires us to love our enemies, and to pray for them, as truly as for our friends. In short, he requires *universal benevolence*; whereas Freemasonry requires no such thing. Its oaths, which are its law, simply require its members to be just to each other. I say just, for their boasted benevolence is simply the payment of a debt.

They do, indeed, promise to assist each other in distress, and to help each other's families, provided they fall into poverty. But on what condition do they promise this? Why, that a certain amount is to be paid into their treasure as a fund for this purpose. But his, surely, is not benevolence, but the simple payment of a debt, on the principles of mutual insurance.

This I have abundantly shown in a former number. Again, the *motives* presented in Freemasonry to secure the course of action to which they are pledged are by no means consistent with the law or the Gospel of God. In religion, and in true morality, everything depends on the motive or reason for the performance of an action. God accepts nothing that does not proceed from supreme love to Him and equal love to our fellow men. Not merely to our brother Masons; but to our neighbor — that is, to all mankind. Whatever does not proceed from love and faith is sin, according to the teachings of the Bible. And by love, I say again, is meant the supreme love of God and the equal love of our neighbor.

But Masonry teaches no such morality as this. The motive urged by Masons is, to honor Masonry, to honor the institution, to honor each other. While they are pledged to assist each other in distress; to keep each other's secrets, even if they be crimes; and to aid each other, whether right or wrong, so far as to extricate them from any difficulty in which they are involved; yet they never present the pure motives of the Gospel. They are pledged not to violate the chastity of a brother Mason's wife, sister, daughter, or mother; but they are not pledged by Masonry, as the law and Gospel of God require, to abstain from such conduct with any female whatever. But nothing short of *universal* benevolence, and *universal* morality, is acceptable to God.

But again: it has been shown that Masonry claims to be a saving institution; that this is claimed for it by the highest Masonic authorities; and that this claim is one set up by itself as well. But an examination of Freemasonry shows that it promises salvation upon entirely other conditions than those revealed in the Gospel of Christ. The Gospel nowhere inculcates the idea that any one can be saved by obedience to the law of God. "By the deeds of the law shall no flesh be justified" is the uniform teaching of the Bible. Much less can any one be saved by conformity to Masonic law, which requires only a partial, and therefore a spurious, morality. The Bible teaches that all unconverted persons are in a state of sin, of total moral depravity, and consequent condemnation by the law of God: and that the conditions of salvation are *repentance* and a total renunciation of all sin, *faith in our Lord Jesus Christ,* and *sanctification* by the *Holy Spirit.* Now these are by no means the conditions upon which Freemasonry proposes to save its members. The teachings of Freemasonry upon this subject are summarily this: Obey Masonic law, and live.

Now, surely, whatever promises heaven to men upon other conditions than those proposed in the Gospel of Christ is a fatal delusion. And this Freemasons can not deny, for they profess to accept the Bible as true. Freemasonry lays no stress at all upon conversion to Christ by the Holy Spirit. It presents no means or motives to secure that result. The idea of being turned from sin to holiness, from a self-pleasing spirit to a supreme love of God, by the preaching of the Gospel, accompanied by the Holy Spirit, is not taught in Freemasonry.

It nowhere recognizes men as being justified by faith in Christ, as being sanctified by faith in Christ, and as being saved as the Gospel recognizes men as being saved.

Indeed, it is salvation by Masonry and not salvation by the Gospel, that Masonry insists upon. It is another gospel, or presents entirely another method of salvation than that presented in the Gospel. How can it be pretended by those who admit that the Gospel is true that men can be saved by Freemasonry at all? If Freemasons are good men, it is not Freemasonry that has made them so; but the Gospel has made them so, in spite of Freemasonry. If they are anything more than self-righteous, it is because of the teachings of the Gospel; for certainly Freemasonry teaches a very different way of salvation from that which the Gospel reveals. But, again, the prayers recorded in Freemasonry, and used by them in their lodges, are not Christian prayers; that is, they are not prayers offered in the name of Christ.

But the Gospel teaches us that it is fundamental to acceptable prayer that it be offered in the name of Christ. Again, as we have seen in a former number, the teachings of Freemasonry are scandalously false; and their ceremonies are a mockery, and truly shocking to Christian feelings.

Again, Freemasonry is a system of gross hypocrisy. It professes to be a saving institution, and promises salvation to those who keep its oaths and conform to its ancient usages. It also professes to be entirely consistent with the Christian religion. And this it does while it embraces as good and acceptable Masons hundreds of thousands who abhor Christianity, and scoff at the Bible and everything that the Bible regards as sacred. In a Christian nation it professes to receive Christianity as a true religion; in Mohammedan countries it

144

receives the Koran as teaching the true religion; in heathen countries it receives their sacred books as of as much authority as that which is claimed in Christian countries for the Bible. In short, Freemasonry in a pagan country is pagan, in a Mohammedan country it is Mohammedan, and in a Christian country it professes to be Christian; but in this profession it is not only grossly inconsistent, but intensely hypocritical.

Notwithstanding all the boasts that are made in its lower degrees of its being a true religion, if you will examine the latter through to the end, you will find that, as you ascend in the scale of degrees, the mask is gradually thrown off, until we come to the "Philosophical Lodge," in the degree of the "Knights Adepts of the Eagle or Sun;" in which, as will be seen, no concealment is longer attempted. I will make a short quotation from this degree, as any one may find it in "Light on Masonry."

Requisitions to make a good Mason.—If you ask me what are the requisite qualities that a Mason must be possessed of to come to the center of truth, I answer you that you must crush the head of the serpent, ignorance. You must shake off the yoke of infant prejudice, concerning the mysteries of the reigning religion, which worship has been imaginary and only founded on the spirit of pride, which envies to command and be distinguished, and to be at the head of the vulgar in affecting an exterior purity, which characterizes a false piety joined to a desire of acquiring that which is not its own, and is always the subject of this exterior pride and unalterable source of many disorders; which, being joined to gluttonness (sic), is the daughter of hypocrisy, and employes every matter to satisfy carnal desires and raises to the predominant passions altars upon which she maintains without ceasing the light of iniquity, and sacrifices continually offerings to luxury, voluptuousness, hatred, envy, and perjury.

FREEMASONRY

Behold, my dear brother, what you must fight against and destroy before you can come to the knowledge of the true good and sovereign happiness! Behold this monster which you must conquer — a serpent which we detest as an idol that is adored by the idiot and vulgar under the name of religion!" — See "Light on Masonry," pp. 270,271. 8th edition.

Here, then, Masonry stands revealed, after all its previous pretensions to being a true religion, as the unalterable opponent of the reigning or Christian religion. That it claims to be a religion is indisputable; but that it is not the Christian religion is equally evident. Nay, it finally comes out flat-footed, and represents the reigning or Christian religion as a serpent which Masons detest, as an idol which is adored by the idiot and vulgar under the name of religion.

Now let professed Christians who are Freemasons examine this for themselves. Do not turn away from examination of this subject.

And here, before I close this article, I beg to be understood that I have no quarrel with individual Masons. It is with the system that I have to deal. The great mass of the fraternity are utterly deceived, as I was myself. Very few, comparatively, of the fraternity are at all acquainted with what is really taught in the higher degrees as they ascend from one to another. None of them know anything of these degrees any further than they have taken them, unless they have studies them in the books as they are revealed. I can not believe that Christian men will remain connected with this institution, if they will only examine it for themselves and look it through to the end. I know that young Masons, and those who have only taken the lower degrees, will be shocked at what I have just quoted from a higher degree. I was so myself when first I examined the higher degrees. But you will inquire how, and in what sense, are we who have only taken the lower degrees responsible for the oaths and teachings of the higher degrees, which we have not taken. In a future number I shall briefly answer this question. Most Freemasons, and many who have been Masters of lodges of the lower degrees, are really so ignorant of what Masonry as a whole is, that when they are told the simple truth respecting it, they really believe that what you tell them is a lie. I am receiving letters from this class of Freemasons, accusing me of lying and misrepresentation, which accusations I charitably ascribe to ignorance. To such I say, Wait, gentlemen, until you are better informed upon the subject and you will hold a different opinion.

I have quoted from Salem Town showing that he claims that Solomon established the institution by divine authority — that Town claims for it all that is claimed for Christianity as a saving religion. I might show that others of their standard writers set up the same claim. Now I am unwilling to believe that these writers are hypocrites. It must be that they have been imposed upon as I was. They were ignorant of the origin of Freemasonry. Perhaps this was not strange, especially as regards Mr. Town; for until within the last half century this matter has not been searched to the bottom. But certainly there is now no excuse for the ignorant or dishonest assertions that are so often made by Freemasons. Such pretenses palmed off, as they now often are, upon those whose occupation or other causes forbid their examination of the subject, ought to arouse the righteous indignation of every honest citizen. I say it ought to do so; yes, and it must do so, when we see our dear young men lured by false pretenses in crowds into this snare of Satan. They get drawn in and committed, and, as we see, are afraid to be convinced of their error and become uncandid (sic) and will not honestly examine the subject. They will shun the light when it is offered. Can men be saved in this state of mind?

CHAPTER XVI

THE ARGUMENT THAT GREAT AND GOOD MEN HAVE BEEN AND ARE FREEMASONS, EXAMINED

It is the universal practice of Freemasons to claim as belonging to their fraternity a great many wise and good men.

As I have shown in a former number, Masonry itself claims to have been founded by Solomon, and to have been patronized by St. John. Their lodges are dedicated to St. John and Zerubbabel, as I have shown; and Solomon figures more or less prominently in a great number of their degrees. Now it has already been shown by their highest authorities that this claim of having been founded by Solomon and patronized by St. John is utterly without foundation. Strange to tell, while it claims to have always been one and identical, and that it never has been changed, still on the very face of the different degrees it is shown that the great majority of them are of recent origin. If, as their best historians assert, Speculative Freemasonry dates no further back than the eighteenth century, of course, the claim of Freemasons that their institution was established and patronized by inspired men can command no respect or confidence.

But, if this claim is false, what reason have we to have confidence in their assertions that so many great and good men of modern times were Freemasons. Investigation will prove that this claim is to a very great extent without foundation. It has been asserted here with the utmost confidence, over and over again, that Bishop McIlvaine was a Freemason. But having recently been written to on the subject, he replied that he never was a Freemason.

Again, it is no doubt true that many men have joined them, and, when they have taken a sufficient number of degrees to have the impression entirely removed from their minds that there is any secret in Freemasonry worth knowing, they have become disgusted with its shams, its hypocrisies, its falsehoods, its oaths and its ceremonies, its puerilities and its blasphemies; and they have paid no further attention to it.

Freemasons have paraded the fact that Gen. Washington was a Mason before the public. The following conclusion of a letter from him will speak for him, and show how little he had to do with Masonry. Before his death he warned the whole country to beware of secret societies. The letter alluded to is dated "Mt. Vernon, September 25, 1798." Here we have its conclusion. It needs no comment:

> I have little more to add than thanks for your wishes, and favorable sentiments, except to correct an error you have run into of my presiding over the English lodges in this country. The fact is I preside over none, nor have I been in one more than once or twice within the last thirty years. I believe, notwithstanding, that none of the lodges in this country are contaminated with the principles ascribed to the society of the Illuminati.
> Signed, George Washington

I might quote numerous instances in which good men have at first hesitated, and finally refused to go any further in Masonry, and have threatened to expose the whole of it to the world. Whoever will read Elder Stearns' little books on Masonry will find examples of this.

But why should Freemasons lay so much stress on the fact that many good men have been Freemasons? It has always been the favorite method of supporting a bad institution to claim as its patrons the wise and good. This argument might have been used with great force, and doubtless was, in favor of idolatry in the time of Solomon and the prophets. Several of the kings of Israel were idolaters, as well as the queens and the royal family generally.

The great mass of the prophets, and religious teachers, and great men of the nation, lapsed into idolatry. Nearly all the learning, and wealth and influence of the whole nation could be appealed to as rejecting Christ. Those who received him were but a few fishermen, with some of the lowest of the people. Now what a powerful argument was this! If the argument of Masons be of any value, how overwhelming an argument must this have been against the claims of our Lord Jesus Christ!

Why the rejecters of Jesus could quote all the great men of the nation, and the pious men, and the wise men, as decidedly opposed to his claims! The same was true after his death and resurrection for a great while. The question would often arise: "Do any of the rulers believe on him?"

An institution is not to be judged by the conduct of a few of its members who might have been either worse or better than its principles. Christianity, *e.g.*, is not to be judged by the conduct of particular professed Christians; but by its laws, its principles, by what it justifies and by what it condemns. Christianity condemns all iniquity. It abhors *covering up iniquity.* In the case of its greatest and most prominent professors, it exposes and denounces their sin, and never justifies it. But Masonry, on the other hand, is a secret work of darkness. It requires its members to taken an oath to cover up each other's sins. It requires them to swear, under the most awful penalties, that they will seek the condign punishment of every one who in any instance violates any point of their obligation. It, therefore, justifies the murder of those who betray its secrets.

Masons consistently justified the murder of Morgan, as everybody in this country knows who has paid any attention to the subject.

This is not inconsistent with their principles. Indeed, it is the very thing demanded, the very thing promised under oath.

But again: This same argument, by which Masons are attempting to sustain their institution, was always resorted to sustain the practice of slaveholding.

FREEMASONRY

Why, how many wise and good men, it was said, were slaveholders. The churches and ecclesiastical bodies at the North were full of charity in respect to them. They could not denounce slaveholding as a sin.

They would say that it was an evil; but for a long time they could not be persuaded to pronounce it a moral evil, a sin. And why? Why, because so many doctors of divinity were slaveholders and were defending the institution. Because a large portion of the church, of nearly every denomination, were involved in the abomination. "They are good men," it was said; "they are great men — we must be charitable."

And so, when this horrid civil war came on, these great and good men, that had sustained the institution of slavery, sustained and stimulated the war.

Many of them took up arms, and fought with desperation to sustain the institution. But what is thought now at least throughout all the North, and throughout all the Christian world — of the great and good men who have done this thing? Who does not now admit that they were deluded? that they had anything the Spirit of Christ? that they were in the hands of the Devil all along?

The fact is, this has always been the device of those who have sustained any system of wickedness. They have taken pains, in one way and another, to draw into their ranks men of reputation for wisdom and piety, men of high standing in Church and State. A great many of those who are claimed by Freemasons to be of their number never were Freemasons at all. Others were entrapped into it, and turned a "cold shoulder" upon it and paid no more attention to it; but were ever after claimed as Freemasons.

But there are great multitudes of Freemasons who have taken some of the degrees, and have become heartily disgusted with it. But knowing that Freemasons are under oath to persecute and even murder them if they publicly renounce it and expose its secrets, they remain quiet, say nothing about it,

152

and go no further with it; but are still claimed as Freemasons. As soon as public sentiment is enough aroused to make them feel safe in doing what they regard as their solemn duty, great numbers of them will no doubt publicly renounce it. At present they are afraid to do so. They are afraid that their business will be ruined, their characters assailed, and their lives at least put in jeopardy.

But it should be understood that, while it may be true that there are many pious and wise men belonging to the Masonic fraternity, yet there are thousands of learned and pious men who have renounced it, and thousands more who have examined its claims, and who reject it as an imposture and as inconsistent either with Christianity or good government.

It is sometimes said: "Those men that renounced Masonry in the days of Morgan are dead. There are now thousands of living witnesses. Why should we take the testimony of the dead instead of that of the living? The living we know; the dead we do not know."

To this I answer, first: There are thousands of renouncing Masons still living who reiterate their testimony on all proper occasions against the institution. Many of them we know, or may know; and they are not dead witnesses, but living. Now, if it was wickedness that led those men to renounce Freemasonry and publish its secrets, how is it that no instance has ever occurred in which a seceding Freemason has renounced and denounced his renunciation, and gone back into the ranks of Freemasons? I have never heard of such a case. It is well for the cause of truth that this question has come up again before the Masons that renounced the institution in the days of Morgan were all dead. It is well that hundreds and thousands of them are still alive, and are still living witnesses, bearing their steady and unflinching testimony against the institution.

But, again: The present living witnesses who testify in its behalf, let it be remembered, are interested witnesses. They

153

still adhere to the institution. They are under oath not to speak against it, but in every way to support it. Of what value, then, is their testimony in its favor?

The fact is, we have their secrets published; and these books speak for themselves. Let the living or the dead say what they may, the truth is established that these books truly reveal Masonry; and by this revelation let the institution stand or fall.

If any thing can be established by human testimony, it is established that Bernard's "Light on Masonry" has revealed Masonry substantially as it is. Bernard is still living. He is an old man; but he has recently said: "What I have written I have written on this subject. I have nothing to add, and I have nothing to retract." And there are still hundreds and thousands of men who know that he has published the truth. How vain and frivolous, then, is the inquiry, "Why should we not take the testimony of living rather than of dead witnesses?" The prophets and apostles are dead. Why not take the testimony of living skeptics that we know? Some of them are learned and respectable men. Alas! if dead men are not to be believed!

CHAPTER XVII

MASONIC OATHS ARE UNLAWFUL AND VOID

Because 1st, they are forbidden by Christ. Matt. v 34-37. Whatever may be said of oaths administered by magistrates for governmental purposes, it can not be reasonably doubted that this teaching prohibits the taking of extrajudicial oaths. But Masonic oaths are extrajudicial.

2. Because they are awfully profane. "Thou shalt not take the name of the Lord thy God in vain." Exod. xx. 7. Certainly both the administering and taking of these oaths are taking the name of God in vain.

3. Because they swear to do unlawful things.

THE SIN MUST BE CONFESSED

1. We have seen that all Masons swear to conceal all the secrets of Masonry that may be communicated to them. This is rash, and contrary to Lev. v. 4, 5:

Or if a soul swear pronouncing with his lips to do evil, or to do good, whatsoever it be that a man shall pronounce with an oath, and it be hid from him; when he knoweth of it, then he shall be guilty in one of these. And it shall be, when he shall be guilty in one of these things, that he shall confess that he hath sinned in that thing.

2. They swear to conceal each other's crimes. This we have seen. This is a conspiracy against all good government in Church and State. Is not this wicked?

3. They swear to deliver a brother Royal Arch Mason out of any difficulty and to espouse his cause so far as to extricate him from the same, if in their power, whether he be right or wrong. Is not this wicked? How this oath must lead to the defeat of the execution of law. It has defeated the ends of justice often, as every intelligent Mason may and ought to know.

4. They swear to give political preferment to a Mason, because he is a Mason, over one of equal qualifications, who is not a Mason. This is swearing to be partial. But is it not wicked to be partial? Can an oath to be partial make partiality a virtue? By swearing to do wrong can a man make it his duty, and, therefore, right to do wrong? No indeed.

5. They swear to persecute all who violate Masonic oaths as long as they live — to ruin their reputation, derange their business, and, if they go from place to place, to follow them with representations of being worthless vagabonds. Is not this a promise under oath to do wickedly? Suppose those who violate Masonic oaths are enemies of Masonry, as well they may be, and as they ought to be, is it right to seek, in any way, to ruin them? Is this loving an enemy? Is not such persecution forbidden by every precept of both law and Gospel? Hence the declaration by the pen of inspiration: "Recompense to no man evil for evil....If thine enemy hunger, feed him; if he thirst, give him drink; for in so doing thou shalt heap coals of fire on his head." — Rom. xii. 17-20. And it is in direct opposition to the requirement. Matt. v. 44: "But I say unto you, Love your enemies, bless them that curse you, do good to them that hate you, and pray for them which despitefully use you, and persecute you."

6. They swear to seek the death or condign punishment of all who violate Masonic oaths. This we have seen! Is it not murder in intention, and, therefore, really murder, whether they succeed or not? To be sure it is.

7. They swear to seek revenge and to take vengeance on those who violate Masonic oaths and to avenge the treason, as they call it, by the death of the traitor. This, also, we have

seen. Now, is not this the perfection of wickedness? Ought not Masons to be put under bonds to keep the peace?

8. They swear to support Freemasonry, an institution, as we have seen, that ought not to exist in any community. These are only some of the reasons for pronouncing the oaths of Freemasonry utterly unlawful.

MASONIC OATHS ARE NULL AND VOID

1. Because they are obtained by fraud. The candidate for the first degree is assured by the master, in the most solemn manner, when the candidate is on his knees and about to take the oath, there is nothing in it inconsistent with his duty either to God or to man. But he finds, after taking and reflecting upon it, that he has made promises inconsistent with his duty both to God and man. This, of itself, makes the oath null.

2. They are void because they pledge the candidate to sin against God and man. 1st By swearing to commit a sin, a man can not make it his *duty*, and, therefore, *right* to do *wrong*. He can not make *sin holiness*, or *crime a virtue*, by taking an oath to do it. Forty men took an oath that they would neither eat nor drink until they had killed Paul. Were they under moral obligation, therefore, to kill him? If they were, it was their *duty*. If it was their *duty*, their killing him would have been a *holy* act. Who does not see the absurdity of this? To keep a wicked promise or oath is only adding sin to sin. But it may be said that we are required to perform our vows. Yes, when we vow to do what is right, but not when we vow to do what is wrong. This is not only the doctrine of the Bible, but, also, of all the able writers on moral philosophy. It is, indeed, a self-evident truth. An oath to do wrong is sin. To perform it is adding sin to sin. All oaths to do wrong, or to refrain from doing right, are *null*.

157

FREEMASONRY

ALL FREEMASONS OUGHT TO
RENOUNCE THEIR MASONIC OATHS

1. Because they are profane and wicked.

2. Because they ought to repent the taking of them.

3. But repentance consists in heart-renunciation of them. A man can not repent of, without forsaking them.

4. If not repented of and forsaken, *i.e.*, renounced, the sin can not be forgiven.

5. Heart-renunciation must produce life-renunciation of them.

6. A sin is not repented of while it is concealed and not confessed to those who have been injured by it.

7. A sin against society or against individuals can not be forgiven, when just confession and restitution are withheld.

8. Masonic oaths are a conspiracy against God and man, and are not repented of while adhered to.

9. They are adhered to, while heart-renunciation is withheld.

10. Refusing to renounce is adherence.

11. Adherence makes them partakers of the crimes of Freemasons — "partakers of other men's sins." Because, to adhere is to justify their oaths and the keeping and fulfillment of them. But to justify their crimes, the murder of Morgan for example, is to partake of the guilt of his murderers.

12. While a Mason adheres his word can not be credited on questions relating to the secrets of Masonry.

13. Nor can his testimony be believed against one who has violated Masonic oaths, because he is sworn to ruin his reputation, and to represent him as a worthless vagabond.

14. An adhering Mason is a dangerous man in society. If he does as he is sworn to do, is he not a dangerous man? If he does not do what he is sworn to do, and yet does not renounce his oath, he is a dangerous man, because he violates an oath, the obligation of which he acknowledges. Is not he a dangerous

man who disregards the solemnity of an oath? But, perhaps, he is convinced that he ought not to do what he has sworn to do, and, therefore, does not do it, but still he adheres in the sense that he will not confess and renounce the sinfulness of the obligation. Is not that a dangerous man who sees the wrong of an oath and will not renounce it.

15. While he adheres to his Masonic oaths, he ought not to be trusted with the office of a magistrate. How should he, if he means to perform his Masonic vows?

16. Nor, while he adheres, should he be trusted with the office of sheriff, marshal, or constable. If he intends to perform his Masonic vows, it is madness to trust him with an office in Church or State.

17. If and while he adheres, he ought not to be received as a witness or juror when a Freemason is a party. This has been ruled as law.

18. Nor should he have power to appoint officers, as he will surely unduly favor Masons.

19. Nor should he have the control of funds and the bestowment of governmental patronage. This he will certainly abuse, if he keeps and performs his vows.

20. Nor should he be intrusted with the pardoning power. I wish it could be known in how many instances Freemasons have been pardoned and turned loose upon the public by governors and presidents who were Freemasons, and who were sworn to deliver them from any difficulty, whether right or wrong.

21. Nor should he be a post-master, as he will surely abuse his office to favor Masonry, and to persecute anti-Masons, if he keeps his vows. Of this we are having abundant proof.

22. While he adheres, his testimony against renouncing Masons ought not to be credited, because he has sworn to ruin their reputation and their business, and, until their death, to represent them to others as worthless vagabonds. Is a man's testimony against another worthy of credit, when he is thus sworn to hold him up to the world? It is the greatest injustice

to credit the testimony of one who has taken and adheres to this oath, if he testifies against a renouncing Mason.

23. Those Masons who have taken and adhere to the vow to thus persecute, and the vow to avenge the treason of violating Masonic oaths by the death of the traitor, should be held to bail to keep the peace. If they intend to perform their vows, they are eminently dangerous persons, and should be imprisoned or held to bail. Let no one say that this is harsh. Indeed, it is not. It is only common sense and common justice. Only remember what they are sworn to do, and that they *intend* to perform their vows, and then tell me is it safe and just that such men should be at large, and not even be put under bonds not to fulfill their vows. We must take the ground, either that they will not fulfill their vows, or we must hold that they ought not to be at large without adequate bail. I am aware that some will say that this is a harsh and extreme conclusion. But pray let me ask do you not feel and say this because you do not believe that there is *real danger* of Freemasons doing what they have sworn to do? If they have sworn as Bernard and others represent, and if they really intend to fulfill their vows, and if you admit this, is my conclusion harsh and extreme? When no occasion arises, calling for the fulfillment of their horrid oaths, they appear to be harmless and even good citizens. But let any man read the history of the abduction and murder of Morgan, as found in "Light on Masonry," and see how many men were engaged in it. Let him understand now this horrid murder was justified by the Grand Lodge, and by many respectable citizens. Let him ponder the fact that the men engaged in that affair were accounted respectable and good citizens; that a number of them were men high in office and in public confidence, and that the conspiracy extended over a wide territory, and then let him say whether, if an occasion arise demanding their action, they will prove to be law-abiding citizens, or, if they will not, as they have often done before, set at naught any law of God and man, and, if need be, reach their end through the blood of their victim.

But some will say that this is representing Freemasonry as *infamous,* and holding it up to the *disgust, contempt,* and *indignation* of mankind. I reply, I have not misrepresented it, as it is revealed in the books which I have been examining. Remember, it is with Masonry as there revealed that I have to deal. If a truthful representation of it excites the *contempt, disgust,* and *indignation* of the public toward it — if to rightly represent Freemasonry is to render it *infamous,* I can not help it. The fault, if any, is not mine. I have revealed nothing, I have only called attention to facts of common concern to all honest citizens. Let the infamy rest where it belongs.

CHAPTER XVIII

WHY FREEMASONS RESORT TO THREATS AND REFUSE TO DISCUSS THEIR PRINCIPLES

There are many aspects of this subject that need to be thoroughly considered by all men. For example, the bearing of this institution upon domestic happiness is of great importance.

The stringent secrecy enjoined and maintained at the hazard of one's life, is really inconsistent with the spirit of the marriage contract. It is really an insult to a wife for a husband to go and pledge himself to conceal from his wife that which he freely communicates to strangers. Suppose that wives should get up lodges, spend their money and their time in secret conclave, absent themselves from home, and swear to keep their proceedings entirely from their husbands; and suppose that such organizations should be made permanent, and extend throughout the length and breadth of the land, would husbands endure this? Would they think it right?

In short, if wives should do what husbands do, should not husbands rebel, think themselves abused, and insist upon such a course being entirely and forever abandoned? Indeed they would! How can a man look his wife in the face after joining a Masonic lodge? I have recently received several letters from the wives of Masons complaining of this: — that their husbands had joined the lodge and paid their money, and were spending their time, and concealing their doings and their principles from their wives. This is utterly unjust. It is shameful; and no honorable man can reflect upon it without feeling that he wrongs his wife.

Of late, partly to appease women, and partly to give the female relatives of Masons certain signs and tokens by which they may make themselves known as the wives or daughters, sisters or mothers, of Freemasons, they are conferring certain side degrees upon women. Of this Freemasons themselves — that is the more honorable among them — are complaining as an innovation, and as a thing justly to be complained of by outsiders. And observe that they ask, what if these daughters or sisters of Masons, who are taking these side degrees, should marry men who are not Masons, and who are opposed to the institution, — what would be the consequence of this? You administer, they say, the degrees for the sake of preserving domestic peace; and here, on the other hand, it would produce domestic discord.

But again, it should be considered that Masonry is an institution of vast proportions, and of such a nature that it will not allow its principles to be discussed.

It works in the dark. And instead of standing or falling according to its character and tendencies, when brought to the light, when thoroughly discussed and understood by the public, it closes the door against all discussion, shrouds itself in midnight, and its argument is assassination. Now, what have we here in a republican government? A set of men under oath to assist each other, and even to conceal each other's crimes, embracing and acting upon principles that are not to be discussed!

Immediately after the publication of the first number of my articles in the *Independent,* of the subject of Masonry, I received a threatening letter from the city of New York, virtually threatening me with assassination. I have since received several letters of the most abusive character from Freemasons, simply because I discuss and expose their principles. Now, if their principles can not bear the light, they never should be tolerated. It is an insult to any community for a set of men to band themselves together to keep each other's secrets, and to aid each other in a great variety of ways, and refuse to have their principles known and discussed, whilst their only argument is a dagger, a bullet, and a bowie knife, instead of truth and reason. Indeed, it is well-known throughout the length and breadth of the land that Masonry is so determined not to have its principles discussed, that men are afraid to discuss them. They expect from the very nature of Masonry, and from the revelations that it has made of itself, to be persecuted, and perhaps murdered, if they attempt to discuss the principles and usages of that institution. Now, is such a thing as this to be tolerated in a free government? Why how infinitely dangerous and shocking is this!

Everything else may be discussed. All governmental proceedings, the characters of public men, all institutions of learning, all benevolent societies, and indeed everything else in the world may be discussed, and criticized, and held up for public examination; but Masonry, forsooth, must not be touched. It must work in the dark. All the moneys received by charitable institutions must be reported; and the manner in which they dispose of every dollar that they receive must be held up before the public for examination. Every one sees the importance of this, and knows that it is right. But Freemasonry will make no report of its funds. They will not tell us what they do with them. They will not allow themselves to be called in question. No, that institution must not be ventilated upon pain of persecution unto death.

Now, it is enough to make a man's blood boil with indignation that such an institution as this should exist in the land. And what is most astonishing is, that members of the Christian Church, and Christian ministers, should sympathize with, and even unite themselves to, such an institution as this.

Suppose the church should conduct in this manner, and the Christian Church should receive its members in secret, and such oaths should be administered to them. Suppose Christianity would not allow its principles to be discussed, would not allow itself to come to the light, should use threats of assassination, and should actually resort to assassination to establish itself, and should thus create a feeling of terror throughout the whole world so that no man would dare to speak against it, to ventilate it, and show up its principles, — what would be said of Christianity, should it, like Freemasonry, take such a course as this?

The fact is, that Freemasonry is the most anomalous, absurd, and abominable institution that can exist in a Christian country; and is, on the face of it, from the fact that it will not allow its principles to be discussed and divulged, a most dangerous thing in human society. In nearly all the letters that I am receiving on this subject — and they are numerous — astonishment is expressed, and frequently gratitude and praise to God, that a man is found who dares publicly to discuss and expose the principles of the institution. Now, what is this? Have we an institution, the ramifications of which are entwining themselves with every fiber of our government and our institution, our civil and religious liberties, of which the whole country is so much afraid that they dare not speak the truth concerning it?

What is this, thrust in upon human society and upon Christian communities, that can not be so much as discussed and its principles brought to light without threats of persecution and assassination? What honest man can witness such a state of things as this in our government without feeling his indignation enkindled?

Everything else may be discussed, may be brought to the light, may be held up to the public for their verdict; but Freemasonry must not be touched. Other institutions must stand or fall in the light of reason and of sound morality. If they are sustained at all they must be sustained by argument, by logic, by standing the test of thorough criticism. But Masonry must stand, not by argument, not by logic, not by sound reason, but must be sustained by persecution and murder. And so universally, as I have already said, is this known and assumed, as to strike men in every part of the land with such terror, that they dare not speak their minds about it.

And now, are we in this country to hold our peace? to hold out our hands and have the shackles put upon them? Is the press to be muzzled, and the whole country to be awed and kept under the feet of this institution, so that no man shall dare to speak his mind? God forbid! "Every plant," says Christ, "which my heavenly Father hath not planted shall be rooted up." The works of darkness shall be dragged to the light; and the power of this institution must be broken by a thorough expose of its oaths, its principles, its spirit and tendency. Afraid to speak out against such an abomination as this! Remember that he that would save his life by concealing the truth, and refusing to embrace and defend it shall lose it.

Again, *Freemasonry is a most intolerant and intolerable despotism.*

Let any one examine their oaths, and see what implicit obedience they pledge to the great dignitaries, and Masters, and High Priests of their lodges, and they will see what an institution this is in a republican government. There is no appeal from the decision of the Master of a lodge. In respect to everything in the lodge, his word is law. In a recent number of the *"National and Freemason,"* which fell into my hands, the editor asserts that there is no appeal to the lodge from the decision of the Master of the lodge, and that he should allow none. In the ascending scale of their degrees, they swear to render implicit obedience to the grand lodges, and the higher orders above them, and this beforehand. They are not allowed to question the propriety of those decisions at all. They are not allowed to discuss, or to have any voice or vote in regard to those decrees. There is not in the world a more perfect and frightful despotism than Freemasonry is from beginning to end. Now, think of the great number of Freemasons in this country that are becoming accustomed to yield this implicit obedience to arbitrary power, a one man power, running through every lodge and chapter throughout the whole entangled system. And this institution is penetrating every community, selecting its men, and enforcing their obedience to arbitrary power throughout this whole republican country. And will not the country awake to this great wrong and this great danger? A friend of mine, a minister of the Gospel, writes me that he had been himself a Mason. He was urged to join the institution, as I was myself; but he renounced it many years ago, and supposed that it was dead. But some fifteen years since he found it reviving in the neighborhood where he was living, and he preached a sermon exposing it. That very week they burned him in effigy at his own gate; and that even now he could not preach against it and expose it without being set upon and persecuted he knows not to what extent.

And this, then, is the way for Masons to meet this question! If allowed to go on they will soon resort to mobs, as the slaveholders and their sympathizers did; and it will be found that Masonry can not be spoken against without mobs arising to disperse any assembly that may meet for the examination of the subject. If fifteen years ago a minister of the Gospel could be burned in effigy before his own gate, for bringing this institution to the light, and if now threats of assassination come from the four winds of heaven if a man speaks or writes the truth concerning it, if let alone how long will it be before it will have its foot upon the neck of the whole nation, so that it will be sure to cost any man his life who dares to rebuke it?

But why do Freemasons take this course? Why do they decline to discuss, and resort to threats of violence? I answer first, for the same reason that slaveholders did the same.

Many years ago John Randolph, with a shake of his long finger, informed the Congress of the United States, that slavery should not be discussed there. At the South they would not allow tracts to be circulated, nor a word to be spoken against the institution. They resorted to every form of violence to prevent it. And who does not know the reason why? Their abominable institution would not bear the light, and they knew it right well. Freemasons know very well that they can not justify their institution before an enlightened public. I mean, those of them who are well-informed know this.

Multitudes of them are so ignorant as to feel quite sure that they are right, and that their institution is what it professes to be. The well-informed among them know better; and those who would naturally be expected to discuss the question, if it were discussed, know that they can not stand their ground. They can not justify their horrid oaths, with their barbarous penalties. They know that they can not establish their false claims to great antiquity.

The ignorant or dishonest among them will vapor, and set forth their ridiculous pretensions to antiquity; and will try to persuade us that God was a Freemason when He created the Universe, and that all the ancient worthies were Freemasons. But the well-informed among them know perfectly well that there is not the shadow of truth in all this pretension, and that their claim to great antiquity is a lie, and nothing but a lie, from beginning to end. They know also that the claims of the institution to benevolence are false, and can not be sustained, and that there is not a particle of benevolence in their institution.

Again, they know very well that the claim of Masonry to be a saving religion is a false claim; and that its claim to be substantially the Christian religion is without the least foundation. They know also that its professions are false in regard to the truth of history; and that its claim to be a depository of the sciences and arts is without foundation.

They know very well that Masonry has no just claims to be the light of the world in regard to any of its pretensions. They know that the secrecy which it enjoins can not be defended, and that it has no right to exist as a secret, oath-bound institution. They know that this oath-bound secrecy can not be justified before an enlightened public; that there is nothing in Freemasonry to justify their oaths or penalties, and that there is nothing in it that deserves the respect of the public.

They are well aware that they can not justify their pompous titles, their odious ceremonies, their false teachings, their shameful abuses of the Word of God; and they are ashamed to attempt to justify the puerilities on the one hand, or the blasphemies that abound on the other.

Any one who will examine Richardson's "Masonic Monitor," will find in it diagrams of the lodges and of many of the ceremonies; and if anybody wishes to see how ridiculous, absurd, and profane many of their ceremonies are, let him examine that work.

The reason of their declining all discussion, and resorting to threats of violence, is manifest enough. It is sagacious in them to keep in the dark, and to awe people, if they can, by threats; because they have no argument, no history, no anything that can justify them in the course they take.

Shame on an institution that resorts to such a defence as this? But it can not live where the press and speech are free; and this its defenders know right well. If freedom of speech is allowed on the subject, and the press is allowed to discuss and thoroughly to ventilate it, they know full well that the institution can not exist. The fact is, that Freemasonry must die, or liberty must die. These two things can not exist together. Freemasons have already sold their liberty, and put themselves under an iron despotism; and there is not one in a thousand of them that dares to speak against the institution, or really to speak his mind.

I have just received a letter from one of them, which reads as follows: "Dear Sir, — I merely write you as a man and professed Christian to say that you are doing God service in your attacks upon the institution of Masonry. I am a Mason, but have long since been convinced that it is a wicked, blasphemous institution, and that the Church of Christ suffers from this source more than from any other. You know that the oaths and scenes of the lodge are most shamefully wicked; and a Christian man's character, if he leaves them, is not safe in the community where he lives. You can make what use you please of this; but, perhaps, my name and place of residence had better not be made public for I fear for my property and my person." This is the way that multitudes of Freemasons feel. They have sold their liberty, and they dare not speak out. Shall we all sell our liberties, and allow Masonry to stifle all discussion by a resort to violence and assassination? Threats are abundant; and they go as far as they dare do in executing their threats.

In some places, where Freemasons are numerous and less on their guard, I am informed that they do not hesitate to say that they intend to have a Masonic government, *peaceably if they can.* That this is the design of many of the leaders in this institution, there can be no rational doubt in the minds of those who are well informed. The press, to a great extent, is already either bribed or afraid to speak the truth on this subject; and, so far as I can learn, there are but few secular or religious papers open to its discussion. Now, what a state of things is this! A few years ago it was as much a man's life was worth to write anything against slavery, or to speak against it, in the Southern States. And has it come to this, that the North are to be made slaves, and that an institution is to be sustained in our midst that will not allow itself to be ventilated? For one I do not feel willing at present to part with my liberty in this respect — although I am informed that a Mason, not far from here, intimated that I might be waylaid and murdered. It matters not. I will not compromise the liberty of free speech on a question of such importance to save my life. Why should I? I must confess that I have felt amazed and mortified when so many have expressed astonishment that I dared to speak plainly on this subject, and write my thoughts and views.

Among all the letters that I have received on this subject, I do not recollect one in which the writer does not admonish me not to publish his name. And this in republican America! A man's life, property and character not safe if he speaks the truth in regard to an institution which is aiming to overshadow the whole land, and to have everything its own way! as the

171

writer of the letter from which I have just made an extract says, that a man's character is not safe if he speaks the truth concerning Freemasonry. Is not this abominable?

So well do I understand that Masons are sworn to persecute, and to represent every one who abandons their institution as a vile vagabond, an to say all manner of evil against him, that I do not pretend to believe what they say of that class of men.

When the question of Freemasonry was first forced upon us in our church, and I was obliged to preach upon the subject and read from Bernard's "Light on Masonry," I found before I got home that Elder Bernard had been so misrepresented and slandered that people were saying, "He is not a man to be trusted." Who does not know that whoever has dared to renounce that institution, and publish its secrets to the world, has either been murdered, or slandered and followed with persecution in a most unrelenting manner?

CHAPTER XIX

RELATIONS OF MASONRY TO THE CHURCH OF CHRIST

We are now prepared to consider the question of the relation of Freemasonry to the Church of Christ. On this question I remark:

1st. God holds the church and every branch of it, responsible for its opinion and action in accordance with the best light, which, in his providence, is afforded them. This, indeed, is law universal, equally applicable to all moral agents, at all times and in all places. But at present I consider its application to the Church of God. If any particular branch of the church has better means of information, and therefore more light on moral questions, than another branch, its responsibility is greater, in proportion to its greater means of information. Such a branch of the church is bound to take a higher and more advanced position in Christian life and duty, to bear a fuller and higher testimony against every form of iniquity, than that required by less favored and less informed branches of the church. They are not to wait til other branches of the church have received their light, before they bear a testimony and pursue a course in accordance with their own degree of information.

2d. While Masonry was a secret, the church had no light, and no responsibility respecting it. Although individual members of the church, were Freemasons, as a body, she knew nothing of Masonry; therefore she could say nothing of it, except as its results appeared to be revealed in the lives of individuals; and, in judging from this source of evidence, the church could not decide, if the lives of the members were good or bad, whether it was Freemasonry that made them so; because, of its nature, designs, principles, oaths, doctrines, secret practices, she knew nothing. Hence God did not require the church to bear any testimony on the subject as long as Masonry was a secret. The world did not expect the church to take any action, or to bear any testimony on the subject, as long as Masonry was a thing unknown, except to the initiated. In those circumstances the unconverted world did not expect any testimony from the church and they had no right to expect it. The well-known fact, that many professed Christians were Freemasons, was then no disgrace to the Church of God, because the character of Freemasonry was not known.

3d. But the state of the case is now greatly changed. Freemasonry is now revealed. It is no longer a secret to any who wish to be informed. Its nature, character, aims, oaths, principles, doctrines, usages, are in print, and the books in which they are revealed are scattered broadcast over the land. As long ago as 1826, Wm. Morgan published verbatim the first three degrees of Masonry. That these degrees were faithfully published as they were known, and taken in the lodges, no man can truthfully deny. Two, or more spurious editions of this work have been published, for the sake of deceiving the public. To obtain a correct edition of this work is at present difficult. Just previous to the publication of this work, Elder Stearns, a Baptist minister, and a high Mason, one who had taken many Masonic degrees, a man of good character who is still living, had published a volume entitled "An inquiry into the nature and tendency of Speculative Freemasonry." In 1860 the same author published a volume entitled "Letters on Freemasonry, addressed chiefly to the Fraternity," with an appendix. He has recently published another volume, entitled "A new chapter of Freemasonry." Soon after the publication of Morgan's book, already referred to, a body of seceding Masons, appointed a committee of sixteen, if I do not mistake the number, upon which committee were several ministers of Christ, to prepare and publish a correct version of forty-eight degrees of Freemasonry. Elder Bernard had taken a large number of degrees, I know not exactly how many. The degrees ordered to be published by this committee were carefully collected and arranged and published under the following title, "Light on Masonry.'" A collection of all the most important documents on the subject of Speculative Masonry, embracing the reports of the western committees in relation to the abduction of Wm. Morgan, proceedings of conventions, orations, essays, etc., etc., with all the degrees of the order conferred in a Master's lodge as written by Capt. Wm. Morgan, all the degrees conferred in the Royal Arch Chapter, and Grand Encampment of Knights Templar, with the appendant orders as published by the convention of seceding Masons, held at Leroy, July 4th and 5th, 1828. Also, a revelation of all the degrees conferred in the Lodge of Perfection and fifteen degrees of a still higher order with seven French degrees, making forty-eight degrees of Freemasonry, with notes and critical remarks by Elder David Bernard, of Warsaw, Genesee County, New York, once an intimate Secretary of the Lodge of Perfection. This book soon passed through seven editions. An eighth, but an abridged edition, has been recently published in Dayton, Ohio." Since the publication of Bernard's book, a volume has been published, entitled "Richardson's Monitor of Freemasonry;" being a practical guide to the ceremonies in all the degrees conferred in Masonic Lodges, Chapters, Encampments, etc., explaining the signs, tokens and grips, and giving all the words, passwords, sacred words, oaths, and hieroglyphics used by Masons. The ineffable and historical degrees are also given in full. By Jabez Richardson, A.M. In this book are published sixty-two Masonic degrees, with diagrams of lodges, and drawing representing their signs and ceremonies. Brother Avery Allyn has also published a large number of Masonic degrees. The question of the reliability of these works, I have discussed in a previous number. I am a little more particular in naming them in this place, for the information of those who have not seen the books. The substantial accord of all these authors, and their reliability, seems to be established beyond all reasonable question. Now, since these revelations are made, and both the church and the world are aware of what Masonry really is, God demands, and the world has a right to expect, that the church will take due action and bear a truthful testimony in respect to this institution. She can not now innocently hold her peace. The light has come. Fidelity to God, and to the souls of men, require that the church, which is the light of the world, should speak out, and should take such action as will plainly reveal her views of the compatibility or incompatibility of Freemasonry with the Christian religion. As God's witnesses, as the pillar and ground of the truth, the church is bound to give the trumpet no uncertain sound, upon this question, that all men may know, whether, in her judgment, an intelligent embracing and determinate adhering to Freemasonry are compatible with a truthful profession of religion.

4th. The Church of Christ knows Masonry through these books. This is the best and most reliable source of information that we can have, or can reasonable ask. We have seen in a former number, that Freemasons do not pretend that Freemasonry has been substantially altered since the publication of these books, that we have the most satisfactory evidence that it has not been, and can not be substantially changed. Let it therefore be distinctly understood, that the action and testimony of the church respects Freemasonry as it is revealed in these books, and not as individuals may affirm of it, pro or con. By these books we know it. By these books we judge it, and let it be understood that whatever action we take upon it, or whatever we say of it, we both act and speak of Masonry as it is here revealed, and of no other Masonry or thing, whatever. To this course, neither Masons nor any one else can justly take exceptions. From all the testimony in the case, we are shut up to this course. Let not Freemasons complain of this. These books certainly reveal Masonry as it was forty years ago. If it has been changed, the burden of proof is of them, and inasmuch as they make no pretense that Masonry has been reformed, and in view of the fact, that they still maintain that they embrace all the principles and usages of ancient Freemasonry, we are bound to speak our minds of Freemasonry as these books reveal it.

5th. Judging then, from these revelations, how can we fail to pronounce Freemasonry an anti-Christian institution? For example, 1st. We have seen that its morality is unchristian. 2d. Its oath-bound secrecy is unchristian. 3d. The administration and taking of its oaths are unchristian, and a violation of a positive command of Christ. 4th. Masonic oaths pledge its members to commit most unlawful and unchristian deeds. *a.* To conceal each others crimes. *b.* To deliver each other from difficulty whether right or wrong. *c.* To unduly favor Masonry in political actions and in business transactions. *d.* Its members are sworn to retaliate, and persecute unto death, the violators of Masonic obligation. *e.* Freemasonry knows no mercy, but swears its candidates to avenge violations of Masonic obligation even unto death. *f.* Its oaths are profane, the taking of the name of God in vain. *g.* The penalties of these oaths are barbarous and even savage. *h.* Its teachings are false and profane. *i.* Its design is partial and selfish. *j.* Its ceremonies are a mixture of puerility and profanity. *k.* Its religion is Deistic. *l.* It is a false religion, and professes to save men upon other conditions than those revealed in the Gospel of Christ. *m.* It is an enormous falsehood. *n.* It is a swindle, and obtains money from its membership under false pretenses. *o.* It refuses all examination, and veils itself under a mantle of oath-bound secrecy. *p.* It is a virtual conspiracy against both Church and State. No one, therefore, has ever undertaken, and for the plainest reasons none will undertake, to defend Freemasonry as it is revealed in these books. Their arguments are threats, calumny, persecution, assassination. Freemasons do not pretend that Freemasonry, as revealed in these books, is compatible with Christianity. I have not yet known the first Freemason who would affirm that an intelligent adherence to Freemasonry, as revealed in these books, is consistent with a profession of the Christian religion. But we know, if we can know anything from testimony, that these books do truly reveal Freemasonry. We have, then, the implied testimony of Freemasons themselves, that the Christian Church ought to have no fellowship with Freemasonry as thus revealed, and that those who adhere intelligently and determinately to such an institution have no right to be in the Christian Church. In our judgment we are forced to the same conclusion, we can not escape from it, we wish it were otherwise, we therefore sorrowfully, but solemnly, pronounce this judgment.

6th. Every local branch of the Church of Christ is bound to examine this subject, and pronounce upon this institution, according to the best light they can get. God does not allow individuals, or churches, to withhold action, and the expression of their opinion, until other churches are as enlightened as themselves. We are bound to act up to our own light, and to go as far in advance of others as we have better means of information than they. We have no right to say to God that we will act according to our own convictions, when others become so enlightened that our action will be popular and meet their approval.

Again: Those individuals and churches, who have had the best means of information, owe it to other branches of the church, and to the whole world, to take action and to pronounce upon the unchristian character of Freemasonry, as the most influential means within their reach of arousing the whole church and the world to an examination of the character and claims of Freemasonry. If churches who are known to have examined the subject withhold their testimony; if they continue to receive persistent and intelligent Freemasons; if they leave the public to infer that they see nothing in Freemasonry inconsistent with a creditable profession of the Christian religion, it will be justly inferred by other branches of the church, and by the world, that there is nothing in it so bad, so dangerous and unchristian as to call for their examination, action, or testimony. Before the publishing of Morgan's book the Baptist denomination, especially, in that part of the country, had been greatly carried away by Freemasonry. A large proportion of its eldership and membership were Freemasons. A considerable number of ministers and members of other branches of the Christian Church had also fallen into the snare. The murder of Wm. Morgan, and the publication of Masonry consequent thereupon in the books I have named, broke upon the churches — fast asleep on this subject — like a clap of thunder from a clear sky. The facts were such, the revelations were so clear, that the Baptist denomination backed down, and took the lead in renouncing and denouncing the institution. Their elders and associated churches, almost universally, passed resolutions disfellowshiping adhering Masons. The denomination, to a considerable extent, took the same course. Throughout the Northern States, at that time, I believe it was almost universally conceded that persistent Freemasons, who continued to adhere and co-operate with them, ought not to be admitted to Christian churches. Now it is worthy of all consideration and remembrance, that God set the seal of His approbation upon the action taken by those churches at that time, by pouring out His Spirit upon them.

Great revivals immediately followed over that whole region. The discussion of the subject, and the action of the churches took place in 1827-'8 and '9, and in 1830 the greatest revival spread over this region that had ever been known in this or any other country. They knew Masonry, as we know it, by an examination of those books in which it had been revealed. We have the same means of knowing Freemasonry, if we will use them, that those churches and ecclesiastical bodies had. We have the highest evidence that the nature of the case will admit, that God approved of their decision and action. In the brief outline that I have given in the preceding pages, I have endeavored to show truthfully, so far as my space would allow, what Freemasonry really is, and if it is what these books represent it to be, it seems to me clear as noonday, that it is an anti-Christian institution. And should the question be asked, "What shall be done with the great number of professed Christians who are Freemasons?" I answer, Let them have no more to do with it. Again, let Christian men labor with them, plead with them, and endeavor to make them see it to be their duty to abandon it. These oaths should be distinctly read to them, and they should be asked whether they acknowledge the obligation of these oaths, and whether they intend to do the things that they have sworn to do. Let it be distinctly pressed upon their consciences, that all Masons above the first two degrees have solemnly sworn to conceal each other's crimes, murder and treason alone excepted, and all above the sixth degree have sworn to conceal each other's crimes, without an exception. All above the sixth degree have sworn to espouse each other's cause and to deliver them from any difficulty, whether they are right or wrong. If they have taken those degrees where they swear to persecute unto death those who violate their obligations, let them be asked whether they intend to do any such thing. Let them be distinctly asked whether they intend still to aid and abet the administration and taking of these oaths, if they still intend to countenance the false and hypocritical teachings of Masonry, if they mean to countenance the profanity of their ceremonies, and practice the partiality they have sworn to practice. If so, surely they should not be allowed their places in the church.

CHAPTER XX

CONCLUSION

In concluding these pages I appeal to Freemasons themselves. Gentlemen, I beg you to believe that I have no personal ill-will toward any member of your fraternity. Many of them are amongst my personal acquaintances, and some of them nearly related to me.

I have written of Masonry, I pray you to remember, as revealed by Wm. Morgan, also Avery Allyn, Elders Bernard and Stearns, and Mr. Richardson. That these authors truly reveal Masonry I am certain, so far as I have personal knowledge of it. That they truly reveal the higher degrees I have as good reasons for believing, as of any fact to be established by human testimony. You can not justly expect me to doubt the truthfulness of these revelations. You must be aware that God will hold me responsible, and demand that I should, in view of the testimony, yield my full assent to the credibility of these authors. You must know that God requires me to treat this subject in accordance with this revelation. Now, gentlemen, no one of your number has attempted to show that these books are not substantially reliable and true. No one of you has appeared to publicly justify Masonry as revealed by these authors. You must be aware that no man can justify it. No respectable author amongst you has attempted to show that Freemasonry has undergone any essential improvement, or modification since these revelations were made; but on the contrary the most recently published Masonic authorities assert or assume that Masonry has not been changed, and that it is still what it ever has been, and that it is insusceptible of change, as I have proved it to be. Now, my dear sirs, what ought you to expect of me? To hold my peace and let the evil overrun the country until it is too late to speak? Believing, as I most assuredly do, that these works truly reveal Masonry, could I be an honest

181

man, a faithful minister of Christ, and hold my peace in view of the alarming progress that this institution is making in these days. In your hearts you would condemn and despise me if, with my convictions, I suffered any earthly considerations to prevent my sounding the trumpet of alarm to both Church and State. Would you have me stultify my intelligence by refusing to believe these authors; or, believing them, would you have me cower before this enormously extended conspiracy? Or would you have me sear my conscience by shunning the cross, and keeping silence in the midst of the perils of both Church and State? And, gentlemen, can you escape from the conclusions at which I have arrived. Granting these works to be true, and *remember I am bound to assume their truthfulness* can any of you face the public and assert that men who have intelligently taken and who adhere to the horrid oaths, with their horrid penalties, as revealed in these books, can safely be trusted with any office in Church or State? Can a man who has taken, and still adheres to the Master's oath to conceal any secret crime of a brother of that degree, murder and treason excepted, be a safe man with whom to entrust an office? Can he be trusted as a witness, a juror, or with any office connected with the administration of justice? Can a man who has taken and still adheres to the oath of the Royal Arch degree be trusted in office? He swears to espouse the cause of a companion of this degree when involved in any difficulty, so far as to extricate him from the same, whether he be right or wrong. He swears to conceal his crimes, *murder and treason not excepted.* He swears to give a companion of this degree timely notice of any approaching danger that may be known to him. Now is a man bound fast by such an oath to be entrusted with office? Ought he to be accepted as a witness, a juror — when a Freemason is a party, in any case — a sheriff, constable, or marshal; ought he to be trusted with the office of judge or justice of the peace? Gentlemen, you know he ought not, and you would despise me should I not be faithful in warning the public against entrusting such men with office. But further: Take the large class of men who have sworn, under the most awful penalties, to take *vengeance* on all who violate Masonic obligations; to seek their condign punishment; to kill them; to persecute them, and to ruin them by representing them wherever they go as worthless vagabonds. Now, gentlemen, I appeal to you, is a man who is under a most solemn oath to kill or seek the death of any man who shall violate any part of the Masonic oaths a fit person to be at large amongst men? Why, who does not know that Freemasons are in the habit of violating various points and parts of their Masonic oaths, and are not Freemasons bound by oaths to kill them, or seek their death? There are many seceding Masons throughout the land. Adhering Masons are under oath to seek to procure their death. Now if they adhere to their oaths and thereby affirm that they design to fulfill their vows, if any opportunity occurs, ought they not to be imprisoned or put under the heaviest bonds to keep the peace? No one can face the public and deny this, admitting as he must that their oaths are truly recorded in these books. No one can think this conclusion harsh unless he assumes contrary to all evidence, either that no such oaths have been taken, or if they have, and are still adhered to there is no danger that these vows will be fulfilled. Take these books and say wherein have I dealt harshly or uncharitably with Freemasonry as herein revealed? Ought a Freemason of this stamp to be fellowshiped by a Christian Church? Ought not such an one to be regarded as an unscrupulous and dangerous man? I appeal to your conscience in the sight of God, and I know that your moral sense must respond amen to the conclusions at which I have arrived. Be not offended with my telling you the truth in love. We must all soon meet at the solemn judgment. Let us not be angry, but honest.

EPILOG

FREEMASONRY'S RETALIATION AGAINST THE CHURCH

© 1998 by John Daniel

Every Mason should cast his lot with the Church; to help vitalize it, liberalize it, modernize it and render it aggressive and efficient; to do less is treason to your country, to your Creator, and to the obligation you have promised to obey.[1]

Scottish Rite *New Age Magazine*
January, 1926

The Masonic murder of Captain William Morgan in 1826 so aroused Americans against Freemasonry that it nearly toppled the Fraternity. In the Masonic book, *10,000 Famous Freemasons*, William Denslow informs us of the devastation wrought the Brotherhood: "The Anti-Masonic Movement gave rise to the Anti-Masonic party, 141 Anti-Masonic newspapers in the U.S., and almost killed Freemasonry in America.... Families, churches, and communities were split; Freemasons by the thousands publicly disavowed their memberships. Lodges and grand lodges went underground. In New York there were 500 lodges, but by 1834 there were only 49."[2]

Of the 50,000 Masons in America when Morgan was killed, there were only 5,000 by 1834. Many of the 45,000 who had quit the lodge, publicly disavowed their membership, causing 2,000 lodges to close their doors. The remaining lodges went underground to plan a strategy against the church — not to destroy the Church, but to infiltrate it and turn it lukewarm.

A century following Morgan's 1826 Masonic murder, Freemasonry was ready to weaken the effect of the gospel. In 1926 it gave the order to infiltrate the Church in America. Its method

185

was subtle, yet powerful; attend church, say the right words to sound Christian, take communion, join the Church, get elected to a ruling position, then "render" the Church "aggressive and efficient" for Masonic use.

As memory of the past faded, Freemasonry bragged of its comeback. Denslow continued: "This was the low point, and from there on recovery was fast and the growth permanent. By 1860 New York had 432 lodges and 25,000 members; 10,000 more than in 1820."

In 1861, the year the Civil War began, the nationwide count of Freemasons had grown to 200,000. During the war over a hundred military lodges were formed.[3] By the end of the war, there were 500,000 Masons throughout America.[4] When the soldiers returned home, they helped with the order's period of rapid growth. By 1900 there were over 800,000 members.[5]

As stated in the "Introduction," and as these statistics prove, war increases Masonic membership because of mutual protection on both sides.

In the Masonic book, *House Undivided: The Story of Freemasonry and the Civil War*, author Allen E. Roberts confirms that "over 300 generals in the Union and Confederate armies were members of the Craft — plus an uncountable number of other officers and men,"[6] all obligated by Masonic oath to protect each other from harm.

Roberts tells of instances in which Masons wearing blue joined hands in peace and harmony with those clad in gray, while the sound of guns and the din of battle were heard all around them. He relates stories on both sides of the conflict in which captured spies, generals, foot soldiers, cavalry, etc., were shown Masonic partiality by releasing them when they displayed the grand hailing sign of distress.

Had such partiality been displayed between brothers in Christ, it would have been considered an act of treason. It would therefore appear that if all men were Masons there would be peace on earth. And indeed, Roberts suggests this very idea throughout his book.

The facts, however, are to the contrary. Freemasonry itself instigated this most horrific war for two self-centered reasons: (1) to increase its membership, which was so drastically depleted by the Anti-Masonic Movement; and (2) to stop the intrusion of Christians into politics.

The first reason is self-evident by the rapid rise in membership prior to, during, and after the conflict. The second reason (to stop the intrusion of Christians into politics), is found in a veiled threat by 33rd degree Mason Love S. Cornwell, who at the time was Grand Master of the Grand Lodge of Missouri. During his 1856 annual address to Grand Lodge, he said:

> [Political] parties are being formed of every political cast.... [D]emagogues, through religious fanaticism [meaning anti-Masonic Christians], are endeavoring to elevate themselves to honor and distinction, by the agitation of questions that should rarely ever be discussed, expecting to ride upon the whirlwind, and guide the storm that will place them in a position they are frequently poorly qualified to fill. *The great trouble will be that the storm may not only carry them, but also the innocent, into civil war, anarchy and confusion.*[7]

Cornwell's last statement connects our Civil War to anti-Masonic activity. But, is he suggesting "religious fanatics" caused civil war, or is he threatening retaliation by Freemasonry with civil war? The answer will be evident as we progress in our study.

The devastating blow landed by the Anti-Masonic Movement caused the 5,000 remaining diehard Masons to call on European Freemasonry to come to its aid. Six Supreme Council meetings were held in Paris, France from 1841 to 1845 to determine how to remedy the Masonic problem in America.[8] Their decision was to put into practice their motto, Order out of Chaos.

The Supreme Council would create the chaos. As the American populace focused on the crisis, American Freemasonry

187

would rebuild its ranks. After the crisis the same Supreme Council would bring Masonic order out of its own created chaos.

The chaos was the Abolitionist Movement,[9] which split both the nation and church denominations north and south. In 1837 the Presbyterians split. In 1840 the Methodists split. And in 1845 the great division in the Baptist denomination created the Southern Baptist Convention.

After the crisis the Masonic idea of "order" was to return to their original agenda; control of government, business, banking, schools, and churches. It would take a while to accomplish this aggressive agenda, but the common saying in European revolutionary lodges was, "It may last for many years, perhaps a century; in our ranks the soldier dies, but the war is continued."[10]

Subsequent evidence suggests that the Masonic conspiracy to recapture America and render the Church impotent had eight phases, all of which were planned and controlled by the Fraternity, as we shall document as we progress:

1. Create a civil crisis that will distract the Church away from its anti-Masonry, so that Freemasonry can rebuild it ranks.

2. Turn primary and secondary schools, which are presently under the control of parents, into public schools funded by the government, and under the control of Freemasonry.

3. Manipulate public school teachers through a union controlled by Freemasonry.

4. Infiltrate the Church with materialism by creating easy credit through central banking.

5. Create a Masonic-controlled mega-church association to control mainline denominations.

6. Infiltrate the pastorate with infidels.

7. Infiltrate the church with Masons.

8. Stack the Supreme Court with anti-American Masons who are willing to reinterpret the Constitution, so that Christian principles can never be taught in public schools.

188

These eight phases are listed in the order they occurred histor-ically, not necessarily as they had been planned. As much as possible we shall stick with the historic order. In some cases we may deviate to connect phases that relate.

Proof that Freemasonry was the force behind instigating our Civil War is impossible to find in Masonic publications, because the Fraternity blatantly destroyed the evidence. Accord-ing to former 33rd degree Freemason Dr. Jonathan Blanchard, who lived through this crisis, "the Southern lodge-rooms worked up the most unjustifiable and infamous war on record. The Southern people were dragooned into it by leaders secretly sworn to obey Masonic leaders, or have their throats cut."[11] Blanchard continues that evidence of these treasonous facts was purposely destroyed by burning fifty-nine years of Masonic records on the eve of the Civil War.

Other evidence, however, abounds from many sources, and is detailed with abundant documentation in volume 3, chapter 4 of *Scarlet and the Beast.* The reader is encouraged to read this work for an unmistakable involvement of Freemasonry in instigating and sustaining the Civil War, as well as the after-math. We shall give only a synopsis here.

After the Morgan Affair and the anti-Masonic fervor that followed, Freemasonry was dealt a devastating blow. That blow came by way of revival. As you have already read in the words of Finney as written in his book, when the Holy Spirit convicted the hearts of 45,000 Masons to renounce Freemasonry, the greatest revival the world had ever witnessed up to that time occurred in this land.

The Brotherhood, however, was not dead. And with its come-back it returned with a vengeance. Of the 5,000 remaining diehard Masons still retaining membership in underground lodges, a larger percentage were now of the most evil character found anywhere on the face of the earth. No one within their Order had the moral courage to restrain them. We shall mention only a few in this synopsis of a universal Masonic effort to return America to the grip of Freemasonry.

FREEMASONRY

The most evil of these Masons were General Albert Pike (1809-1891), 33rd degree Moses Holbrook (?-1844), and Holbrook's private secretary, a Scottish Rite Mason by the name of Longfellow. Holbrook, a Jew, was Sovereign Grand Commander of the Supreme Council at Charleston, and one of the nine creators of the 33rd degree at Charleston in 1801.

In 1843, Holbrook and Longfellow were attempting to penetrate the inner shrines of Freemasonry with the doctrine of Satanism. Both had studied thoroughly the occult sciences and enjoyed discussing with Pike the mysteries of the Jewish *Cabala*, but were unable to convert the general to Satanism.[12]

Pike was opposed to a Satanic Rite in Freemasonry because he, as a Luciferian, refused to believe Satan and Lucifer were the same personality. "Satan," he said, "is the figment of the imagination of Christians. Lucifer is God, and unfortunately Adonay [the God of the Bible] is also God. For the eternal law is that there is no light without shade, no beauty without ugliness, no white without black, for the absolute can only exist as two Gods.... Thus, the doctrine of Satanism is a heresy; and the true and pure philosophic religion is the belief in Lucifer, the equal of Adonay; but Lucifer, God of Light and God of Good, is struggling for humanity against Adonay, the God of Darkness and Evil."[13] Three decades later Pike rewrote the Scottish Rite rituals in his 1871 book, *Morals and Dogma.* In it he states that the true light of the world is Lucifer.

Every Mason raised to the 3rd degree is given a copy of Pike's *Morals and Dogma.* The 1990 January issue of the Scottish Rite *New Age Magazine* states that *Morals and Dogma* is a "Mason's guide for daily living."

In this book (from pages 69 to 741), Pike gradually builds his Luciferian doctrine so as not to shock the reader early on, and perchance lose him as a disciple. The following quote is a medley of six excerpts from between these pages:

Masonry is a search after Light.... What light is, we no more know than the ancients did.... Light was the first Divinity worshipped by men.... To the

190

ancients, it was an outflowing from the Deity.... The earliest Indian and Persian Deities are for the most part symbols of celestial light.... Lucifer, the Son of the Morning! Is it he who bears the Light, and with its splendors intolerable blinds feeble, sensual, or selfish Souls? Doubt it not.... [T]his is the Light for which all Masonic journeys are a search....[14]

When Pike was debating Satanism with Longfellow and Holbrook, he had not yet joined Freemasonry, but rather was a member of the Oddfellows.[15] Yet, young Pike had so impressed the European Illuminati with his research into their Luciferian doctrine that he was appointed to carry their torch into the American lodges. Consequently, Pike, and those who followed him, rebuilt American Freemasonry on the principal doctrine that Freemasonry's Great Architect of the Universe is the Fallen Angel.[16]

One of the techniques used for restructuring and rapidly expanding American Freemasonry was to push initiates up the ladder of degrees as fast a possible. This is still practiced today — only in America. We shall use Albert Pike's meteoric rise in Freemasonry as an example of how it works.

Pike was not a Southerner, but rather a Northerner. The precise year he became a Mason is not recorded, but as an Illuminatus he was placed under the tutelage of 33rd degree General Caleb Cushing (1800-1879). Cushing then sent Pike south to take control of the Southern Jurisdiction of Scottish Rite Freemasonry in preparation for civil war.[17]

In August of 1850, at age 40, Pike was raised to 3rd degree in Western Star Lodge No. 2, Little Rock, Arkansas. On March 20, 1853, two weeks after Cushing was appointed Attorney General of the United States, he sent word to Pike to go to Charleston, South Carolina, and there receive the Higher degrees. In one day Pike received all the Scottish Rite degrees (4-32) from Albert G. Mackey. In 1857 he received the 33rd degree in New Orleans. On January 3, 1859, Pike was elected

FREEMASONRY

Sovereign Grand Commander of the Southern Jurisdiction of Scottish Rite Freemasonry.[18]

In six years Lucifer-worshipping Pike was raised from 3rd degree to 33rd degree and ruled the largest body of Scottish Rite Masons in the world. Tens of thousands more were raised as rapidly to fill the void of those lost to the Anti-Masonic Movement. Now, compare this rapid rise by degrees to that of Captain William Morgan. When Morgan wrote his book, he, after having practiced the Craft for thirty years, was only a Royal Arch Mason (13th degree).

What is most astounding is that the two jurisdictions of Scottish Rite Freemasonry (north and south) cooperated to incite the great rebellion. Rebel Mason Albert Pike was the Yankee selected to head the "Southern Rebellion." He took his orders from Yankee Freemason Caleb Cushing, and received funding from British Masonic bankers.[19] When he called for the secession of eleven southern states, the governors of those states had no choice but to secede, for they were all Masons under obligation to obey their Masonic superior, or have their throats cut.[20]

Developing the Masonic intrigue between the Northern and Southern Jurisdictions of Freemasonry to provoke civil war is too lengthy to reproduce here. Interested readers are referred to *Scarlet and the Beast*, volume 3, chapter 4 for a detailed, and well documented account.

Suffice it to say that Freemasonry was desperate for membership. If the agenda of illuminated Freemasonry was to move forward in America, recruitment was of utmost importance. War guaranteed that rapid expansion. In fact, when the draft went into effect for the Civil War, it was the general consensus of the population that Freemasonry was behind it — that draftees were required to present themselves to local lodges to sign up. Although Freemasonry denies this assertion today, angry mobs of citizens did sack Lodges across the land and destroyed all papers so they would not have to participate in what was generally known as "Freemasonry's war."[21]

If the rumor were true that Freemasonry instigated the draft, let's consider the benefit to the Fraternity. Phase one was to "Create a civil crisis that will distract the Church away from its anti-Masonry, so that Freemasonry can rebuild the ranks." The abolitionist movement and civil war was the crisis. How better to rebuild its ranks during war than to offer the federal government access to Masonic lodges to sign up draftees. Not only could recruits be enlisted, they could also be initiated, with the guarantee attached that they had a better chance to return home after the war.

Whether the rumor was true or not, the fact remains that by the end of the war, Freemasonry had increased it ranks from 5,000 to 500,000. In addition, many of these veterans were high-Masons, meaning they had advanced to at least the 32nd degree. This was accomplished in the same manner in which Albert Pike was rapidly advanced from 4th to 32nd in one day.

With the end of the Civil War, phase one was complete. Phase two was to turn parent-controlled and -funded primary and secondary schools into Masonic-controlled public schools funded by the state. Investigative journalist Paul Fisher, in his book, *Behind The Lodge Door,* has summarized the goals of Freemasonry in America in creating and promoting a system of compulsory public education: (1) The destruction of all social influence by the Church and religion generally, either by open persecution or by so-called separation of Church and State; (2) To laicize or secularize all public and private life and, above all, popular education; and (3) To systematically develop freedom of thought and conscience in school children, and protect them, so far as possible, against all disturbing influences of the Church, and even their own parents — by compulsion if necessary.[22]

Freemasonry actually began its takeover of schools in 1809, seventeen years before the Morgan Affair. It was a state-by-state Grand Lodge effort, which began in New York. Grand Lodge of New York initiated the drive to fund what they called Free Schools. *Mackey's Encyclopedia of Freemasonry* informs us that "Brother Dewitt Clinton founded the New York Free

FREEMASONRY

School Society, which later became the Public School Society of New York.... He was Chairman of the Board of Trustees and very active until his death in 1828."[23]

Dewitt Clinton, as you recall, was at this time a member of the Columbian Illuminati Lodge. He served as Grand Master of the New York Grand Lodge from 1806-1820, and was a two-term Governor of the state during the Morgan Affair.[24]

At first Masons stood on street corners to collect donations to fund the Free Schools. In 1817, the Free School System was formally established under state supervision, and further support from the Masonic Fraternity was no longer required.[25]

As designed, the character of teaching in New York schools significantly changed from supernaturalist philosophy to naturalist philosophy. Consequently, the Northeast was liberalized a century before the rest of America.

In 1841 Freemasonry in several states began to build and fund its own colleges to compete with Christian colleges that had sprung up as a result of the Second Great Awakening. However, Freemasonry found it too costly and corrupting to continue, since "large funds, amassed for such purposes, must of necessity be placed under the control and management of comparatively few, it will have a corrupting influence, promote discord, and bring reproach upon the Craft."[26]

The public schools of phase two coincided with phase three, which was to control school teachers through unionization. During the Second Great Awakening in America, most parents were Bible-believing Christians, who insisted teachers of their children be of the Christian faith and teach the precepts of Holy Scripture, primarily the Ten Commandments.

Scottish Rite Freemasonry usurped that role in 1857 by founding the National Education Association, better known as the NEA.[27] Not until this teacher's union had been sufficiently liberalized did the Scottish Rite Supreme Council relinquish its control of the NEA's powerful Secretariat. Today the liberal NEA, with over two million members, is one of Freemasonry's strongest lobby organizations.

In 1920 Freemasonry made its next move to solidify federal control of public schools. That year the Southern Jurisdiction of Scottish Rite Freemasonry openly declared itself in favor of the creation of a Department of Education with a Secretary in the President's Cabinet. The secretary, of course, would be a Mason. Freemasonry takes sole credit for the passage of the Smith-Tower Educational Bill, which also furnished Federal Aid to the Public Schools.[28]

After the passage of this bill, Freemasonry declared its belief in compulsory attendance of all children to Public Schools, including children of Christian parents. Through its *New Age Magazine*, the Scottish Rite gave orders to all Masons to be active on school boards and to encourage parents to make the public schools so efficient that their superiority over all church schools should be so obvious that every parent will have to send their children to the public schools.[29]

At that time 33rd degree Earl Warren was Grand Master of the Grand Lodge of California. He had not yet received his appointment as Chief Justice to the Supreme Court. In his 1936 annual address to the Brethren in California, he said, "the education of our youth...can best be done, indeed it can only be done, by a system of free public education. It is for this reason that the Grand Lodge of California, ever striving as it does to replace darkness with light, is so vitally interested in the public schools of our state.... By destroying prejudice [meaning Christianity] and planting reason in its place it prepares the foundation of a liberty-loving people for free government."[30]

Phase eight, although belated, was part of phases two and three. It called for stacking our Supreme Court with Masons who would reinterpret our Constitution so that nothing in the Holy Scriptures would ever be taught again in public schools. Franklin Delano Roosevelt, a 32nd degree Mason, was the man who performed the task. As President, one of his functions would be to appoint justices to the Supreme Court when a seat was vacated by death or resignation. World War II would distract attention from his Masonic appointments. By the time he died in 1945, Roosevelt had appointed five justices, all of whom were his Scottish Rite buddies. The remaining four shared liberal views.

From 1941 to 1971, five to eight Masons sat on the Supreme Court in any given year.[31] Their first agenda was to change the First Amendment's freedom of religion guarantee to "separation of Church and State." To alter an Amendment would be an act of treason. Therefore, the Masonic justices simply ruled that separation of church and state was "implied" in the First Amendment.[32]

The First Amendment to our Constitution reads as follows: "Congress shall make no law respecting an establishment of religion, or prohibiting the free exercise thereof; or abridging the freedom of speech, or of the press; or the right of the people peaceably to assemble, and to petition the Government for a redress of grievances."

Our forefathers passed the "Bill of Rights" in 1791, which were the first ten amendments. The First Amendment was written so that freedom of religion and freedom of speech go hand-in-hand. It mentions nothing of "church."It is a deistic instrument that permits any and all religions to be practiced openly and verbally in this land of "freedom."

There are many religions, but only one Church. "A wall of separation between church and state" are words from the mouth of Thomas Jefferson alone — never written in our Constitution. These words are significantly different words than "separation of religion and state." Separation of religion and state are words discussed in the atheistic minds of the French revolutionists while writing their 1791 constitution, which provided for the creation of a system of free, public secular education, with the final result that no religion, Christian or otherwise, is taught in French public schools to this day.[33]

The constitution of the former Soviet Union was significantly different from its French counterpart. It specifically separated "church and state," which meant that all religions could be

196

practiced openly in the former Soviet Union except Christianity.[34] Likewise, the reinterpretation of our First Amendment by the Masonic-stacked Supreme Court specifically separates "church and state," not "religion and state." Therefore, humanism, evolution, New Age, all of which are fundamental doctrines in pagan religions, can be, and are taught in our public schools. Christianity alone is forbidden!

When Justice Robert H. Jackson (a 32nd degree Mason), was questioned about the Supreme Court's interpretation, he said, "the Constitution and its amendments are what the judges say they are."[35] As a result of this treasonous interpretation of the First Amendment, not only was our government forbidden to fund church schools, it paved the way for outlawing prayer and Bible reading in those same schools.

Another problem that confronted Freemasonry's control of public schools was the vast number of small school systems throughout our land that were controlled by parents. Consolidation was Freemasonry's solution. Therefore, after World War II, the Fraternity began lobbying government to consolidate the public school system. James B. Conant, a 33rd degree Mason and member of the NEA's Educational Policies Commission, was sent on a public speaking tour to promote consolidation. In advance of Conant, the Scottish Rite openly advertised to all school systems to compel parents to attend the meetings. In Lodge, Freemasonry secretly ordered all Masons to attend. After the tour, parents throughout the United States marched to the polls and voted themselves out of control of what their children would be taught. As planned by Freemasonry, 259,000 parent-controlled public school districts were consolidated into 1,600 NEA-controlled districts.[36]

After consolidation parents were no longer intimate with teachers. As planned, both became alienated by the larger body — the NEA. Gradually but surely the Masonic-controlled NEA became adversarial towards parents. Although the Parent-Teacher Association (PTA) was formed to bridge the gap, it pales in strength to Freemasonry's revolutionary teachers' union.

197

FREEMASONRY

A sobering statement made by NEA past-president Katherine Barrett articulates the weakness of the PTA and the strength of the new revolutionary role of teachers: "The teacher will be the conveyor of values, a philosopher. Teachers no longer will be victims of change [meaning controlled by parents]; we will be agents of change."[37]

Recall Paul Fisher's earlier statement in his "summarized goals of Freemasonry in America" on page 193: Freemasonry's plan is "To systematically develop freedom of thought and conscience in school children, and protect them, so far as possible, against all disturbing influences of the Church, and even their own parents — by compulsion if necessary."

In 1959 Freemasonry published in its *New Age Magazine* its victory over parents: "Every Mason becomes a teacher of Masonic philosophy to the community, and the Craft is the missionary of the new order, a liberal order, in which Masons become high priests. We proclaim that this Masonic philosophy which has brought forth a New Order has become a reality by the establishment of the public school system, financed by the State."[38]

In the same decade as consolidation, Freemasonry began selecting the textbooks that were to be used in the new public school system. The February 1959 issue of the Scottish Rite *New Age Magazine* announced an "Evolution of American Education" to Masons throughout the nation and "mandated that members of the Fraternity disseminate Masonic materials in public schools." They were instructed to "take that role seriously."[39] And indeed they did. From 1959 to 1964, the Scottish Rite began selecting textbooks for the consolidated school systems.[40]

In 1964 the fatal blow to our youth was landed by the Masonic-stacked Supreme Court when it outlawed Bible reading and prayer in public schools. In its place the NEA taught a "new morality" called "situation ethics."[41] The supreme Court then legalized pornography. In time, free and open sex became the order of the day for our school children. To curtail the problem of so many unwed mothers, the Supreme Court authorized abortions, then authorized children to have abortions without parental consent, then authorized schools to distribute contraceptives to children without parental consent. Today, immorality pervades every walk of American society, including the Christian community.

In 1968 Freemasonry sounded its victory trumpet in its *New Age Magazine*: "The keynote of Masonic religious thinking is naturalism which sees all life and thought as ever developing and evolutionary.... The Bible is not today what it once was. Current higher criticism has made obsolete the idea that the Bible is a unique revelation of supernatural truth."[42]

This brings us to phases 4-7, Freemasonry's direct attack against the evangelical Church in America to turn it lukewarm. Phase four was planned to turn the heart of America to materialism. A wealthy society would naturally turn the churches materialistic.

Albert Pike initiated the plan. He knew that if Freemasonry was to survive in America, the Fraternity would have to curtail the forward progress of the evangelical Church. Universal Freemasonry assisted, as it had during the planning of our Civil War. In October of 1885, Pike took his plan to the floor of an international convention held in Paris, France for all the 33rd degree Supreme Councils of Scottish Rites of the world. Each delegate received an outline of his speech, which spelled out the destruction of Christianity in America. In Orphic terms the document and Pike's speech reads as follows:

> Supernaturalism [meaning Christianity], authority [meaning European monarchies], and anti-Masonic activity [in the U.S.A.] must be destroyed. [Freemasonry shall accomplish this by] materialism of conscience, of education, and of the state. This must be imposed upon the family, the nation, and on humanity. 'By every means, whatever they may be, one must Impose first on the Family, and then on the Nation in order to achieve the aim of Imposing on Humanity.'[43]

199

FREEMASONRY

The instrument used for the imposition of materialism of conscience in America was central banking.[44] It would give the public easy access to credit so that it could benefit immediately from material things. Masonic bankers would likewise benefit on the addictive nature of credit, piling loan upon loan and interest upon interest, making them wealthy.

Even before the Paris convention, the totally Masonic-staffed Rothschild bank in London, England wrote a letter to the Masonic bankers of New York explaining how the plan would benefit them:

> The few who understand the system will either be so interested in its profits, or so dependent on its favors that there will be no opposition from that class, while on the other hand, the great body of people, mentally incapable of comprehending the tremendous advantages that capital derives from the system, will bear its burdens without complaint, and perhaps without even suspecting the system is inimical to their interests.[45]

Material success came to Freemasonry in 1913, as it lobbied and pushed through Congress the passage of the Federal Reserve Act.[46] This Act established a permanent central bank on our soil, which gave Americans easy access to credit, culminating in the materialism of conscience in our nation today. This affluence-grabbing conscience was carried into our churches by wealthy benefactors. Hence, Freemasonry is indirectly responsible for turning the hot evangelical Church of the 1800s into the materialistic and lukewarm Church of the 1900s, which Church is in need of nothing — including in need of no Lord and Savior, Jesus Christ, Who stands outside the church door knocking for reentry (Rev. 3:20).[47]

This brings us to phases 5-6, which is the infiltration of the Church by infidel pastors, and the creation of a national organization that would control mainline churches.

In 1907 illuminated Freemasonry in America financed Dr. Harry F. Ward, a professor at the Union Theological Seminary, in founding the Methodist Foundation of Social Services. Ward's job was to teach bright, young men to become so-called ministers of Christ and place them as pastors. Rev. Ward taught them how to very subtly and craftily preach to their congregations that the entire story of Christ is a myth, to cast doubts on the divinity of Christ, to cast doubts about the Virgin Mary. In short, to cast doubts on Christianity as a whole. It was not to be a direct attack, but much of it by crafty insinuation that was to be applied, in particular, to the youth in the Sunday Schools.[48]

In 1908 the Methodist Foundation of Social Services changed its name to the Federal Council of Churches. By 1950, the Federal Council of Churches was becoming suspect as being a Communist front, so it changed its name to the National Council of Churches.[49]

In 1975 former 33rd degree Freemason Rev. Jim Shaw exposed the link between Freemasonry and the NCC:

> A preacher in the National Council of Churches is really not "in" until he is a Mason. I have served in lodge with them. I have a list of many NCC pastors who are working for the Masonic monster with all the strength they have. They are not interested in the Lord Jesus Christ, though they pretend to be.[50]

In January 1983 the *Reader's Digest* exposed the National Council of Churches in an article entitled "Do You Know Where Your Church Offerings Go?" The article revealed, among other things, that over $1 million dollars of churchgoer's money in 1981 was sent by the NCC to political activist organizations, such as the PLO, communists in Latin America, Asia and Africa, and to several violence-prone fringe groups in the United States. The article also accused the NCC of rewriting the Bible to conform to a male/female-god religion, "so as to eliminate reference to gender, or as an alternative, to spread the gender around." Jesus no longer would be identified as the son of God, but rather as the child of God.[51]

The United Methodist Church, the largest contributor to the NCC, has the highest density of Masons and Masonic pastors per capita than any other denomination. Hence, it was the first to fall away. The Associated Press reported on December 10, 1983 that the governing body of the United Methodist Church in Nashville, Tennessee had approved guidelines on biblical and theological language that suggest that fewer male nouns and pronouns be used in referring to Jesus. In 1986 the Rocky Mountain Region of the United Methodist Church adopted a new policy prohibiting ministry candidates from referring to God as exclusively male in church paperwork and interviews. The policy allows the historical Jesus to be called He, but prohibits any exclusively male reference to a divine or messianic Jesus. The policy also calls for phrases such as Divine Light, a Masonic term, to be used in place of Father, King, or Lord. Candidates are allowed to refer to God as Mother and Father, or as He and She.[52]

The National Council of Churches then began to work on our youth. On May 9, 1989, *USA Today* reported that the NCC supports a provision in the Congressional Child-Care Bill that says parents who receive federal subsidies may send their children to programs in churches that avoid religious instruction.

On May 22, 1989, in the "Religion" section of *Time* magazine, Dr. Richard Mouw of California's Fuller Theological Seminary is quoted as saying that the mainline churches that are members of the NCC are now teaching "magic and the occult and the New Age. There's a return to a premodern world view."

A Masonic pastor of the First Congregational Church of Salt Lake City sums up the attitude of many Masonic pastors and Masonic laymen of today. He is quoted in the Masonic book *The Craft and the Clergy*, written by 33rd degree Freemason

Rev. Dr. Forrest Haggard, as saying, "I am in a mighty army of men who have committed themselves to minimize the importance of moral and ethical teachings."[53]

This brings us to phase seven, the Masonic infiltration of American churches. In 1926, the Scottish Rite published an article in its January *New Age Magazine* telling Masons to join Christian churches. It was an order coming directly from the Supreme Council at Charleston, South Carolina, the headquarters of Universal Freemasonry. Written by W.B. Zimmerman, the article entitled "Let There Be Light," stated that every Mason "should cast his lot with the Church — to help vitalize it, liberalize it, modernize it and render it aggressive and efficient — to do less is treason to your country, to your Creator, and to the obligation you have promised to obey."[54] Each Mason was to follow these instructions as directed by his local lodge.

A Mason's obligation is more powerful than any law of the land. Under oath he obligates himself to carry out all orders given him by the Masonic hierarchy. Consequently, following the publishing of this article in 1926, Masons throughout the United States flocked to join local Protestant churches. In time these Masons worked their way into church leadership. And in time they turned the evangelical churches materialistic and lukewarm.

Freemasonry's insidious war waged by local lodges against local evangelical churches is detailed in the "Appendix" with four testimonies from Southern Baptist pastors. But, don't be discouraged, for these pastors will inform us of how we can win this battle. Matthew 16:18 is our encouragement: "upon this rock [Jesus Christ] I will build my church; and the gates of hell shall not prevail against it."

FREEMASONRY

Epilog Notes

1. Paul A. Fisher, *Behind the Lodge Door* (Washington, DC: Shield, 1988) pp. 186-187.
2. William R. Denslow, *10,000 Famous Freemasons*, vol. 3 (Trenton, Mo.: Missouri Lodge of Research, 1959) pp. 230-231.
3. "Busy Brotherly World of Freemasonry," *Life Magazine* (8 Oct., 1956) p. 120.
4. Allen E. Roberts, *House Undivided: The Story of Freemasonry and the Civil War* (Richmond, Va.: Macoy Publishing and Masonic Supply Co., 1961) p. 32.
5. "Busy," p. 120.
6. Roberts, p. ix.
7. Roberts, p. 10.
8. John Daniel, *Scarlet and the Beast*, vol. 3 (Tyler, Tx.: Jon Kregel, Inc, dba JKI Publishing, 1995) p. 63-70.
9. Daniel, vol.3, chapter 4. Detailed documentation from several Masonic sources confirms that European Freemasonry trained Mason John Brown's abolitionists on revolutionary tactics.
10. Edith Starr Miller, *Occult Theocrasy* (1933; Hawthorne CA: The Christian Book Club of America, 1980) p. 431.
11. Jonathan Blanchard, *Scottish Rite Masonry Illustrated*, vol. 2 (?1840s-1860s; Chicago: Charles T. Powner Co., 1979) p. 484.
12. Miller, pp. 210-213, quoting Albert Pike's daughter, Mrs. Liliana Pike Room. Following is a quote from Mrs. Room: Speaking of her father, Albert Pike, she says, "I will state here what he told me himself.... Pike and [Albert Gallatin] Mackey received the visit of Longfellow... the intimate friend and private secretary of Moses Holbrook, then Sovereign Commander of the Supreme Council of Charleston. The intimacy between Longfellow and Holbrook (a Jew) became quickly serious as both had thoroughly studied the occult sciences and enjoyed discussing the mysteries of the Cabala.... While

exchanging views on the Cabala, they had formed the project of creating a Satanic rite in which the adepts would be instructed in Black Magic. But Holbrook, the Grand Master of the Supreme Council of Charleston, who had already composed a suitable ritual and sacrilegious mass call Adonaicide Mass, died, retarding the fulfillment of the project.... Pike, who had himself already thought of introducing Luciferianism into the inner shrines of Scottish Rites Freemasonry, would not take a definite stand, so Longfellow addressed himself directly to the Grand Master John Honour. He [Honour] seemed indifferent to the subject on the grounds that one could not introduce Satanism into the Supreme Council of Scottish Rites without the knowledge of his lieutenant-commander, Charles Furman, who was opposed to changes of this kind."

13. Miller, pp. 220-221.
14. Albert Pike, *Morals and Dogma* (1871; Richmond, Va.: L.H. Jenkins, Inc., 1942) pp. 76, 252, 321, 601, 660, 741.
15. Miller, p. 210; quoting Pike's daughter: "He became an Oddfellow, some time in the forties, and in 1850 entered the Masonic Fraternity."
16. John Daniel, *Scarlet and the Beast*, vol. 1, chapter 14, entitled "Lucifer — God of Freemasonry."
17. Daniel, vol.3, pp. 63-70.
18. Denslow, vol. 3, p. 341
19. Daniel, vol. 3, pp. 63-70. Detailed documentation of the funding of our Civil War by European Masonic bankers is in this chapter.
20. Blanchard, p. 484.
21. Roberts, pp. 137-139
22. Fisher, p. 40.
23. Albert G. Mackey, *Mackey's Revised Encyclopedia of Freemasonry*, vols. 1-3 (1909; Chicago: The Masonic History Company, 1950) vol. 2, pp. 817-818; vol. 3, p. 1199.

FREEMASONRY

24. Denslow, vol. 1, pp. 226-227.
25. Mackey, "Public Schools," vol. 2, pp. 817-818.
26. Mackey, vol.1, pp. 217-218. Understand that Masonic colleges were run by Masons, and their funds controlled by Masons. Can Freemasonry not prevent corruption within its own ranks? What a statement to make of itself — the organization that claims to teach the highest standards of morality in secret, then openly exemplify the same in life-style! Compare Freemasonry's colleges with their counterpart. Christian colleges have stood the test of time, still exist today, and without corruption. This prompts the question: "Which religion teaches morality and lives morally — Freemasonry or Christianity?"
27. Daniel, vol. 1, p. 243.
28. Mackey, vol. 2, p. 817.
29. Mackey.
30. Fisher, p. 176.
31. Fisher, Appendix A.
32. Fisher, p. 134.
33. "Education, Systems of (Religious and other factors — types of educational systems and their characteristics)," *Encyclopaedia Britannica: Macropaedia* 1984.
34. "Education, Systems of."
35. Fisher, p. 134.
36. Daniel, vol. I, pp. 245-246.
37. Ralph A. Epperson, *The Unseen Hand* (Tucson, Az.: Publius Press, 1985) p. 490.
38. Fisher, pp. 56-57.
39. Fisher, p. 57.
40. Fisher.
41. *The Random House Dictionary of the English Language* defines "situation ethics: a view of ethics that deprecates (belittles) general moral principles while emphasizing the source of moral judgments in the distinctive characters of specific situations."

A member of the NEA told this author that at an NEA teachers' conference she was informed that teachers would lose their jobs if they taught right from wrong, because that would be a "religious doctrine." They were instructed to pose a "situation" to students and permit them to judge right from wrong. The "situation" suggested was to ask the students how many get an allowance? Is the allowance adequate for your needs? If not, what do you do to get an increase in allowance? When the teacher returned to her classroom, she asked these questions. One student was not getting enough allowance. To get an increase, he told his Dad that lunch money had increased to $3.50. The teacher responded, "But, Johnny, lunch money is only $1.75." Johnny responded, "I know that, but my Dad doesn't." The teacher was not permitted to tell Johnny he was deceptive, and thus wrong. She could only ask the students their opinion. To Johnny's response, a full one-third of the class agreed with Johnny, saying that he was justified in his action, because his father was stingy. This is a perfect example of "situation ethics."

42. Fisher, p.57
43. Miller, pp. 709-710.
44. M.W. Walbert, *The Coming Battle: A complete History of the National Banking Money Power in the United States* (Chicago: W.B. Conkey Co., 1899) entire.
45. Epperson, p. 157.
46. Daniel, vol. 3, chapter 5. With detailed documentation from many sources, including Masonic.
47. Rev. 3:20 has been illustrated by others as Christ knocking on the heart's door of an unsaved person. Many souls have been won to Christ as a result. However, this Scripture is taken out of context when used in this manner. To understand how author John Daniel treats this Passage within context, refer to his 7-cassette tape series entitled "Secret Societies and their infiltration of the Seven Churches of Revelation." This

series of seven messages is also an excellent study of Church history.

48. Myron Fagan, *The Illuminati*, two cassette tapes recorded 1967. For sale through JKI Publishing.
49. Fagan.
50. Rev. Jim Shaw, *Pastors in the National Council of Churches who are in Freemasonry*, audio tape, 1970s. In the library of John Daniel.
51. Rael Jean Isaac, "Do You Know Where Your Church Offerings Go?," *Reader's Digest* (January 1983) pp. 120-125.
52. Peter Lalonde, *Omega-Letter* (December 1986) p. 3.
53. Daniel, vol. 1, p. 254, quoting Dr. Haggard.
54. Fisher, pp. 186-187.

CR∞

APPENDIX

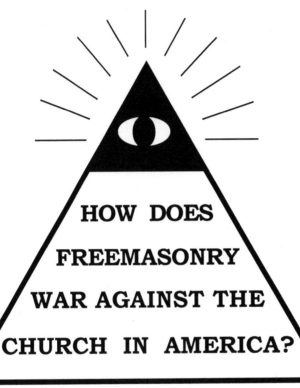

How Does

Freemasonry

War Against the

Church in America?

This is their **resemblance** through all the earth.
Zechariah 5:6

Personal testimonies of what happened to four evangelical Southern Baptist Pastors who dared preach the gospel, who dared disciple their flock, and who dared shed the LIGHT of God's Holy Word on the doctrines of Freemasonry.

Zechariah 5:6
This is their **resemblance** through all the earth.

Strong's Concordance KJV
"resemblance" #5869 in Hebrew is written
'ayin.
It is a primitive root word meaning
"an eye."

Zechariah 5:3
"This is the **curse** that goeth forth
over the face of the whole earth."

Strong's Concordance KJV
"curse" #423 in Hebrew is written
'alah,
meaning **"oath."**
It comes from #422, a primitive root word meaning
"to adjure, usually in a bad sense."

*The Random House Dictionary
of the English Language* defines **adjure:
to bind under oath, often with the threat of a penalty."**

Zech. 5 is a false religion, which is a "resemblance" of Solomon's Temple in Zech. 3-4; more specifically, a singular eye, which is a "resemblance" of the "seven eyes" of the Lord in Zech. 3:9 and 4:10. It represents all mystery religions and secret societies that counterfeit the Jewish religion. In Rev. 2:9 and 3:9, Christ refers to these mock Jewish temples as "synagogues of Satan."

Freemasonry claims to be a "resemblance" of Solomon's Temple. Freemasonry binds its initiates under oath with the threat of penalty. Its god is represented by the "All-Seeing Eye," which is a "resemblance" of the "seven eyes of the Lord." Therefore, according to Scripture, Freemasonry is a "synagogue of Satan."

APPENDIX

Satan Works Hardest Where God's Work Is Succeeding
by Stoney Shaw

After graduating from seminary, I spent two years as an associate pastor and eight years as a Baptist campus pastor, before moving to my pastorate at a Southern Baptist Church in St. Louis, Missouri. My life there was like a ten year honeymoon. We completed a $4 million building program ($3.4 million paid), while consistently giving 21 percent to the cooperative program of the Southern Baptist Convention, Association ministries, and state mission offerings.

Although my leadership style is redemptive in nature, I was also a strong leader in other ways, and those who ministered under me were truly innovative. We had precept Bible studies, AWANA for children, discipleship and outreach ministries. We went to the foreign fields, the inner city, mission trips, and had a prison ministry second to none.

Trouble began when I brought in a number of growth ministries, such as Life Action Crusades, Exchanged Life Conference (Dr. Charles Solomon), Resolving Personal and Spiritual Conflict Seminars (Dr. Neil Anderson), Institute in Basic Life Principles (Bill Gothard), Major Ian Thomas, Precept Training, and many others. There were some who did not like all of this and resented our building being used by so many different people, like men's Bible Study Fellowship.

Another element in our church was opposed to the church's historical stand on divorce, remarriage, and the holding of leadership positions in the church. The church, as well as I, interpreted the Scriptures to mean that a divorced man could not be a deacon or in a called staff position. This definitely caused a "spirit of contention" in our fellowship.

At this time my wife and I had some financial difficulties that ultimately led us to confess before the church that we had

211

financially overextended ourselves. We sought their forgive-ness. It turned out to be a beautiful, redemptive experience. Ninety-five percent of the members showed their compassion, love and forgiveness.

Although the church ministered God's grace toward us in our time of need, there were some who would not forgive, causing again, a "spirit of contention." Among those who would not drop their burden of bitterness, each contention was heaped upon another. Freemasonry served as the last and greatest issue of contention. The element within the church that was in continual opposition to all our righteous standards and spiritual growth programs also supported Freemasonry. Therefore, the issue of Freemasonry provided the catalyst for bringing my ministry to a close and ruining a fine church.

It began when one of our godly Sunday School teachers challenged his class to sever themselves from any of their past dealings with the occult, cults, or false religions. On the list he handed out were many things that Christians should not be affiliated with, including Freemasonry.

Some of the older members of the class were Masons, and took offense. Some verbally attacked the teacher. The teacher then began a self-study of Freemasonry. What he discovered troubled him greatly. He wrote a letter challenging the deacons to study the subject and make a decision whether or not Masons should serve in positions of spiritual leadership in the church.

I had just returned from the June 1992 Southern Baptist Convention in Indianapolis, where Freemasonry had become an issue at our convention. I shared this with our Board of Deacons, and the chairman asked me to educate them on the subject. At that time I knew nothing about Freemasonry, nor what a Mason was, nor if there were Masons in my church. As I began collecting resources, studying and investigating Free-masonry, I was appalled! Then I thought, "This can't be true." No Christian would be involved with secret pagan rituals that would condone praying around an altar saying that all people, regardless of their religion, could hold hands and pray to the God of a thousand names, the great architect of the universe! After an in-depth study consisting of reading books, listening to audio tapes, interviewing former Masons, and viewing video tapes of their rituals acted out by former masons who had seen the clear Light of Jesus Christ as the true LIGHT of the world, I came to realize that Freemasonry was truly a false religion!

After several months of study, the deacons dealt with the issue of Freemasonry by voting 24-1 that it was incompatible with Christianity. The dissenting vote was a middle-aged man who had gone through the York Rite and did not believe there was any conflict between Masonry and Christianity. (The York Rite is Templar Freemasonry with 13 degrees, as opposed to Scottish Rite Freemasonry with 32 degrees.)

This York Rite Mason, instead of being open and truthful with his fellow deacons, neither denied nor confirmed what we discovered. He preferred to keep deep, dark secrets of things to which he had made "death oaths," even before he knew to what he was committing. This amazed me!

Ultimately he became a strong opponent of my ministry, and opposed me as pastor. By his side was a Mason who had gone through the thirty-two Scottish Rite degrees. Together these two men gathered around them many of their friends, and the antagonism escalated to a higher level. Letters began to come in challenging what the deacons had done. They were asking questions whether or not the church should be involved in issues such as Freemasonry. Antagonism turned to ridicule. We were asked if we were going to start investigating all groups, such as the Boy Scouts, the Democratic Party, and many other organizations. I patiently answered each letter and challenged the people to study the material on Freemasonry and learn for themselves what it was all about.

Meanwhile, the deacons worked up a resolution that said a "Mason could not be a deacon or a called staff member." The resolution was presented to the church for a vote. Six months after the issue had first come up, a special business meeting

FREEMASONRY

was called. I was confident when I entered the sanctuary, because I believed we had done a superb job of educating members.

Was I in for a surprise! The chairman of the deacons, as well as some other deacons, had a "failure of nerves." They had studied Freemasonry as much as I. They were resolved that it was occultic, therefore not compatible with Christianity. But, they worried what their resolution would do to the church. Consequently, I was "set up" by the chairman of the deacons, who opened the meeting by saying, "Pastor, you're going to have to be the 'point man,' because you know more about this than we do." At first I thought this was a compliment. Later I realized that he and many other deacons were not intending to give a defense for their resolution. They wanted me to carry the fight alone!

Of course, this worked against me as it appeared that I the pastor was against "godly Masons." Only two deacons out of twenty-eight stood with me and gave a defense during the debate. I was forced to stand again and again against the Masons. I just could not let what some of them said go unchallenged. Once, while trying to respond, I was literally shouted down by the Masonic element.

I was deeply hurt. To be shouted down in my own church after having faithfully lead and protected this flock for twelve years was almost more than I could bear. However, God was gracious and He sustained me throughout the evening. I praise Him for some of the good laymen and laywomen who stood and made a defense against the Masons.

Finally, the vote was taken — 150 - 58 that Freemasonry was incompatible with Christianity. Had the hour not been so late, many younger couples would have stayed. I believe their vote would have caused a 4-1 ratio instead of the 3-1.

Although it appeared we had won, I was amazed that so many good Christians voted against the resolution. How could they not see that the pagan foundation, questionable history, dark secrets, and the terrible death oaths of Masonry were wrong? How could they vote against a Godly pastor? How could they vote against our spiritual leadership? How could they vote against a resolution that would protect the Church of the Living God from the fiery darts of the wicked?

I had endeavored to keep the discussion a "truth issue" and not a "personality issue." The Masons and their friends, however, had carefully made it a personal issue between them and the pastor. And they had succeeded! The deacons failed the congregation by not giving spiritual leadership before the very body they had committed to protect and serve. They also harmed themselves by not publicly standing with their pastor on such a vital issue.

The next few weeks were difficult for me as I thought through all that had happened to my family, my church, and to me. My mind reflected on all the attacks that had come my way because of this whole ordeal. One event that hurt me the most occurred when one of our senior adults, who had been a very good friend over the years, personally attacked and threatened me while I was teaching a Sunday School class on the dangers and ungodly nature of Freemasonry. Oh, that we would defend Christianity as fervently.

There were others. One lady, to whom my staff, my wife and I had ministered quite extensively, accosted me after a church service with these words, "Once you were a giant in my eyes! Now you are a pygmy." The letters, phone calls, pointed visits, and conversations became a daily affair!

Then the looks, the whispers, the innuendoes, avoidances, and lack of love and fellowship began to increase. As gossip flowed like a river, everyone appeared to be joining "camps." Although the Masons had lost the vote, they persistently spread discord among the brethren, and relentlessly attacked me and all who supported me.

Then my ideas began to be attacked, especially at business meetings. Anything my opponents could dig up from the past would be thrown up at me in a variety of ways. Opposition rose to such a level that nothing was happening in the church for the glory of God. Although the majority in the church supported me, I was not permitted to exert the strong leadership needed to deal with the disruptive element. Nor would the deacons take the leadership required to deal with the situation. So, all we had was spiritual anarchy!

Because I had put twelve years of my life, time, energies, and money into that church, I struggled to keep the church from disintegrating. I constantly challenged our people not to let anything get between us except Jesus — and to let Jesus be Jesus in all of our relationships. But the rebellious nature of Freemasonry rode roughshod over those godly principles and ultimately caused deep conflict in the church. It became open season on the pastor.

At this point I knew I must resign and move on, or my family and I would be emotionally destroyed. The Spirit's leading was not to split the church since the church had voted against Freemasonry. On February 26, 1992, I resigned. Two months later I started a new kind of church, one built on the cell church model.

As I look back on those tumultuous days, I have come to realize that Satan will use any means to destroy God's church and His people.

The Aftermath

Several Mason's names have been resubmitted to be deacon candidates. A 32nd degree Mason is now chairman of the personnel committee that oversees a godly staff. Two pastors have already turned down the pastoral search committee. As a result, there has been some soul searching by some of the membership. For example, to make the church more attractive to a potential pastor, they tried to change the bylaws to give more spiritual authority to the pastor. But spiritual anarchy continues unchecked, since the Masonic element overruled.

They have no desire to be under the spiritual authority of anyone, especially a godly pastor!

The evil agenda of Freemasonry, and the selfish agenda of those who permitted it to happen, ruined a good church. To this date Masons still churn dissension in the fellowship. Consequently, the church continues to decline in membership as deception and delusion reign. It is amazing to see good men and women just holding on while the self-centered, rebellious spirit of Masonry tightens its grip on the church.

What I have learned through all of this

Truth Matters. Without the truth of God's Word over every matter in life, we will be deceived! I believe the weakness in the church today is that people do not accept truth. We have multitudes as "hearers" of the Word, not "doers" of the Word. If we are not "doers," we deceive ourselves. This leads to "double mindedness." A double-minded man cannot know the things of God; thus, he is left to the ways of the world, the flesh, and the devil. This is "Ever coming to knowledge, but never coming to the truth!" Without truth we will be deceived. What else can explain Freemasonry's dominant hold on the church today?

We must stand for the truth no matter what! Today we have too many hireling Pastors who are afraid of the consequences. We also have too many defeated pastors with the Elijah syndrome. "Woe is me; I am the only one left in all of Israel who loves the Lord." But that is not true! God always has His faithful remnant! Since leaving that church, God has seen fit to give me a church with an international ministry. In Grace Fellowship International I have found a remnant of Godly people willing to stand for truth. Today I have more joy teaching, preaching, and leading this small, but enlightened God-fearing, Bible-obeying, flock of God than I would have in a large "deceived flock" with a self-centered, rebellious spirit. Yes, the large flock brought more denominational recognition and fanfare, but the

217

small faithful remnant brings deep satisfaction, close fellowship, authentic caring with agape love, and a hunger to know
God's Word, and obey it no matter what!

We did not go far enough. I personally believe that if Masons
refuse to reject Masonry, they should not be allowed to be church
members. Jesus never intended for his church to be divided.
A Mason has a divided heart! Would we allow a Mormon to
join our church and still practice Mormonism? Of course not!
Jesus permits no rival. Masonry offers a rival relationship. Jesus
confronted this kind of confusion in Matthew 6:24, "No man
can serve two masters: for either he will hate the one, and love
the other; or else he will hold to the one, and despise the other.
Ye cannot serve God and mammon."

I believe church-attending Masons should reject and demit
from the lodge or they should be disciplined according to Matthew 18. God told the children of Israel to take the land and
clean out the evil inhabitants. They did not, and today we are
still dealing with the problem they refused to confront!

Until Freemasonry is cleaned out of our churches, the spirit
of rebellion and witchcraft will infect and disease the body of
Christ. The Church will struggle with division and double-
mindedness. Instead of building upon the foundation of Christ,
the Church will build with "wood, hay and stubble." These
works will be burned up in the end time!

As a pastor I thought we were doing so many wonderful
things. AWANA, Precepts, Prison Ministry, internal programs
were all attracting people from other churches. But, we were
seeing few come to a saving knowledge of Jesus Christ. Of
course, this pleased Freemasonry. So long as we kept busy
doing all these good "things," Freemasonry never rebelled. But,
when we brought in Bill Gothard, Exchanged Life Concepts,
Freedom in Christ Ministries, and Life Action Crusades, Freemasonry grumbled and griped about these life-changing ministries. Freemasonry is all for good programs, but not for
anything that will cause people to commit their lives to Christ.
This is the rebellious spirit of Masonry.

APPENDIX

My advice to pastors who wish to set the Body of Christ apart from Freemasonry

Prepare yourself and your staff. At first I did not know what Masonry was, nor who in my church were Masons. So, I prepared myself. I accumulated the resources, then studied to show myself approved, a workman not to be ashamed. I did research into the primary documents and writings of the lodge. I personally interviewed and debated Masons and counseled with former Masons and other experts in the field. I made long distance phone calls, watched hours of video and counseled with cult experts.

Educate your leadership. I educated the deacon body for two months. Out of twenty-eight deacons, one was a Mason. He was the lone dissenting vote. We did not go on a witch hunt in the church looking for Masons, because we wanted it to be a truth issue, not a personality issue.

Challenge your spiritual leadership to take a stand. The deacon body took a Saturday afternoon and evening, and through gut-wrenching debate, came up with a resolution to take to the church that a man could not be a Mason and be a deacon, pastor, or staff member. Be sure your leadership is ready to take the lead in this battle. It is a proven fact that staff members can only take so many skirmishes before they are shot between the eyes. Therefore, prepare them emotionally and spiritually for the onslaught. Warn them of the retaliation of Masons. Some may be threatened with the exposure of secret sins. Others may be threatened with losing their secular jobs. Freemasonry is all-encompassing in almost every community in America. Make sure your deacons fully understand that this is a spiritual battle between God and Satan, and that God is already the victor.

Educate the church body. After educating the deacons, the deacons themselves asked me to educate the church. I accomplished this through printed materials, audio cassettes, videos,

219

personal teaching, and casual conversation. This must be done with complete thoroughness. Do not leave this task to someone else. I personally believe that the pastor should stay on top of this all the way. Do not assume that once you teach them that there will be understanding and acceptance. Keep taking them back to Scripture.

The only thing I did not do, and would change if I had it to do over again — I would have had the deacons invite all Masons in the congregation to come together with the staff and deacons to discuss the issue privately before bringing it to the church body. This will prepare you in advance for all their objections.

Set a time for open discussion and a vote. Our discussion and vote was on a Sunday night. If I had it to do over again, I probably would do it on a Sunday Morning, when most of the congregation is present. When we are dealing with sin, we should take it seriously! Be sure you have lay leadership ready to respond and stand united with you.

Don't be afraid to use the pulpit. You are the shepherd. It is your God-given duty to protect the sheep. Don't be a fearful shepherd and run when the Masonic wolves circle the fold, else the sheep will scatter. During this period I preached out of Colossians and other important passages trying to lay a foundation of how to handle truth vs. the lies of Satanic darkness and deception. Take opportunities to frequent Sunday School classes. Go out to lunch with people who have questions and who desire to discuss the issue. Caution! Never go to lunch, or have a private meeting without a knowledgeable and qualified supporter with you as a witness to the conversation.

Stoney Shaw

Buzy Projects!

by Stewart Bedillion

While pastoring a church in Arkansas, I was asked to take a church that was on a spiritual and numeric decline. I accepted the call, and in November 1990, I became pastor of the First Baptist Church of Columbia, Louisiana. For the first few months, the chairman of the Pulpit Committee regularly visited my office telling me what I could or could not do. He was especially opposed to door-to-door evangelism. Soon I learned that a group of other men shared his views. They criticized most of the former pastors and even explained in detail how they had "railroaded" a full-time youth pastor out of the church. His removal was so slick, they said, that no one in the congregation knew what was happening. Their message was clear, "Do what we want, or we will do the same to you."

They kept me so busy carrying out their plans, projects, and agendas that I had little time to listen to God. When I would move in the direction I felt God wanted, one of them would show up with all kinds of plans and projects. I was continually derailed from God's leading.

There was small numeric growth with these activities, but the church was spiritually dead. Worship was oppressive, as if a dark cloud hovered over the services. Throughout this time the chairman of the Pulpit Committee repeatedly gave me a funny handshake. I had no clue what he was doing.

Finally, God began to speak to me that I needed to listen to His direction, not the direction of these men. His Words were so clear, "Concentrate on worship, revival, evangelism, and making disciples."

When I first began to emphasize worship, I sensed resistance from the Minister of Music, who proudly wore his Masonic ring and tie tac. Several months later, however, he went through a spiritual crisis and prayed to receive Christ. Two weeks later he gave his testimony in church.

After his testimony, I stood to invite others to come forward and receive Christ. I was shocked at what I saw. Although there

221

FREEMASONRY

was rejoicing on a few faces, most were hostile — so hostile that it sent chills up and down my spine. As I looked at their faces, I identified them as Masons and their Eastern Star wives. "This is demonic," I thought.

When I started two discipleship groups, there was tremendous resistance within the deacon body. One deacon, who was also a Mason, tried to wreck every session. When I emphasized a personal relationship with Jesus, he became combative and hostile. He argued so much during Wednesday night Bible study that I had to switch to straight preaching.

Hungry for fellowship, I had been praying for months for a soul-winning partner. God answered that prayer when the Music Minister expressed a desire to go out witnessing. We went from house to house sharing Jesus, and quietly, without fanfare, his Masonic ring and tie tac disappeared. He told me that God had convicted him about being a Mason, and that he had formally renounced Freemasonry through a letter of resignation sent to the lodge.

Gradually, a group in the church began to catch a vision for having a personal walk with Jesus, learning discipleship, and evangelism. The church services began to change. I could feel God's presence in every service. The Masons, however, were not rejoicing. The one who had so frequently given me the Masonic handshake, called my home and threatened me that if I didn't get the Minister of Music "calmed down," the deacons would "take care of him."

As one group in the church grew closer to Jesus, another group became increasingly resistant toward what God was doing, and hostile toward me as pastor. Seven couples began forming a wall of resistance. Of the seven couples, two individuals were not Masons, nor members of the Eastern Star. One was a Seventh Day Adventist, and the other's father was a 32nd Degree Mason.

During this same period, a sister church was experiencing a touch of God, with the same resistance from Masons. Not willing to participate in the battle, several couples left that church

APPENDIX

and came to ours. They openly acknowledged that they had been upset because the Masons had squelched the moving of God in that church. The Masonic group in our church immediately began a verbal attack against the newcomers.

One Mason summoned me to his house and warned me that the newcomers could cause trouble in our church because of their attacks on Masonry. He revealed that he was a Mason and that there was not going to be a discussion of Freemasonry at First Baptist. He warned that a previous pastor had tried to deal with the Masonry issue in the church and had created problems as a result.

I located the former pastor and learned that he had maintained a bookstore which contained several books exposing Freemasonry. One night someone broke into the store and stole all the books on Masonry.

"If Freemasonry is just a harmless men's fraternity, why get upset about a few books? Why all the scrambling to hide books and refuse to even discuss Masonry? If Masonry is of God, let's bring everything out in the open and see what wonderful things God has done in Masonry. But if it is not of God, then there are many reasons to operate in darkness and secrecy." These were my thoughts.

It was at this time we began experiencing demonic manifestations during the services. Usually the demons would surface when I preached on our victory over Satan through the blood of Christ. Any aspect of victory in the Christian life or salvation messages would stir up the demons. During a series of messages on revival, and the filling of the Holy Spirit, there was considerable agitation. All of those with demonic manifestations were either Masons or Eastern Star wives.

Hostility toward me began to increase, all directed by the Masons. Deacons' meetings became nothing more than open season on the pastor. Again, led by the Masons.

Finally, the man who had given me numerous Masonic handshakes came to my office, tearing into me about the spiritual atmosphere that was developing within the church. As he was

223

verbally attacking me, suddenly a force, as it were, came out from him and hit me. Evil surrounded me. I sensed oppression. Within two days the oppression became deep depression.

All that week I read books on spiritual warfare to educate myself on what was happening. By Sunday a black cloud of spiritual oppression had settled over the entire church. I told no one of my encounter with the Mason, yet several people verbally expressed that things were different in the church.

This oppression continued for eight months, while life for me and my family was a living hell. It was as though sharks could smell blood and were coming in for the kill. Vicious attacks by the Masons were leveled against me and my family, and against all who supported me.

I became so physically ill that I had to enter the hospital for two weeks. The church decided to give me a three-month sabbatical, which at first seemed compassionate. It soon was evident that this generous action was a disguise to buy time, so that the Masons could remove me from the church.

When I returned from my sabbatical, the deacons informed me that I was no longer pastor — that the church would have to vote me back in. This was one of those instances in which a few deacons decided their own agenda privately. No one else knew what was going on. This is the way Satan works — always in the dark, in secret, behind closed doors. Satan lost temporarily. The vote was never taken and I was permitted to resume preaching.

Two months later, at a monthly business meeting, the Masonic group succeeded in voting me out. The members voting against me included many who had rarely come to church, and some I had never seen before! I was not permitted to speak, and the meeting was so hostile that I thought I was going to be mobbed. Those who were yelling, screaming, and jumping out of their seats were one and all Masons and their Eastern Star wives.

Shortly after leaving First Baptist I had a counseling session with Dr. Mark Bubek, who is well known both nationally and internationally for his experience in spiritual warfare. After hearing about the man who regularly harassed me in my office, his first question was, "Is he a Mason?" He confirmed that I had been under heavy demonic attack.

I never preached against Masonry, so the attack was not a counterattack. It was simply that the spirit behind Freemasonry opposes anything God-sent, Christ-exalted, Spirit-empowered that brings revival to the church. Yes, the Masons reacted negatively to my messages on grace. They were infuriated when I suggested man could not earn his way to heaven. They were not opposed to inviting people to church. They were opposed to the evangelism that was taking place in church, once the visitors arrived. And they were greatly offended by the fact that people in the church were going door-to-door in the community, asking people if they knew that they had eternal life. The Masonic message is one that abhors a Christian life that has Jesus Christ at the center.

The Masons in Columbia regard First Baptist as an extension of their lodge. Well, they have preserved that extension, for today First Baptist has disintegrated into a handful of men and women, primarily the Masonic and Eastern Star group. The price of their success was the destruction of a house of God, and the persecution of its pastor and many God-fearing people. Such is the spirit and purpose of Freemasonry.

Stewart Bedillion

What are pastors to do? First, take a stand on Freemasonry. Second, write your position in a letter and mail it to your national headquarters.

Freemasonry:
The Trojan Horse in the Church
by Pierce Dodson

In Greek mythology the Trojan horse was the means by which the Greeks successfully brought their army into the city of Troy. It was an act of subterfuge. The Greeks hid their soldiers inside the wooden horse and left it outside the city. The Trojans, thinking it a trophy, took it inside the gates, not knowing their enemy was within. At night, while they slept, the Greeks emerged from the horse, opened the city gates to the waiting army and took the city captive.

The Trojan horse of Freemasonry brought the enemy into two churches I served as pastor. I was born and raised in a Southern Baptist home in Tennessee. At the age of nine I was converted to faith in the Lord Jesus Christ. After receiving a call to the ministry, I attended Southern Baptist Seminary in Louisville, Kentucky, graduating with a master of divinity in theology.

While in seminary I was pastor of a church in which I had a fruitful ministry. Fourteen years later I accepted a call to a prominent small town church in the county seat of my home state of Tennessee. My homecoming was marked by two events that occurred during the first week I was on the field.

First, a man and his wife came to my office to inform me that a couple of Satanists were harassing their daughter at school. Second, I learned of a stabbing in the community that involved someone in the occult. I wondered what I had gotten myself into by taking a church in this community.

As I familiarized myself with my new surroundings, I discovered other troubling signs. On main street was a liquor store named Lucifer's. The town cemetery had a section called "Masonic Gardens." In it a miniature lodge stood. Inside were lodge chairs arranged as found in an actual lodge. On the marble altar was a marble Bible.

It was not long before I was aware that six of my eighteen deacons belonged to the Masonic Order. A few weeks later I

226

was talking with two ladies in the church office. When our conversation turned to Masonry, one lady commented that her husband was a Mason. I took little thought to the ramifications of the discussion. Although I was critical of Freemasonry, she seemed not to be offended. I later learned that she had told her husband.

Some time later I preached a two-part message on the exclusive nature of the Gospel of Jesus Christ. Although I did not mention Freemasonry by name, my message stood in stark contrast to Masonic doctrine. The husband of the lady who visited me was in the congregation. He apparently understood that I had contradicted the theology of Freemasonry. However, instead of confronting me, he called one of my deacons who was his lodge brother.

At our next deacons' meeting a foreboding spirit fell on me. The deacon who had been called was visibly angry and generally rude toward me throughout the meeting. I had an idea what had triggered his hostility and it was confirmed the next night when he called me by phone. After I said "hello," he began shouting accusations that I had called Masonry a cult. I shouted back that indeed I had. After we both calmed down, we ended our conversation in prayer.

I realized this was not the end of the matter. I felt I needed support from others to combat the spirit of Freemasonry. I quickly educated some members of the flock by clandestinely distributing anti-Masonic literature published by John Ankerberg.

A prominent member of the church privately revealed to me that some years earlier she had a vision that Satan was holding the church in his grip. She compared the vision to a Sherwin Williams paint logo, where the can is upside down pouring paint over the globe of the earth. I immediately understood her vision to be Freemasonry "gripping" our church.

The next event in my saga had to do with the John Ankerberg booklet I had distributed. It was given to the wrong person, who in turn brought it to one of the Mason deacons. I got a

FREEMASONRY

phone call Sunday afternoon and was told there would be a deacons' meeting after the Sunday night service. The caller asked if I knew about it. I responded that I hadn't been informed, but that I suspected the Masons might be behind it. Apparently, the pastor was not welcome to that secret meeting.

That night we were scheduled to celebrate the Lord's Supper. Fortunately, one of the deacons had enough courage to stand up to one of the Mason deacons and ask, "How can we take the Lord's Supper and then have a secret meeting behind our pastor's back?"

That was a pretty good question! Maybe I shouldn't have been surprised. After all, Satan had set a precedent about two thousand years ago. Judas Iscariot, one of the twelve disciples, had likewise planned a clandestine meeting after the first Lord's Supper.

My deacons' clandestine meeting was probably meant to roast me in absentia. But, when the question was raised at the evening service, I was given a last minute invitation.

After the service I went upstairs to a room where the deacons and I sat down. A few of the deacons did not know what the meeting was about. However, most of the Mason deacons did. You might say it was their meeting.

We all were seated around the room against the wall. The Ankerberg literature I had distributed was produced, and when confronted about it by a Mason deacon, I got up and took a seat in the middle of the room facing them all. I spoke of famous preachers who had opposed Masonry, such as Finney, and D.L. Moody. One of the Masons tried to shut me up. To his surprise, another deacon told him to "shut up and let the man speak."

The meeting was tense. Near the end I was asked if I could work with the Masons. I responded I could probably give an answer, but I would prefer to wait until a later time. I closed the meeting with prayer. Afterwards, one deacon remarked to some of his peers that he would give up being a deacon before he would give up his lodge membership.

228

During the next few weeks, tensions mounted among church members. Even the townsfolk were discussing the problems at our church. One Mason visited a deacon and questioned his stand regarding me. I speculated the Masons were mustering forces to oust me. But, I stood my ground.

One Wednesday night the title of my sermon was "Standing Alone." As I looked out over the congregation I sensed the opposition was not ready. I preached the sermon, with no reaction from the audience.

The following Sunday morning a Mason-deacon took me aside and asked if I had made a decision about being able to work with the Masons. I answered, "The issue here is truth."

The Mason responded, "What is truth for you is not necessarily truth for me."

I was under intense pressure to make a decision. If it was not in their favor, I knew I could not stay at that church. Should I force their hand, or should I resign? My emotions were on a roller coaster. First, I thought I would try to last thirty days and see if something could be worked out. After all, my wife and I had bought our first house. We had two young children, and had not yet made the first payment. I quickly discarded the thirty-day idea and wondered if I could hold out two weeks. No, I'll resign tonight. I was not going through this any longer.

I called the deacon chairman, requesting a meeting with the deacons before the evening service. I did not tell him the purpose of the meeting. When I resigned, no one tried to stop me, not even my supporters.

That night the youth were presenting a musical entitled "The Big Picture," based on Romans 8:28. The theme was that we do not understand our trials while we are going through them. We must wait till later to see the big picture. I could see God's hand in the timing of my resignation.

When the youth finished their program, I got up, and without anger or animosity, read my resignation from a prepared text. I did not mention Freemasonry. I simply stated that there was

FREEMASONRY

a situation in the church which made it impossible for me to fulfill my calling to the ministry of the Gospel and my calling as pastor of the church.

Some people looked shocked, others cried. Many came to the front to speak with me. I stayed up until four o'clock the next morning conversing with friends.

Friendships forged in the flames are the strongest, and I am grateful for Christian friends who stood with us. We also got support from our former church members back in Kentucky, which was an added blessing.

Our house went back on the market before the first payment was made. When I resigned, I had no idea how or if I would be offered any severance pay. But, praise God! He prepared a table before me in the presence of my enemies. One of the non-Mason deacons recommended that the church pay my salary for the next six months. I am probably one of the few preachers on record who was paid longer not to be pastor of a church than to be pastor.

Since our house did not sell for 18 months, we were forced to remain in that small town. I believe God used our house to make our presence a constant reminder to the town of what had happened at that church. He was not going to allow the rebellious spirit of Freemasonry in the church to be swept under the rug.

A few weeks after my resignation, my family and I spent a Sunday visiting churches in a nearby city. One church had a guest speaker that morning. His text was Genesis 50:19-21.

And Joseph said unto them, Fear not; for am I in the place of God? But as for you, ye thought evil against me, but God meant it unto good, to bring to pass, as it is this day to save much people alive. Now therefore, fear ye not; I will nourish you, and your little ones. And he comforted them and spoke kindly to them.

230

I had honestly selected that church with the idea of talking with the guest speaker after the service. God, however, wanted to say something first. That night we attended another church in the same town. The pastor, a friend of mine, had no idea we were coming. When he got up to preach, he announced that the Lord had impressed upon him to change his text to Genesis 50:19-20!

Twice in one day! Thank you Lord! God wanted my wife and me to understand that he had a purpose in all that was taking place and that he would provide for us.

Six months after my resignation, just as the severance pay was running out, I was asked to do some fill-in preaching at a church two hours away. This led to a position of interim pastor. The pulpit committee knew of the circumstances at my previous church, but the congregation did not. After about five months I agreed to permit the pulpit committee to submit my name as a candidate for the pastorate. Several members of the church, however, had ties with my former church and learned of my confrontation with the Masons. Now the issue of Freemasonry had begun to be a problem at their church.

When the deacons learned of my stand on Freemasonry, they requested a meeting to discuss the matter. I shared my position and showed the Jeremiah film on Freemasonry, "From Darkness to Light." Although none of the deacons were Masons, one was sympathetic to Freemasonry and told some Masons what had transpired at the meeting. They were not happy with the film and made it known.

Although these Masons were fewer in number than those at the former church, they still were able to stir up considerable dissension. When it came time to vote on a date of my official candidacy, the Masons came out en masse, and history began to repeat itself. As if on cue, all the Masons in one accord rose out of their seats and headed for the front. One pointed a finger at me and called me a trouble maker. He challenged me to meet with all the Masons. I agreed, so long as the deacons and pulpit committee could be present. "No!" he exclaimed. "I want a meeting with you and the other Masons." He never got his meeting.

When challenged, Freemasonry will show its true colors. After the service, a dear lady asked me if I could be in any physical danger. I replied that I could be. I told her that the history of Freemasonry has had its share of violence, in spite of its denials.

In the days following, the Masons worked hard to discredit me. One of them was so strong against me that he told a deacon "I would lay down my life to keep that man from becoming pastor of this church." After my candidate message, the vote was taken. The majority was in my favor, but not by much.

Realizing that not all the "no" votes were Masons, I struggled with the decision to accept their call. Many had been intimidated by the whole mess, and simply did not want to rock the boat. They opposed me only because they felt it best for the church. I decided to decline their call, but stay on as interim pastor.

The next day one of the Masons presumptuously took my name off the church sign, not realizing I was still interim pastor. When he discovered I was still there, you should have seen the look on his face. He and the other Masons had to put up with me for another three months until the church called a full-time pastor.

I left that church in November 1992 and have chosen not to accept another pastorate. However, I was seriously considered by a church early in 1997. But, lightning struck again! A member of the church had a Masonic brother-in-law back in the first church where my nightmare began. The Mason got his non-Mason brother-in-law to oppose me. His opposition to my candidacy was successful. Since then, the non-Mason has had a change of mind and regrets his opposition.

In some respects I am a pariah in my own denomination. I have been branded by this issue, in which my position is the correct one, the Christian one. I was mistreated, but not mistaken. My family and I have paid a high price, but don't regret it. We thank God for the privilege of suffering for His Name's sake. Meanwhile, our Lord has given me great opportunity to evangelize in foreign countries. I have been to Russia, Trinidad, and three times to Romania. These nations are wide open to the gospel.

In America's churches, however, evangelism will continue to be hindered so long as Masons are permitted to join the church and have a vote, or hold ruling positions in our assemblies. Freemasonry is at war with the gospel of Jesus Christ. This battle cannot be understood apart from the knowledge of spiritual warfare. I have shown how Freemasonry's battle was waged against me. Simply stated, "work with the Masons" and everything will be alright.

Working with the Masons means that you as a pastor must first allow their Trojan horse to be rolled into the church. Inside the hollow belly of the horse is the enemy disguised as many good "projects" that keep everyone so busy that evangelizing the community is almost impossible. Each time you try to evangelize, the horse will kick. If you are persistent, either you will be kicked out of the church by their vote, or you will resign, or the Masons will leave.

The effectiveness of Freemasonry in the Southern Baptist Convention, or any other denomination for that matter, is whether or not pastors, the majority of whom are not Masons, are backed by their denomination in their effort to keep the Trojan horse of Freemasonry out of the church.

Pastors, for the sake of the pure gospel of Jesus Christ, I urge you to take a stand on Freemasonry and write your denominational headquarters of that stand.

Pierce Dodson

Standing For Truth

by Daniel D. Carlen

I first came to Masonville, Tennessee (not its real name) in 1983 to visit family. We made the trip each year for four years, and each time we passed an old decrepit church badly in need of tender loving care. I would drive by the old church and wonder what sort of people worshipped there. What vision they possessed. And did they not know how the building and its appearance on the outside spoke volumes about the people on the inside? The church had no sign, no identification, just a tired old building casting a weary shadow. Little did I dream that four years later I would become pastor of that church.

Over those four years my curiosity grew, and I sensed a tremendous need for someone to reclaim the church building for the glory of God. Occasionally a family member would mention someone special in that congregation, and I developed a distant prayerful attachment for the church and its people.

At that time I was contented teaching Bible to ninth graders at a Christian school. Our two children were born during this time and we sensed God's blessings were pouring down upon us.

Meanwhile, a small country church near our home needed a pastor and asked me to fill in. I had long known my spiritual gift as pastor-teacher (Ephesians 4:11). My bi-vocational ministry at this small church awakened an unspeakable desire to serve full-time. When they asked me to be their pastor, I accepted the call.

During this time my father-in-law in Kentucky had developed lung cancer and our trips to and from Kentucky were long, very tiring, and much too infrequent. We began to seek God's guidance and will about pastoring full-time and whether it was God's will to get closer to the grandparents back in Kentucky.

Many of my relatives had copies of my resume, and one of them in Masonville gave it to a member of the First Baptist Church. It was the same decrepit church I had first seen four years previous, only now I knew its name.

234

To my surprise the church contacted me, and we arranged to meet in June of 1987. By previous agreement I brought a message at another small country church so the Pastoral Search Committee could hear me.

After the service we met with the Search Committee at a local restaurant. They seemed to have no idea what to ask or where to begin. They did want to know how much I would need to be paid. Sensing a need to guide the interview, I went over a few of my essential beliefs as a pastor.

First, I believe God's Word is inerrant and inspired of God in all 66 books.

Second, I believe God had assigned the church His vision and work, which He graciously asks us to join. He wants us to make disciples and lead people to follow Jesus Christ as Lord and Savior (Matthew 28:19-20). This was not Jesus' opinion, but His command.

Third, I knew my gift as pastor-teacher and I explained this meant pastoring the sheep, taking the oversight of their souls, teaching them God's truth and leading by example in service for the Kingdom of God and His glory (Ephesians 4:11ff). I was a teacher not a preacher and I explained the difference.

I instructed them not to consider extending a call to me unless they wanted a pastor-teacher, not a preacher. They assured me they wanted a pastor-teacher and asked me to speak to the congregation Sunday morning and evening. When my family and I arrived at the church, I was given a tour of the facilities. The inside was worse than the outside, with the exception of the auditorium, which had recently undergone a face-lift. The education and fellowship space needed painting. For a church membership roll of over 500, there were two tiny bathrooms. For the aging membership there was a cheap ugly carpet in the halls that was dangerously wrinkled. Outside doors stuck and were difficult to open. When it rained, the doors and windows leaked, and ceiling tile was falling down in the nursery, which had one tiny bathroom.

FREEMASONRY

They needed a pastor, and my heart was touched by the need. When they called us to be their pastor, we prayed about the decision, discerned that God was speaking to us, and began preparations for a move to Tennessee.

Year One

As I walked to the pulpit that Sunday morning in August 1987, there appeared to be about 100 in the congregation. I thanked the Lord and began my ministry in Masonville. The church grew spiritually and numerically. Slowly new souls were added to the Kingdom. It was a joyful honeymoon period.

My first inkling of trouble was at our first deacon's meeting. It was time for deacon rotation, and a motion quickly passed for the same men to serve another year. The meeting was all business, and clearly these men ran the church and controlled the money like a board of directors — not as servants. I noted a need for a deacon retreat and deacon ministry for the near future.

I took the first year getting to know people, while attending to the most urgent physical needs of the grounds. We needed a sign out front to identify who we were. We needed to fix up and remodel the education facility. As the work slowly progressed, a new excitement was in the air, and our aging congregation and building were experiencing new life.

As I settled into the community, I began inviting folks to the church. Many would laugh "Why bother, you won't be there long." I learned that First Baptist had a reputation of moving their pastors after a few short years. I committed to trust God no matter and seek out those He would have me disciple.

Deceitful Winds Of Change

After a year we had paid off all church debt, established a building fund, and created a Long-Range Planning Committee. Then one Sunday a man and his family visited our church. Something in me immediately went on the alert, but I stilled the small voice and thanked them for their visit. They were back the next Sunday and announced they would be moving to the community. The husband would be managing a local business. They seemed friendly enough. Besides, I learned he was a deacon in another Baptist church in a town not far from Masonville. (I shall refer to him as Deacon Doe). Several of the deacons wanted to bring him onto the deacon body right away. One deacon had moved, and there was a vacancy. The church constitution, however, required that any deacon transferring in must wait a year before he would become eligible to serve. I held my ground on this point, and the deacons finally agreed. He could, however, serve on a committee and was asked to be on the Building Committee.

Deacon Doe visited each Sunday School class, saying he wanted to check out all the adult classes to see where he and his wife might best fit in. After a few months they settled in a class that met in the corner off the basement education area and included several deacons and the mayor of Masonville.

The church continued to grow. New classes were started and souls continued to be added to the Kingdom. But something sinister was present. I sensed it, but was blinded to its root. As a pastor I have always tried to look for the good in everyone, just as I desire people look at me. But more than once I dismissed the still small voice that said "beware!"

One instance of change was the reception of a couple who had moved to Masonville from out of state. The wife began to attend regularly and the husband occasionally for special services. Our bylaws allowed us to receive non-Southern Baptist as members if they professed faith in Christ and had been baptized by immersion. Having interviewed her and being assured of her faith in Christ (as far as I could ascertain), I asked the church what was their favor. She was allowed to become a voting member. Shortly thereafter our treasurer resigned and the Finance Committee chairman in a panic recommended this lady. I counseled against this move, stating that she was too new to our church. After much protest I went against that still small voice and acquiesced. She accepted on the condition she could keep the books in her place of business. We agreed, and she took over the church financial records.

I sensed an icy wind blowing, but could not determine from what direction. Things seemed all right outwardly, but something ominous was out there. What could it be? Souls were steadily being added to the Kingdom, and tithing was up. Maybe it was me. Once again I failed to pray for discernment about the growing oppression.

By my third year Deacon Doe was well entrenched as a deacon, and now chaired both the Building Committee and Long Range Planning Committee. Then a young couple visited and took offense to my teaching on spiritual gifts. They went on a crusade against me, dislodging several faithful members from the church.

Other problems surfaced. I began to notice several overdue bills showing up more regularly. In addition, certain of the deacons were seen meeting with the treasurer — not at her place of business where she kept the books, but at their place of business. In addition, committees were not meeting as they should, and rumors abounded that certain deacons were unhappy with the pastor. Some were setting up cliques. For example, when adult visitors came in, they were ushered off to the adult class where Deacon Doe had become a fixture.

Then a young man came to me and asked if I would disciple him. This is one of my gifts. Disciplining people multiplies my efforts, building more souls for the Kingdom. After the second session he announced he was ready to preach the next Sunday. I told him he was not ready, and urged him to continue studying with me and learn the books of the Bible, basic doctrine, Bible study methods, etc. I promised to reconsider after one year. Visibly upset, he left the office and more rumors drifted back to me that I was running off the membership.

APPENDIX

The Masonic Lodge Connection

One visitation night, a deacon had me park close to the Masonic Lodge of Masonville, proudly pointing to the lodge building and naming six of the current deacons and two inactive deacons who were lodge members. He mentioned that Deacon Doe was Grand Worshipful Master of the Grand Lodge. He was so proud that the First Baptist Church should have such a highly esteemed Mason as a deacon. Not knowing anything about the Masons, I remained unimpressed. But, I filed away the information.

Deacon Doe, a laid back man who said little, was now actively throwing parties and rapidly building a following. At this time I just so happened to wander through the Baptist Book Store in Nashville, Tennessee and my eyes fell on a book by Tom McKenney entitled "Deadly Deception." The book was a biography of Jim Shaw, a former 33 degree Mason. Mr. Shaw had received Christ as Lord and Savior, and the Holy Spirit led him to demit (letter of resignation) from the lodge. He dedicated the rest of his life warning non-Masons and Masons alike of the false and deceptive spiritual teachings of Freemasonry.

I took the book home and could not put it down until I had finished reading it. Immediately I called the author, Tom McKenney. His advise and prayer were invaluable. While reading the book, I recalled that my grandfather had been a Mason. He had wanted me to come into the lodge. But I was always suspicious of anything secretive and fraternal. Now I needed information and facts from more than just McKenney's one book, and my grandpa was dead.

I called my brother who owned a used bookstore in New Jersey. After hearing of my discovery and need for original Masonic material, he warned me of the danger, then promptly sent me the books. Works, such as *Morals and Dogma* by Albert Pike; *History of Freemasonry* by Raymond Moore; *A New Encyclopedia of Freemasonry* by Arthur Waite, etc.

FREEMASONRY

At this time I was given a copy of *This Present Darkness* by Frank Peretti. I sensed I was living this story. I passed the book around the church and sent up warning flags to my prayer supporters. Yet it was difficult to know who I could trust. The slightest conversation about the church structure or personnel became a brushfire of criticism. Instead of studying and preparing messages, disciplining, counseling, and visiting, I found myself in meeting after meeting over this accusation or that judgment. The spiritual warfare was raging all around. My wife and I began to feel isolated from those we were called to serve. Casual conversations with us were guarded. When we would talk to people, they seemed always to be looking over their shoulders to see who was watching them.

Drawing Strength For Battle

I read Peretti's book a second time and let it encourage me to pray and seek the victory in Jesus. I learned something about myself. I always prayed standing, sitting, walking, and jogging, but never on my knees. Several passages of Scripture undergirded me in my trial of faith and service, and I had begun to pray more on my knees. I read Psalms 5:1-4, and early in the mornings I would spread my prayer organizer out before the Lord, petitioning Him to "hearken unto the voice of my cry."

While I was doing a study on I Peter for a Sunday morning, this passage leaped off the page: "Foreasmuch then as Christ hath suffered for us in the flesh, arm yourself likewise with the same mind; for he that hath suffered in the flesh hath ceased from sin.... If you be reproached for the name of Christ, happy are ye; for the spirit of glory and of God resteth upon you; on their part he is evil spoken of, but on your part he is glorified." (4:1,14).

Other scripture that blessed and reassured me were Isaiah 12:2-3; 41:10 and Psalms 105:1; 106:1. I camped on Jeremiah

240

33:3 as I called out to God to show me great and mighty things. In Psalms 32:8, I too pleaded for instruction for the things I should say and do. I was in the den with the lions and they weren't asleep — and, "Lord, my name is Daniel."

Strike One

The treasurer controlled the finances and budget, and several times threatened to resign over conflicts with the Finance Committee. In the fall of 1991 she stomped into my office and said, "I quit!" This was the fifth time she had tried to manipulate the Committee. This time I accepted her resignation. I called the Finance Committee chairman to inform him. He went to see her, fearful he would get the books in his lap. He then came to me and said that it was true, she had resigned, but that she refused to turn over the books.

A few days later one of the Masonic deacons was seen at her residence. The following week she asked for a called meeting to consider firing the pastor. She accused me of firing her. Her husband, who I had recently led to the Lord and baptized, seconded her motion. When the congregation voted, no one stood against me. The now "former" treasurer was furious.

I began my own investigation and discovered that some annuity money had never been sent to Dallas. I confronted the Finance Committee chairman and a deacon with the fact that numerous unpaid bills and budget money were not accounted for. The chairman convinced me to let it slide, get a new treasurer, and find out what we could without telling the church for the moment. The church was in such an uproar it would only cause further harm, he rationalized. I acquiesced and took no church discipline.

In the heat of the battle I erred in not seeking wise counsel (Proverbs 1:5). I must say to my pastor friends, sins affecting the entire church body must always be confronted and be revealed to the church body immediately.

FREEMASONRY

Because I did not take such action, the former treasurer did not leave. In her rage she began to attack from behind the scenes. In the midst of all of this, while professions of faith continued to increase, attendance decreased. The building program was virtually dead in the water.

In my daily prayer I was convicted of the need to humble myself and seek an evaluation from the deacon body. The deacon chairman quickly jumped at the opportunity and led the effort. The deacons held a preliminary meeting. Then on a separate date he called me to attend the face-to-face report. My original request was to the active twelve deacons, but they had rounded up six inactive deacons, and I sat facing eighteen men who did not appear ready to offer me tea and crumpets. The room was somber, stark, heavy and acrid. Tension filled the air. It was going to be a long evening.

The chairman let Deacon Doe bring the report. I was given nine positives and over thirty negatives. On the positive I was a good teacher and pastor. Among the negatives, I preached beyond 12 noon too often; I used too much Greek and Hebrew in my sermons; and I generally talked over their heads. I listened and took notes and prayed for guidance and control of my tongue (Proverbs 15:1). The natural tendency is to be defensive, but I wanted to find out what the complaints were and stop the rumor mill by being open and vulnerable. I quickly saw two items I accepted as bona fide complaints. Yes, sometimes I preached beyond 12 noon. I apologized for undo overage. However, if there was a decision for Christ, naturally the time must be extended.

I asked their help in preserving the 35-40 minutes I needed for my sermon. I promised to go over the remainder of the list and seek God's counsel and leading as whether I exceeded my authority or did not fulfill my pastoral duties. I did remind them, however, that I fully intended to preach God's Word.

One of the deacons then suggested that everything that had happened in the last two years was my fault. Several suggested

I think about resigning. I responded, "But none of your written accusations warrant resigning. Please speak the truth and tell me what's going on here."

The room got deathly quiet. One of the Masons said, "We've got to do something!" Silently I prayed, "Lord I'm in your hands, Thy will be done."

The silence was so thick you could cut it with a knife. Finally Deacon Doe, the chief Mason, exploded at me. His face red like fire, pointed his finger in my face and shouted, "We are doing this because we love you! You have to change and let us help you do the ministry!"

The chairman of the deacons could not get out a motion and Deacon Doe seemed hesitant to do so. God had shut the lion's mouth.

The peace that only the Lord can give came over me and I knew His presence. As the meeting dismissed, I thanked them and I knew God's will was done.

I reflected over the evaluation for several days. I noticed the rumor mill did die down during this time and the battle seemed to be at a stand-still. I made arrangements to attend a "Ministering in the Nineties" seminar in Knoxville with my wife. In this Southern Baptist gathering the issue of Masons was skirted. Several pastors spoke as to their being fired and how it transpired. I had an opportunity to share that I was having a problem with the Masons and was concerned with resolving the conflict. In a small group session I shared how I asked for an evaluation by the deacons. The pastors recoiled in shock. One facilitator asked, "By what stretch of insanity possessed you to do that?" So I shared how much I learned and how it gave a chance to hear face to face what the complaints were, instead of by rumor. I was stripped bare for sure, but I sensed some of the pastors were drawn closer because I listened and testified of my willingness to undergo such vulnerability. Most, however, thought I was wrong to have asked for an evaluation. "A pastor just does not do this," I was told. I disagreed. I still believe my action was in step with God's work at First Baptist.

FREEMASONRY

Let's Make A Deal

A few weeks after our return from the seminar, one of the deacons pulled me aside after church and wanted to know if I was coming to the meeting. "What meeting?" I asked. He wasn't sure what it was about, but my not knowing a deacons' meeting had been called made him suspicious something was up. I told him to go to the meeting prayerfully, that I had a hunch I would get a call from the chairman sooner or later.

That afternoon the chairman called and asked that I come over to the church. The deacons wanted to meet with me and make a deal. I told him I'd be right over, but that any unannounced meeting was unconstitutional. I told my wife to get on the phone to church members who were supporters and ask them to pray a hedge.

I first went to my office to get a copy of the constitution, a Bible and a notebook. I did a quick check. Yes, their called meeting without my knowledge was illegal. I prayed Jeremiah 33:3 and Psalms 32:8 and went into the meeting. They were not a happy, spirit-filled looking bunch. I noticed that two active deacons were not present. I sat down by the chairman. All eyes were riveted on me. Anger and tension visibly began to build. With no preliminaries, the chairman proceeded to lay out "the deal."

"We have voted ten to one to ask for your resignation. Your five years of ministry have hurt the church financially, numerically, and spiritually. Option one: If you resign immediately we will recommend severance and full benefits for ninety days. Option two: Refuse and be fired, move out of the parsonage immediately, no severance pay, no insurance after thirty days."

These were not "options." They knew I could find no place to live. They expected me to accept "option one" without question. But, I knew they were in violation of the church constitution and by-laws. The meeting was illegal and hiring and firing of a pastor was never to be done by the deacons but by the congregation. I was becoming extremely angry, and I prayed for self-control. I remember looking around the table and recalling the advice of Dr. Charles Stanley. He said he gets on average one phone call a week from a pastor about to be terminated. "What do I do?" Dr. Stanley replied, "Do you believe God called you to that church? If you do, has God called you to leave? If no, then ask them, why would you want to resign under pressure and go against God's will? What does that say about what you really believe about God?"

This response inspired my decision to the deacons. I focused on their faces and felt a sense of compassion and peace come over me. I thought of their refusal to carry Bibles to Church. I thought of their sins out in the community that had so hurt the ministry of the Gospel. I thought of their lies and deceitfulness, and I knew resigning would neither be best for them, the church, nor me. I knew it was not God's will that I resign. With great emotion I said, "Gentlemen, I do not find at this meeting a body of men worthy to decide God's will for this Church, or my life, let alone my family. I respectfully request a called meeting of the church to decide this matter. The constitution requires a hearing be given on such a decision as this."

To my surprise, they agreed to call a meeting for Wednesday night. It was to be announced at the close of the Sunday night message. One of the deacons got me off to the side and told me he misunderstood the vote and would vote to keep me as pastor. I went home and got the prayer line going. At the close of Sunday night's message I really focused on John 14:6. "And Jesus said, I am the way, the truth, and the Life. No man comes unto the Father but by me." The deacons were livid, vibrating in their pews waiting to announce the called meeting. This was dutifully done and the word went out.

Normally a Wednesday night business meeting in a Baptist Church is strictly for the super committed — the faithful few who have that sense of duty to be there. This Wednesday night meeting proved to be one of two I shall never forget.

FREEMASONRY

The Called Meeting

On Monday I got on the phone to key pastor friends who promised to call other pastor friends. I asked for a prayer cover; that God would be glorified through my family's trial. My wife and I got on our knees the night before the meeting and gave ourselves and our ministry to the Lord. We were ready to depart or willing to stay. We only wanted God's will to be done and Him glorified.

By prior arrangement some close church family members and supporters met half an hour early for prayer to bind Satan and seek God's will. We interceded for those being used of the enemy. After prayer we devised a strategy to control the meeting by motioning an agenda be followed that would be fair to all sides. Since the meeting was about the future of the pastor's employment at First Baptist, a full disclosure of charges had to be presented. Equal time was to be given for those supporting the pastor. This was to be done one person at a time from each side. The constitution required that a 75 percent vote was necessary to call a pastor. It was moved that this percentage be used for dismissal as well. This item failed to pass at the called meeting. The church voted to heed a simple majority. The deck was stacked. A church split was in the making.

By prior arrangement, those who supported me spread out all over the auditorium. We had coveted to pray for peace and God's presence and that Satan be bound. The auditorium was nearly three quarters full. There were people present I had never seen before. Some I had seen maybe once or twice at church in my five years at First Baptist. Many came to vote, but they had never come to grow spiritually or to serve. I thought it strange they would not come to hear me teach, but would come to vote me out. What must it have been like for Jesus on the final day in Jerusalem? Was I imagining, or did I really smell sulfur? Maybe I had been reading too much Frank Peretti.

By prior agreement, my wife and I thought it best for our two small children to be present to hear what was being said about their daddy. We never wanted them to doubt my moral purity and integrity of office. We have never regretted this decision. I believe that when God's man has nothing to hide, his family needs to be a witness to all the proceedings.

The meeting began around 7:00 pm. Some had come earlier to pray. Sometime after the meeting began I heard clanging of metal above us. Then I heard something outside like a steady beep, beep, beep. My children leaned forward and whispered, "Do you hear that?" Phyllis and I said, "Yes." One of my friends was sitting in front of me. I tapped him and his wife on the shoulder and asked if they heard the strange sounds overhead. "No," they replied. Later we learned we were the only ones who heard. But all four of us heard. We believe God's angels and Satan's demons were locked in mortal combat over the outcome of this meeting. How compassionate our God is. Only my family needed to hear the battle for our own assurance that God is our fortress.

The session began with the same former treasurer, the woman who kept the questionable books. She made a motion to terminate me as pastor of First Baptist. Her husband seconded as he had done previously. At that, the discussion began. The deacons would go to the podium and present their case or charge. A supporter would follow and state why the charges needed evaluating — not just on merit, but on who was bringing the charges. If the pastor was being accused of something, how had the deacons sought to help the ministry with regard to financial, numerical and spiritual well-being of First Baptist?

The chairman of the deacons waited his turn almost to the end. I was to follow him. At this point we were two and a half hours into the meeting. No one old or young left to take a break. "Why is it," I thought, "that on Sunday morning any number of adults and/or children would have to parade to the bathroom distracting everyone else, but not tonight?"

FREEMASONRY

I watched the chairman carefully from my spot towards the back. He got out the evaluation the deacons had made of me, which by unanimous agreement of the deacon board was to be kept in confidence. He came to the front and quickly went over my thirty negatives to my nine positives. This he hoped would sway the final vote.

Finally, the chairman said I may speak for thirty minutes. I had taken notes on key points and had perfect rebuttals, including the public exposure of the former treasurer, who appeared to be collaborating with the Masons. But as I slid out of the pew, a still small voice said, "Don't say that."

"Is that you, Lord?" I asked.

Again, I heard, "Don't say that."

I'm in the aisle now headed toward the podium arguing with God. Towards the front row I asked again, this time in desperation, "Lord, what do you want me to say?"

"Tell them your name."

I silently laughed as I stepped up on the platform and touched the all-too-familiar oak podium I had come to love so well. I turned and scanned the faces in the audience. Never had I seen such a crowd except during a revival. Never in five years had I met some of these people, who were here only to decide my future. Their eyes were filled with hate. Over to the side my wife was attending a grieving friend with a Kleenex. There was gentle weeping all around.

I paused for a moment and reflected on something I had perceived was from the Lord during the meeting. Three times, while the naysayers were criticizing my ministry, I heard a whisper, "Hear their pain."

I stood there speechless and began to weep. I asked my dear wife for some Kleenex. As I looked out over the audience, I realized that many present did not even know who I was. Perhaps they did not know Jesus as their Lord and Savior. Perhaps they were blinded by pain, not realizing they were being used of Satan to fight against God's Kingdom work. I was broken with a burden for one and all. I heard their pain. Now I could see it in their eyes.

I had been praying I would be filled with a burden for those in the community who needed Jesus and who opposed Christ's work inside and outside the church. Tonight was an answer to that prayer. They were all sitting in front of me.

"I'm Dan Carlen," I said. "I want to tell you what my Lord and Savior has done for me."

In twenty-five minutes I told them my testimony of salvation, my call to the pastorate, and my call to First Baptist. I closed with James 2:18, "Yea, a man may say, thou hast faith, and I have works; show me thy faith without thy works, and I will show thee my faith by my works."

I then read our Lord's Great Commission in Matthew 28:18-20 and sat down. It was 10:00 PM — time to vote.

Strike Two

The vote was to be a secret ballot. The slips were handed out, and the vote taken. I was at peace, as was my wife and family. Oh how I loved them at this moment. A Godly wife and precious children are truly a gift and blessing from God.

The vote was announced, "Fifty-two against and sixty-seven in favor of keeping the Pastor." Weeping and rejoicing broke out all over the assembly. Many had obviously chosen not to vote at all, but were mere spectators. Who knows, perhaps there were a few angels in disguise who cast a vote.

The chairman of the deacons loudly proclaimed as he left the rear of the church, "Boys we've got our work cut out for us. This isn't over." I knew he was right.

Deacon Doe was standing on the right side of the congregation weeping so hard he was shaking. I didn't think they were tears of joy. After I received the many congratulations, I made my way over to Deacon Doe. I told him I loved him. He cried. I encouraged him to come by and talk with me to try and reconcile to serve the Lord together at First Baptist. Then I asked him if he had ever read *Morals and Dogma* by Albert Pike. He admitted he had read some, actually only a few pages. I named several other Masonic books I had read. He had read only portions of these. I asked him what degree of Freemasonry he held? He was the 18th degree. Then I asked him if he realized that his Christian faith and God's Holy Word took authority over all other human systems of beliefs. Did he not think he needed to go over the belief system of Freemasonry and compare it with scripture? Then I told him it was only in God's Word that he would gain the true Light of a relationship with Jesus. But first he needed to demit (resign) from the Lodge.

At that last statement, he exploded in anger and began shaking his finger at me. His face full red, veins popping, he said it was all my fault. "Get out of here," he shrieked. I calmed him down while my family and friends formed a circle off to the side and prayed. I asked him to join me in the back for prayer, which he did. But there was no peace. I knew it was not over with him.

In the weeks that followed the deacons boycotted the worship hour and skipped other services. They held back their tithe, and after a month it became clear they hoped to freeze me out. By this time Frank Peretti's book was being read and circulated again. Urgent prayer of God's help was needed and we needed His guidance.

Two months later I noticed we had some visitors. There was a sweeter spirit in our services. The new treasurer reported that giving was on the way up. What an exciting time to be a pastor.

Christmas came and went (1992). 1993 held the promise of a fresh new year. What did God have in store for First Baptist and Masonville this year?

The first Sunday I found out. All the deacons and their families were back for communion. I read I Cor. 11:23-32, and stressed the importance of judging self over unconfessed sin (I John 1:9). They took communion anyway. At the close of the service

250

they stood in front of me and smirked. I sensed that at the next opportunity they would once again seek to get me released without a called meeting.

I began to seek earnestly God's will concerning a ministry move. God was saying wait. I began to lead our new committee members to action. Because of certain Masons' blocking committees, the vision to minister and to do God's work was not being carried out. I had no peace about resigning, and no indication of a move being evident, yet ministry was at a standstill. It was difficult to pray and study because of constant interruptions and counseling problems and flare-ups that plagued our congregation. Satan seemed to be beating up on the sheep. Supporters became sick as viruses swept through the city. I had a heavy schedule of travel, as the church just seemed to limp along. Oppression was heavy.

Then one of the deacons met me in the hall and said with a escalating voice, "I wish you would just leave, get on out of here! All this anger and unhappiness — it's all your fault." I got him calmed down and invited him into my office and explained I was seeking God's will. I had sent my resume out some time ago, but God was saying wait. I was to be patient and faithful. I asked him to pray with me that the Lord would turn cursing into blessing and we all might draw closer to him through this time of trials. We parted on peaceful terms, or so I thought.

Later I received a phone call from a member that several deacons were seen up town meeting with the former treasurer. We suspected a third attempt to fire me was in the planning stages.

I was teaching the "Sermon On The Mount" on Sunday night, and God really spoke to me through this study. Many of the Masons came and vibrated at our Lord's words. One Mason deacon had been assigned to sit in the third row right in front of me and hold up his watch for all to see when he thought I should quit. I ignored him and kept on till God led me to stop. I began to wonder how much more of this I could stand. I held on to I Corinthians 10:13. I asked God to help me endure. I felt His assurance.

The new budget was based upon what God had done previously, and a vision budget for what we would trust God to do for 1993. For the first time the finance committee was in majority to adopt such a budget. The deacons were incensed. We had raised over $115,000 for the building fund. We had paid off debt that the church had been paying on for 10 years prior to my coming. Newly trained church members and disciples were filling committee vacancies. Things were building to a conclusion. The tension was so thick you could cut it with a knife. But, God was in control and working.

In spite of the difficulties and oppressive spirit, there was for the moment a sense of renewal in the congregation. The deacon meetings of 1993, however, were short and angry, which helped to encourage their hatred of the pastor. I asked for another deacon retreat at a local park. They accepted. I invited an employee of the Tennessee Baptist Convention to speak to us on conflict resolution. We had a good turn out and a good meeting, but nothing changed.

In the midst of all this we began the process of hiring a part-time youth minister as part of the new vision-oriented budget. This was not well received, but I encouraged the Personnel Committee to continue the interview process. We also had a revival plan on-going. But, attempts to move the Building Committee forward met with opposition from Deacon Doe. The Committee appeared not to want to keep up the old church for fear I would receive credit. I could only persevere and pray to be faithful.

Strike Three — You're Out Of Here

In March of 1993 illness struck hard in our congregation, especially among my supporters. Several other supporters were out of town. There was a strange feeling in the air, a sense of foreboding.

The Personnel Committee arranged for a youth minister candidate from Nashville to meet with the congregation at our regularly scheduled business meeting. Little did we know what an exciting visit he would have. Prior to the meeting, the personnel committee and I met with the candidate. It seemed to go well. When we went into the auditorium, I noticed a few unfamiliar faces. And yes, there were definitely more than the usual for a Wednesday night Baptist business meeting. When I sat in front with our young candidate, I began hearing shuffling in the back. As the moderator walked to the pulpit, one of my friends tapped me on the shoulder and said I should look around. I turned and saw more strange faces.

Now I understood why there was a strange feeling in the air, a sense of foreboding. The word had definitely gone out to call a vote while some of my supporters were home sick and others out of town. Such hate on their faces — shame on the faces of others. I told my candidate youth pastor to hang on, this would be a ride to remember. I apologized to him in advance for what I anticipated would happen. I told him the demons were present to incite these people to vote me out. I could tell by those present and those absent, we would probably lose this time, except God intervene again.

One of my supporters jumped up and ran to the phone. The moderator knew we were mustering our forces. Nervously he tried to push through the agenda. I looked at my watch; 7:15. More shuffling as more strangers appeared. I looked around and was amazed that the church was now half full. Some of my supporters had come, but the count was too few. This would be a barn burner. I maintained a sense of calm and prayed, "Father, Thy will be done."

The preliminaries were finally over and new business was before the church. The former treasurer, who had been attending the Methodist Church since attempting to fire me the second time, jumped up and came forward. The moderator allowed her to make a motion to terminate the pastor, vacate the pulpit immediately, vacate the office in three days, vacate the parsonage in 30 days, and provide for one month separation pay.

"Let's send him on to bigger and better things," she shrieked, pointing in my direction.

This time she had the full backing of the deacons. There was little discussion allowed. An inactive deacon was allowed to come forward to accuse me of missing his mother's funeral. He said I had hurt him deeply. Then others on the Building Committee spoke of my divisiveness. Few stood in my defense. One did, and impressed me very much. It was the candidate youth minister. He boldly asked to be recognized. The church voted to let him speak.

"Please reconsider the motion and seek to work to reconcile on a Biblical basis," he exclaimed. "I have heard no charges meriting such treatment against this man of God."

Someone in the audience shouted, "Sit down!"

As he returned to his seat the moderator gave me ten minutes to speak. "Lord, what should I say?" As I rose from my seat and walked to the pulpit, the Lord impressed on my mind Psalms 106: 3-10. I quoted verse 3, "Blessed are they that observe justice and he that doeth righteousness at all times." I asked them to consider their actions before God and thereby commit it unto the Lord. I sat down. The vote was taken, and I lost by a few votes.

Weeping immediately broke out across the church. One by one, members began to stand and resign their various leadership positions. The Sunday School director resigned. The church secretary resigned. The majority of the Sunday School teachers resigned — and on it went.

In the midst of the tearing apart, I sensed relief. This church had been controlled by an aging populace governed by Freemasons, who viewed church friends, church building, and church property their own. I was an intruder. The Lord had released me from the burden and call to minister to these people. It was now time to move on and trust God in seeking His calling elsewhere.

I made my way back to the office and phoned my wife to tell her the news. She thought I was kidding. Then the office filled with supporters and well-wishers. The group spilled over into the secretary's office. She was there, along with the new treasurer, the Sunday School director and others who had resigned in support. They were in agreement that because the act was so callous and so cold, so ruthless and unchristian, they could not in good conscience continue to attend First Baptist. I was numb.

The moderator, who permitted a motion be made by a member not in good standing, was also the Mayor of Masonville. He dropped by the office, gave me a broad political smile and said, "I am truly sorry." Always the consummate politician, never able to draw a line and say, "Here I stand."

As I conversed with my supporters, I began to feel so weak that I could barely stand. I sensed a tremendous burden to pray. I asked everyone to gather around me. We all knelt. Some in the office, some in the hall. I praised God, thanking Him for the privilege to experience in this small way what Jesus meant by "bearing our cross." This had been a time of experiencing the presence and power of Almighty God. He was more real and personal to me than He had ever been before. I then interceded for the church, praying that cursing would be turned to blessing. I went home to comfort my family.

The Aftermath

I got up the next day and went immediately to the radio station to do one last spot. Normally my spots are taped a week in advance. This time I wanted to do it live, otherwise my radio audience would never know what happened. I wanted to share with them my story before rumors started. I finished by reading Psalms 106, then asked for their prayers.

Immediately the phone rang. This dear Church of Christ lady was crying as she expressed her love for me and my family.

FREEMASONRY

She had listened in every morning. Several from other denominational backgrounds blessed my family with prayers, encouragement, and money over the next critical weeks.

The next few days were a nightmare. We had no time to hurt. We had to pack up the office, send out resumes, minister, counsel, talk till exhaustion masked pain. Then to heap insult on injury, someone put water in the gas tanks of both my cars. Someone else shot my German Shepherd. All the while gracious well-wishers were ringing the phone off the hook. Late at night and early morning hours it was harassing phone calls. When I would pick up the phone, they would hang up. After three weeks of this, we called the phone company about having a tracer put on the calls. Next day we found the crawl space door under our house open. Strangely the calls immediately stopped. We believe our house had been bugged.

We were searching desperately for a place to rent. There was none. We thought of filing suit, but Scripture says we are not to sue our brother. We could only trust God to provide and show us the way.

I attended our regular association meeting, and a dear pastor friend made a motion that my family and I be allowed to move into the vacant association mission house. The board approved (not unanimously), but with more than enough votes. The house was perfect. It had three bedrooms, two baths and a two-car garage in which we could store our furniture until we knew God's will.

With the help of a faithful few, we were moved by the deadline, ending our five-year ministry at First Baptist. The next Sunday a group of church members asked me to speak to them somewhere. We met in a local business cafeteria. A total of 70 attended that first meeting. A large offering was taken on our behalf. Many wanted to start a new church. Instead, I suggested they put the money in an account and wait on the Lord. They asked if I would stay as their speaker until God led us elsewhere. I agreed. They then voted to become an unofficial body of believers meeting for Bible study.

The next week we moved to a different location. After a month, I began to sense my own unresolved bitterness. At our next Bible study, I spoke about reconciliation and the need to apply Matt.18:15-20 and Luke 17:1-6. They responded positively and that night in special session a list of offenses and grievances was drawn up and voted on. The following week the newly formed group went over to First Baptist for the monthly business meeting. Their intention was to seek reconciliation with other church members. At the close of the reading of the offenses, one deacon stood and said, "I think it's time to talk about finger food!"

About 9:00 pm the group returned to our temporary meeting place quite happy, saying, "God wants us to become a church. We have been set free." I had intentionally not gone with them. I remained to pray for reconciliation, but it was not to be any time soon. We joined hands in a circle and prayed for guidance and sought God's help. I was asked to stay on as the group's pastor, but as yet sensed no clear leading. I did agree to become interim pastor until God showed us clearly what He was doing, and what we were to do. Meanwhile, I sent out more resumes.

We got the children situated in a different school, met with their teachers and explained what had happened. God blessed us with wonderful Christian teachers who loved our children through the turmoil of those days. Their grades suffered some, but they continued to do fairly well.

We continued to pray for rental housing. Everything was so expensive. We were getting some help from the new group but not enough to handle the rent on a home or apartment. We just did not know what to do. First, we thought about selling our furniture. We had little, but what we had we wanted to keep if at all possible.

After six months the association needed the house back for a missionary who was coming. They had been so kind and gracious and used of the Lord. However, I explained to them that I could not, nor would not move my family into the street. Some in the association suggested they evict us. Masonic influence was everywhere.

FREEMASONRY

Some Miracles From God

During this test I felt led to spread my family's needs before the Lord, as did Hezekiah. I opened my prayer book and laid it before the Lord. I prayed, "Lord, in Matthew 6, you promised to provide the basics of life; food, shelter, and clothing. We are so thankful for your care. But the enemy is bringing pressure to bear, and Lord we need a place. Lord, we need a home. I can't do it Lord. You must help. We need a house with at least three bedrooms, two baths, and a two-car garage large enough to put an office in. If it be your will, please let me know — and Lord, I need to know this week."

Meanwhile, the Lord had already moved the new church group into a big barn. That's right, a barn. It was a cattle barn fixed up for auctions and other events. When we approached the owner about using the facility for church services, not only did he agree, he paid the utility expenses. Praise the Lord! For two years we met in that barn.

God answered my Hezehiah prayer within the week. He sent two key people into our lives to help us with getting a house; a former Baptist pastor and a mortgage advisor.

For you to understand the miracle, I must first explain my credit record. New employment. No record of house payments or rent payments for the past few years. Cars paid for. In fact, my financial history was so good that I had no credit history. And that's not so good. What a crazy world!

There was a long-ago credit record in Texas, where we had built a small home through a veteran loan. When we moved, we sold the house to another veteran on an assumption. He defaulted after eighteen months. Although I was released from liability, it was still on my record as being a repossession. Now, the story.

The former Baptist pastor was led to resign a church in our association and join our church. He had gone into real estate and thought he could help us find a house. He introduced us to a mortgage advisor, who looked at our "no history" credit. He was sceptical. I suggested that we try a veteran's loan, since I had used that lending institution before. I had no idea that I was flagged on their computers as having a bad loan. When "default" showed up, the mortgage advisor informed us it was hopeless, but that we could appeal. He would do the paperwork and personally hand carry it to the lender. It was denied, so we appealed again, this time to arbitration. VA said it would take eight months to a year to get a slot for arbitration.

It was a time of severe testing. We kept trusting in the Lord (Proverbs 3:5-6). Two weeks later the advisor called and said a miracle has happened. My case had been arbitrated and I had received my benefits back. I could borrow up to $144,000!

A few days later God led us to a house and we closed and took possession. We were moved in just as the missionary arrived to take occupancy of the association mission house. We set up my office in the garage, laying used carpet and hanging plastic walls. Just as I had asked, God gave me a place to study and to write.

This confirmed God's call for me to stay as pastor at the "barn." The Lord blessed this new work. In time the community was ministered to in many ways. Not only have we been blessed with 20.5 acres at a prime intersection, but have just finished a new church building for God's glory. This vision was not mine, but the congregation's, who recognized how God was working to turn cursing into blessing. My prayers are being answered.

To Pastors: Lessons I Have Learned

1. I learned the Bible must at all time be my foundation and my guide. I believe it is inspired and inerrant from Genesis to Revelation in the original language. Because I believe this, I believe God has given me truth. As His servant, though a sinner saved by grace, I must do my best to uphold truth.

Satan does not like truth. He will come against those who stand for it. On this point the Sermon on the Mount comforted me by teaching me that persecution is normal, not abnormal.

If I am upholding truth, what happened to me was to be expected (Matthew 5:3-11), to God's glory (Matthew 5:16, 2 Thessalonians 1:11,12; Hebrews 13:20.2.)

2. I learned to praise God and thank Him for my trials (Psalms 106:1, I Thessalonians 5:18). As a pastor, this is what I teach. But, how much more beneficial my teaching when I personally experienced it. What joy! Oh how I believe this is the interpretation and application of I Peter 4:1.

When I was humbled by this experience, only then did I become a knee-bending pastor. If you are not there, may God grant you the trial to become broken before Him. This is for your own good, the good of your family, the good of your flock, and the good of your ministry, so that souls will be saved for the Kingdom of God. The trials God put me through progressively matured me spiritually, working in me patience as I asked for wisdom without worldly fear (James 1:3 ff.).

3. I learned to trust God at His Word. He told me in 1st Corinthians 10:13 that He would not test me beyond my ability to endure. He was true to His Word. However, I thought my endurance had long since been reached before God did. I praise Him though, for it has since helped me to embrace trials.

This last statement is pregnant in meaning for me and my family. No one starts out to be a martyr, or a "Daniel in the lion's den." Daniel was obedient. God did the rest. In my situation, God did not ask me my thoughts or opinions. He simply asked me to be obedient, and trust Him at His Word.

4. I learned how sinful and fearful I am. My sin was pride, afraid of making mistakes. So God allowed me to make many mistakes. This humbled me. As a result, I learned to apologize and ask forgiveness for my past sins.

I also harbored the sin of bitterness. I had not forgiven those people. So, about a year and a half after I was terminated, I called the interim pastor and told him of my desire to talk to his congregation and forgive them and tell them I love them. That request was denied, but I had tremendous peace that I had taken a new step in my personal healing.

5. I learned I must beware! I must not accept individuals into positions of service in the church without testing them over a period of time (Philippians 3:2).

The present imperative of <u>blepo</u> in this Scripture means to "keep constantly looking around." Be diligent as a guard on duty who sees that the enemy cannot harm God's troops.

In John Daniel's trilogy, <u>Scarlet and the Beast</u>, a whole chapter is devoted to Freemasonry's infiltration of American churches. One example cited occurred in 1926, when an order from the Scottish Rite Supreme Council directed every Mason to join a local church and liberalize it, modernize it, and render it aggressive for Masonic use. Satan knows that as goes the church, so goes America. If the spirited foundation of the church is removed, both the church and the nation will crumble.

Too often we are just happy to have someone who wants to serve anywhere. I have often said a key test of a servant is to begin by cleaning restrooms before moving up. I personally have done this in both a Christian school and a church, and have benefited from it. It has character building. Jesus used the example of washing his disciple's feet as the test of a true servant.

In my former church, Masons did not want the position of deacon so they could serve people. They wanted it for their own agenda, which was to steer the direction of ministry away from evangelism. We pastors are God's watchman to guard against this. It may offend some, but it is necessary.

6. I have learned the importance of support groups. God led me to Tom McKenney, who encouraged me to participate in the "Ministry to Masons Conference." There I met men like Ed Decker, Bill Creel, David Reagan, Steven Tsoukulis, Rev. Pierce Dodson, Rev. Harmon Taylor, David Houghton, and many others — all of whom ministered the love of Jesus to help heal wounds I did not know I had.

In my former church, I had been interceding in prayer for the Masons for two years. I felt that many of them were not saved and truly needed a relationship with Jesus Christ. I thought I had God's perspective on the situation. However, at the Ministry to Masons Conference, I was convicted of my sin of anger and bitterness directed towards these Masons. The Conference helped me to confront this sin and confess it. Only then was I able to pray anew for these men to be delivered from the real enemy — Satan, World, and Flesh.

I also discovered I was not alone in my persecution by Masons. Pierce Dodson and Harmon Taylor's experiences were far worse than mine. How important it is that we stand together and pray a hedge around each other, and praise God, for whose glory we stand (Philippians 1:9-11)

7. I learned that toleration of Masonry, and those who have taken an oath to it, is not Biblical.

If Masons are in the church, toleration by the church is not in its best interest. If they claim to be Christian, they must be confronted according to II Timothy 2:24 and 4:2, and reconciled according to Luke 17:1-6. Our purpose is not to alienate Masons but to reconcile them.

We must first fervently pray in accordance with Acts 26:18 to break down Satan's deceit and blindness. Second, we must learn to "hear their pain."

During the Mason's second attempt to fire me, I plainly "heard their pain." I have since thought often about the words of Jesus on the cross, suffering terribly and saying, "Father, forgive them, for they know not what they do." (Luke 23:34).

Love Masons enough to stand against their blindness, their Satanic deception, and their malice toward you for teaching truth. And when they persecute you (and they surely will), love them enough to forgive them.

8. I learned that a pastor does not need to openly attack Freemasonry from the pulpit.

After I met Dr. Larry Holly at Indianapolis in June 1992, I returned to my church and distributed his books behind the scenes to all the deacons. I asked them for information and cooperation in order to understand their rationale in being a member of an organization that is anti-Christ and one-world government in its belief system. They never responded.

The more I read about Freemasonry, the more I ended the worship service focusing on John 14:6. Jesus is the only way to salvation. On the other hand, Freemasons believe they can be saved by their good deeds. According to Masonic authors, anyone anywhere in the world can believe in any god and be saved, so long as he practices good deeds, such as giving to Masonic charities.

I never taught directly against Freemasonry. I did use the word Freemasonry in conjunction with a concluding study on I John 5:21. John wrote, "Little Children, keep from idols." I developed the word idol and traced the history of false religions and mentioned one such false religion following idolatry is Freemasonry. This was just prior to the second attempt to fire me. Their hatred was so strong at this point, they came out in the open against me.

I present truth. Satan hates truth. He will always come against it (John 8:44). He uses deception (such as taught in Freemasonry), to counter truth. God is greater than Satan. So, praise the Lord and stand for truth!

9. I learned God is good. Romans 8:28 is so true. What a comfort I found in I Peter 4:14 — "If you be reproached for the name of Christ, happy are you; for the spirit and glory of God rests upon you; on their part He is evil spoken of, but on your part He is glorified."

Dear reader, my prayer for you and me is Philippians 1:20. "According to my earnest expectation and my hope, that in nothing I shall be ashamed, but that with all boldness as always, so now also Christ shall be magnified in my body, whether it be by life or by death."

To God be the Glory! Great things He hath done!

Daniel D. Carlen

A "Masonic Agenda?"
What can the Church do about it?

Marlin Maddoux of POINT OF VIEW radio talk show, Dallas, Texas, writes: "Domination of churches by members of the Masonic Lodge is a scandal which cries out for exposure."

Frequent POINT OF VIEW guest Ed Decker, an expert on Masonry, writes of churches "on whose board sits a majority from the Lodge." These are churches "whose deacons or elders share Lodge secrets that are in keeping with their higher allegiance to the Lodge, sworn by blood oaths." Such men "are often the financial backbone of many small congregations."

Ed Decker recounts one frightening story from a pastor of a small rural church: "I always feel at board meetings that there is a second agenda which is not open to me. It's like they get their marching orders from the Lodge on how to conduct the business of the church."

The only written documentation that suggests a secret Masonic agenda against the Church is found in the Scottish Rite's *New Age Magazine*, January issue, 1926, quoted at the beginning of the "Epilog" of this book. Perhaps a former Mason, who has accepted Christ as his Savior and Lord, and who has renounce Freemasonry and its oaths, will one day come forward with proof of such a secret, or second agenda. Until then we have only circumstantial evidence, as revealed in this book.

We can, however, combat Masonic infiltration by adjusting Church Constitutions and Bylaws. For example, people who claim to be Christian, yet practice Hinduism, Buddhism, Mormonism, Freemasonry, etc., "halt [hop] between two opinions" (I Kings 18:21). Hence, they should not be allowed to join the Church, or hold positions in the Church, or be allowed to teach in the Church, or be pastors of the Church.

Pastors, do you think this callous? We are living in the Laodicean Church Period, the age of the voting church, in which congregations, boards, elders, sessions, and deacons rule by vote. Therefore, Christians alone should vote on Church activity, and not idolators with secret agendas that quench the Holy Spirit. ∎

264

RENUNCIATION

OF

MASONIC

OATHS

FREEMASONRY

THE "CURSE" OF FREEMASONRY

English words in [brackets] are from *Strong's Concordance*, KJV

Zechariah 5 describes a mystery religion that counterfeits as Jewish. We find this in verse 6, in which the angel says, "This is their <u>resemblance</u> through all the earth." Resemblance of what? Simply this, a resemblance of the two preceding chapters (3-4), which is Solomon's Temple.

Ayin, the Hebrew word for *resemblance,* is a primitive root word found no place else in Scripture. It can be translated "outward appearance" or "resemblance." Most significantly, its primary meaning is literally and figuratively *"an eye."* Therefore, *Ayin* refers not only to a pagan religion that counterfeits a resemblance of Solomon's Temple in Zech. 4, but also a resemblance of the "seven eyes of the Lord" in Zech. 4:4, 6 & 10.

A better word could not have been selected by the translators of the KJV to reference modern Freemasonry. "Resemblance" refers to the All-Seeing Eye of Freemasonry, as well as its "resemblance" of Solomon's Temple.

In Zech. 5:3 the angel says to the prophet, "This is the curse [Hebrew: *oath*] that goeth forth over the face of the whole earth..." If the Masonic oath is a curse in the earth, it is also a curse in our nation, as well as a curse in the family of every Mason. In verse 5:4 we read: "I will bring it (the curse) forth, saith the Lord of hosts, and it shall enter into the <u>house</u> [Heb: *family*] of the <u>thief</u> [Heb: *deceiver who administers the oath secretly*], and into the <u>house</u> [Heb: *family*] of him that <u>sweareth falsely</u> [Heb: *takes the oath deceitfully*] by my name: and it shall remain in the midst of his <u>house</u> [Heb: *family*], and shall consume it with the timber thereof and the <u>stones</u> [Heb: *children*] thereof."

FOR FREEMASONS AND THEIR DESCENDANTS, A PRAYER OF RELEASE FROM THE MASONIC CURSE

Christians should pray for Masons without judging them. Masons are deceived. And with that deception, they have brought a curse on their family. Therefore, we must bring their sins to God in an attitude of love, petitioning the Father for His mercy, binding in the name of Jesus Christ the spirits of deception, antichrist, witchcraft and death. Please remember that "we wrestle not against flesh and blood [our loved ones], but against principalities, against powers, against the rulers of the darkness of this world, against spiritual wickedness in high places," (Ephesians 6:12). This is a spiritual battle, and should be treated accordingly.

If you are a former Mason and have accepted Christ as your Savior, you must renounce your oaths, else you and your family will continue to be bound by the Masonic curse. The following prayers will assist you in your renunciation.

If you or your spouse are descendants of a Mason, your family is also under the descendant's curse. Exodus 20:5 reads, "Thou shalt not bow down thyself to them (idols), nor serve them: for I the LORD thy God am a jealous God, visiting the iniquity [Heb: *punishment*] of the fathers upon the children unto the third and fourth generation of them that hate me."

To break the descendant's curse, we recommend that from your heart you pray through the following renunciations. Read the renunciations first, so that you know what is involved. After reading them we recommend you pray the renunciations aloud in the presence of a Christian witness or counsellor.

Prayer of Renunciation

"Father God, creator of heaven and earth, I come to you in the name of Jesus Christ your Son. I come as a sinner seeking forgiveness and cleansing from all sins committed against you, and others made in your image. I honor my earthly father and mother and all of my ancestors of flesh and blood, and of the spirit by adoption and godparents, but I utterly turn away from and renounce all their sins. I forgive all my ancestors for the effects of their sins on me and my children. I confess and renounce all of my own sins. I renounce and rebuke Satan and every spiritual power of his affecting me and my family.

"I renounce and forsake all involvement in Freemasonry or any other lodge or craft by my ancestors and myself. I renounce witchcraft, the principal spirit behind Freemasonry, and I renounce Baphomet, the Spirit of Antichrist and the curse of the Luciferian doctrine. I renounce the idolatry, blasphemy, secrecy and deception of Masonry at every level. I specifically renounce the insecurity, the love of position and power, the love of money, avarice or greed, and the pride which would have led my ancestors into Masonry. I renounce all the fears which held them in Masonry, especially the fears of death, fears of men, and fears of trusting in the name of Jesus Christ.

"I renounce every position held in the lodge by any of my ancestors, including Tyler, Master, Worshipful Master, or any other. I renounce the calling of a man Master, for Jesus Christ is my only Master and Lord, and He forbids anyone else have that title. I renounce the entrapping of others into Masonry, and observing the helplessness of others during the rituals. I renounce the effects of Masonry passed on to me through any female ancestor who felt distrusted and rejected by her husband as he entered and attended any lodge and refused to tell her of his secret activities.

YORK RITE: "I renounce the oaths taken and the curses involved in the York Rite of Freemasonry, including Mark Master, Past Master, Most Excellent Master, Royal Master, Select Master, Super Excellent Master, the Orders of the Red Cross, the Knights of Malta, and the Knights Templar degrees. I renounce the secret words of JOPPA, KEB RAIOTH, and HAHER-SHALAL-HASH-BAZ. I renounce the vows taken on a human skull, the crossed swords, and the curse and death wish of Judas, of having the head cut off and placed on top of a church spire. I renounce the unholy communion and especially of drinking from a human skull in some Rites.

SHRINERS: (America only. Doesn't apply in other countries). "I renounce the oaths taken and the curses and penalties involved in the Ancient Arabic Order of the Nobles of the Mystic

Shrine. I renounce the piercing of the eyeballs with a three-edged blade, the flaying of the feet, the madness, and the worship of the false god Allah as the god of our fathers. I renounce the hoodwink, the mock hanging, the mock beheading, the mock drinking of the blood of the victim, the mock dog urinating on the initiate, and the offering of urine as a commemoration.

33rd Degree: "I renounce the oaths taken and the curses involved in the thirty-third degree of Masonry, the Grand Sovereign Inspector General. I renounce and forsake the declaration that Lucifer is God. I renounce the cable-tow around the neck. I renounce the death wish that the wine drunk from a human skull should turn to poison and the skeleton whose cold arms are invited if the oath of this degree is violated. I renounce the three infamous assassins of their grand master, law, property and religion, and the greed and witchcraft involved in the attempt to manipulate and control the rest of mankind.

All Other Degrees: "I renounce all the other oaths taken, the rituals of every other degree and the curses involved. I renounce all other lodges and secret societies such as Prince Hall Freemasonry, Mormonism, The Order of Amaranth, Oddfellows, Buffalos, Druids, Foresters, Orange, Elks, Moose and Eagles Lodges, and the Ku Klux Klan. I renounce the Grange, the Woodmen of the World, Riders of the Red Robe, the Knights of Pythias, the Mystic order to the Veiled Prophets of the Enchanted Realm, the women's Orders of the Eastern Star, and of the White Shrine of Jerusalem, the girl's Order of the Daughters of the Eastern Star, the International Orders of Job's Daughters, and of the Rainbow Girls, and the boys' Order of De Molay, and their effects on me and all my family.

"I renounce the ancient pagan teaching and symbolism of the First Tracing Board, the Second Tracing Board and the Third Tracing Board used in the ritual of the Blue Lodge. I renounce the pagan ritual of the 'Point within a Circle' with all its bondages and phallus worship. I renounce the occultic mysticism of the black and white mosaic checkered floor with the tessellated boarder and five-pointed blazing star. I renounce the symbol 'G' and its veiled pagan symbolism and bondages. I renounce and utterly forsake the Great Architect Of The Universe, who is revealed in the higher degrees as Lucifer, and his false claim to be the universal fatherhood of God. I also renounce the false claim that Lucifer is the Morning Star and Shining One and I declare that Jesus Christ is the Bright and Morning Star of Revelation 22:16.

"I renounce the All-Seeing Third Eye of Freemasonry or Horus in the forehead and its pagan and occult symbolism. I renounce all false communions taken, all mockery of the redemptive work of Jesus Christ on the cross of Calvary, all unbelief, confusion and depression, and all worship of Lucifer as God. I renounce and forsake the lie of Freemasonry that man is not sinful, but just imperfect, and so can redeem himself through good works. I rejoice that the Bible states that I cannot do a single thing to earn my salvation, but that I can only be saved by grace through faith in Jesus Christ and what He accomplished on the Cross of Calvary.

"In the Name of Jesus Christ, I renounce all fear of insanity, anguish, death wishes, and suicide. Death was conquered by Jesus Christ, and He alone holds the keys of death and hell, and I rejoice that He holds my life in His hands now. He came to give me life abundantly and eternally, and I believe His promises.

"I renounce all anger, hatred, murderous thoughts, revenge, retaliation, spiritual apathy, false religion, all unbelief. I especially renounce unbelief in the Holy Bible and God's Word, and all compromise of God's Word. I renounce all spiritual searching into false religions, and all striving to please God. I rest in the knowledge that I have found my Lord and Saviour Jesus Christ, and that He has found me.

"I will burn all objects in my possession which connect me with all lodges and occultic organizations, including those objects of Masonry, Witchcraft and Mormonism, and all regalia, aprons, books of rituals, rings and other jewelry. I renounce the effects these or other objects of Masonry, such as the compass, the square, the noose, or the blindfold have had on me or my family, in Jesus' Name.

"Holy Spirit, I ask that you show me anything else I need to do or to pray so that I and my family may be totally free from the consequences of the sins of Masonry, Witchcraft, Mormonism and Paganism.

Pause, while listening to God, and pray as the Holy Spirit leads you....

Now dear Father God, I ask humbly for the blood of Jesus Christ, your Son, to cleanse me from all these sins I have confessed and renounced, to cleanse my spirit, my soul, my mind, my emotions and every part of my body which has been affected by these sins, in Jesus' Name!

"I renounce every evil spirit associated with Masonry and Witchcraft and all other sins, and I command in the name of Jesus Christ that Satan and every evil spirit be bound and leave me now, touching or harming no one, and go to the place appointed for you by the Lord Jesus Christ, never to return to me or my family. I call on the name of the Lord Jesus Christ to deliver me of these spirits, in accordance with the many promises in the Bible. I ask to be delivered of every spirit of sickness, infirmity, curse, affliction, addiction, disease, or allergy associated with these sins I have confessed and renounced.

"I surrender to God's Holy Spirit and to no other spirit all the places in my life where these sins have been. I ask you, Lord, to now baptize me in your Holy Spirit according to the promises in your Word. I take to myself the whole armor of God in accordance with Ephesians 6, and rejoice in its protection as Jesus surrounds me and fills me with His Holy Spirit. I enthrone you, Lord Jesus, in my heart, for you are my Lord and Savior, the source of eternal life. Thank you, Father God, for your mercy, your forgiveness and your love, in the name of Jesus Christ, Amen."■

PETITION OF WITHDRAWAL FROM LODGE

Lodge #_____

City_____State_____

Gentlemen:

When initiated into the Entered Apprentice Degree, I was induced to swear that, "I will always hail, ever conceal and never reveal any of the secret arts, parts or points of the (supposed) hidden mysteries of Ancient Masonry, which have been heretofore, may at this time or shall at any future period be communicated to me as such." In my ignorance, and being led along line by line, I indulged in the bloody obligation required of me.

Now, however, gentlemen, after having examined the highest documents and authorities of the institution of Freemasonry, and after having found beyond any doubt that the god of Freemasonry is positively not the God of the Bible, and that Freemasonry is in no way compatible with, or complementary to Christianity, I have chosen the following course of action:

Being a Christian, as I am, and confessing the Lordship of Jesus Christ over my life, as I do, and having learned the true purpose and nature of Freemasonry, as well as the true interpretation of its pagan symbols, I proudly present to you my Petition of Withdrawal.

I renounce my association with and obligation to the occult craft of Masonry without the least equivocation, mental reservation, or self-evasion of mind. I do this gentlemen, because the Word of God says:

"Be ye not unequally yoked together with unbelievers: for what fellowship hath righteousness with unrighteousness? And what communion hath light with darkness" (2 Corinthians 6:14).

Please believe me gentlemen, I have no degree of animosity whatsoever toward you, or toward any other man in the Lodge. It was not you that deceived me, it was those in the institution of Freemasonry who know the true designs and purposes of the institution who deceived us both.

Respectfully,

Mr. _____

Date _____

(This letter was composed by former 32nd degree Freemason, C.F. McQuaig, and can be found in *The Masonic Report*.)

BOOK REVIEWS

❧

OTHER BOOKS

&

CASSETTE TAPES

YOU CAN ORDER FROM

JKI PUBLISHING

SCARLET AND THE BEAST

BOOK REVIEWS

"In all my 33 years of study in God's prophetic Word, I have never been as awestruck with any revelation as that which is revealed in *Scarlet and the Beast* I have never seen so much convincing and compelling documentation on the identity of the Beast nation in all my years of study. Never before have I learned so much from one book (except the Bible), and after 900 pages, I hated for it to end! To attempt to explain even a small portion here would be totally impossible. You must read it for yourself." *Dr. John Barela, editor of "Today, The Bible, And You," Tulsa, OK.*

"I have read your 3-volume set of *Scarlet and the Beast* with fascination. It cleared up many questions and is probably the most satisfying and comprehensive work I have seen on the subject." *Dr. Jonathan Henry, Clearwater Christian College, Clearwater FL.*

"I received your three books, *Scarlet and the Beast,* months ago. But, they went on a huge pile of waiting-to-be-read books. Then recently I got a call from Joel Bainerman, who began raving about the books. So, this spurred me to get them down, and now I can't stop reading! Much of the material I knew, as I have read many of your sources, but the way you have put it together; argued through the history; linked all with Scripture; put things into the 'plan of God', etc., blows my mind. I am not even half way through book one yet, and am writing to order all three books for my friend!" *Gemma Blech, Israel.*

"Praise God for using his servant John Daniel in writing *Scarlet and the Beast!* All my questions are answered and loose ends are now tied." *Karen Campbell, Christian public school teacher.*

SCARLET AND THE BEAST

Volume I

The War Between English And French Freemasonry

by John Daniel

Table of Contents

275

the British throne? Why, when and where did Templar Freemasonry become Scottish Rite Freemasonry? Why is the Scottish Rite also known as the Jewish Rite? What historic event in French history justified the Scottish Rite's revolt against the Bourbon dynasty? What role is played by the Illuminati in the war between English and French Freemasonry?

Chapter 5: Rejecting Christianity: Pagan Symbols of Freemasonry and the Illuminati. What is the secret meaning of the Masonic square and compass? What event does May Day commemorate? Why was the Illuminati founded on May 1, 1776? How did the symbol of the Illuminati become the national emblem of the United States of America? What is the significant meaning of this symbol? Where is the USA mentioned in Scripture? What role does the USA play in end-time Bible prophecy? What Scripture in the Bible describes the Masonic All-Seeing Eye?

Chapter 6: Music and Revolution. Can music cause people to revolt against authority? How was music used by French Freemasonry prior to the French Revolution? Why were most of the famous European musicians Masons? Which European musician is specifically noted for composing music for "Masonic use?" Is there a connection between modern British rock-n-roll stars and English Freemasonry? Why are British rock stars infatuated with 33rd degree Freemason Aleister Crowley? What role does the Fallen Angel play in music?

Chapter 7: The Jewish Connection. How did Moses Mendelssohn's writings promote revolution? Why did the Jew Jacob Frank assault orthodox Judaism? What is the connection between Reform Judaism and illuminated Freemasonry? What role do Jewish bankers play in English Freemasonry? Is the Scottish Rite controlled by Jews, or is it a counterfeit "synagogue of Satan?"

Chapter 8: The Jesuit Connection. What role did Freemasonry play in the Jesuit suppression of 1773? What year, and under what circumstances did Freemasonry plan to infiltrate the Catholic Church? Why did Free-masonry pit Protestants against Catholics? What pope did Freemasonry claim as its own? What pope did Freemasonry assassinate? What connection does the South American Catholic Liberation Theology have with Freemasonry?

Chapter 9: Secular Education: A Masonic Blueprint. Did 32nd degree Freemason Karl Marx write the *Communist Manifesto*? What educational legacy did Karl Marx leave the world? When did Freemasonry begin its drive for a public school system in America? What connection is there between Freemasonry and the National Education Association (NEA)? Why did Freemasonry lobby Congress for passage of the Federal Department of Education? What role did Freemasonry play in the consolidation of our public schools during the 1950s? After consolidation, how did Freemasonry select the curriculum to be taught? What is the connection between Freemasonry and the National Council of Churches? On what date did Freemasonry order Masons to infiltrate Protestant Churches and liberalize them?

Chapter 10: Masonic Control of the Media. How did illuminated Freemasonry use pornography prior to the French Revolution? Why was it a prerequisite that Freemasonry be in control of all media resources prior to all European revolutions? Is there proof that Freemasonry controls the news media in America? Do business logos make statements? Can you find the Masonic All-Seeing Eye (either actual or stylized) on the three major television networks? What role does Freemasonry play in pornography today? From 1752-1778 what were the ten steps Freemason Voltaire took to destroy Christianity in old France? What date did these same ten steps begin to be taken against Christians in American?

Chapter 11: First War Between English and French Freemasonry. Was Napoleon Bonaparte a military genius, or were his successes made possible because he was a Mason? What role did British Masonic bankers play in the defeat of Napoleon? What empire at the Congress of Vienna torpedoed Freemasonry's first attempt at world government? What Masonic retaliation was taken against that nation in the 20th century? What is the connection between Freemasonry and Switzerland's neutrality?

Chapter 12: French Freemasonry Tries, and Tries Again. Did communism originate in Russia, or in French Masonic lodges? What is the connection between Freemasonry and the Mafia? How did the Mafia assist in spreading revolution worldwide? How did organized crime play a role in the Italian Revolution? What is the connection between the Mafia and International Freemasonry? When did France first become known as a "Masonic State?"

Chapter 13: The Protocols of the Learned Elders of Sion, not Zion: Where did Zionism originate? Where did Sionism originate? What is the difference between the two? Is Sionism Jewish, or a counterfeit? What role did French Freemasonry play in the Sionist intrigue?

Chapter 14: Lucifer: god of Freemasonry. What famous American Mason created the Luciferian Rite for the 33rd degree Supreme Council? Is there a secret Super Rite above the 33rd degree? Can you prove in Scripture that Satan was once Lucifer? Why does Freemasonry deny the existence of Satan? Does Universal Freemasonry adhere to the Luciferian Doctrine? Is Lucifer good or bad, or good and bad? What does the Supreme Council of Freemasonry say about the God of the Bible when comparing Him to Lucifer?

Chapter 15: Freemasonry and the New Age Movement: What universal Masonic convention in 1889 united Atheists, Spiritists, and Luciferians

Volume I

with Freemasonry? How did English Freemasonry found New Age lodges at the turn of the 20th century without being directly involved? What role did 33rd degree Freemason Aleister Crowley play in the New Age Movement? What is the connection between occult ritual murders and New Age Lodges?

Chapter 16: New Age Movement unites English and French Freemasonry. What role did the British Quatuor Coronati Lodge of Masonic Research play in founding the New Age Movement? What famous New Age Lodges brought the drug culture to America in the 1960s? How does the drug culture unite the two Freemasonries? What New Age Lodge is attached to the United Nations? Who are the prominent American members of this New Age Lodge?

Chapter 17: The First Masonic World War: Why did Universal Freemasonry want world war? How did Universal Freemasonry divide the nations to set the stage for World War One? What six incidents (from 1908-1913), did Freemasonry instigate in its attempt to trigger World War? The seventh incident was successful. What error did Freemasonry make, which tipped off Archduke Francis Ferdinand, causing him to say, "The Freemasons plan to kill me."? The assassins were prosecuted and sentenced in the midst of WWI. During their trial, what lodges were implicated as being involved in plotting the assassination? What lodges furnished the weapons? Which of the assassins said in court, "in Freemasonry murder is justified."? What Mason in Europe solicited help from individuals close to President Woodrow Wilson to bring America into the War? Is it coincidental that these American individuals were one and all Freemasons?

Chapter 18: The Hungarian Masonic Revolution: Following WWI, what was the conflict between British and French lodges in Hungary? Which French lodge formed the Soviet Republic of Hungary on March 21, 1919? What triggered the counter revolution that made Hungary outlaw Freemasonry? What action did the USA take against Hungary for refusing to reinstate Freemasonry? What punishment was administered to Hungary after WWII for outlawing Freemasonry after WWI?

Chapter 19: The Russian Masonic Revolution: What did French Freemasonry know in the mid 1800s about a future Russian Revolution that caused a French Freemason in 1843 to write, "The future smells of Russian knouts, of blood, of impiety and of violent blows."? What Famous Russian Mason and satanist received funds in 1870 from French Freemasonry to foment revolution in Russia? What role was played in the Bolshevik Revolution by French Freemasonry? Why did British Intelligence attempt the assassination of French Freemason Vladimir Lenin? What was the connection between English Freemasonry and Joseph Stalin? What famous British Mason coined the phrase "Iron Curtain" to describe the Soviet Union? What Mason in British Intelligence defected to Russia in 1962 with a British agenda to topple the Soviet Union? Before Gorbachev came to power, why

Volume I

did he meet with high-level Masons in London and Paris? When was Gorbachev made a Freemasonry, before or after he dissolved the Soviet Union?

Chapter 20: The Masonic Ritual Murder of Czar Nicholas II: Why did Russian Freemasons order the death of the Czar and his household? What evidence is there that the murder was a Masonic ritual murder and not simply an assassination?

Chapter 21: Competing for World Governance: The Round Table vs. the League of Nations: French Grand Lodge minutes during 1913 reveal that French Freemasonry was planning a "League of Nations" following the future world war. After the war, why was Woodrow Wilson given the credit? How was the British Round Table used by English Freemasonry to destroy the League of Nations? What is the connection between English Freemasonry and the Council on Foreign Relations (CFR)? Why did Freemason Cecil Rhodes found the Rhodes Scholarships?

Chapter 22: English Freemasonry and the Hitler Project. In the 1870s, how did British Masons prepare the world to accept a Hitler? What New Age Lodge founded by English Freemasonry in 1887 groomed Hitler in the 1920s? What famous Mason founded the Thule Society? How did this Society bring Hitler to power? Why did English Freemasonry support Hitler in destroying European Freemasonry? Why did Hitler rebel against London? What Nazi Mason flew to London in an attempt to negotiate peace?

Chapter 23: Hitler's Destruction of French Freemasonry. Is there evidence in Masonic books that Hitler's war was against French Freemasonry? Why is mention made of six million Jews slaughtered by Hitler, and no mention made of five million Masons slaughtered? What year did Fascist Italy outlaw Freemasonry? What year did Nazi Germany outlaw Freemasonry? What year did Franco's Spain outlaw Freemasonry? What year did Japan outlaw Freemasonry? Why is none of this mentioned in our history books, while abundant documentation exists in Masonic books?

Chapter 24: Yalta, Post-War Masonry, and the United Nations: Is there evidence that the USA provoked Japan into attacking Pearl Harbor? If so, was Freemasonry involved? After WWII, why did the occupation armies of the Allies stack the governments of postwar Germany, Italy, and Japan with Masons? Why did the CIA take a direct hand in rebuilding Freemasonry in Italy? Which of the Americans negotiating with Stalin at Yalta were Masons? How many judges at the Nuremberg Trials were known Masons? Which Nazi at Nuremberg was quoted as saying, "We planned to destroy

Volume I

Freemasonry."? Why were Nazi Masons not given death sentences. Why were some released? Did the Masonic oath prevail over international law?

Chapter 25: The Address of Scarlet. Are modern Masonic revolutions prophesied by Ezekiel and Zechariah? When did Mystery Babylon exit the Catholic Church and enter English Freemasonry? Does Revelation 17-18 shed light on English Freemasonry as Mystery Babylon today? How does Rev. 18:23 expose English Freemasonry's involvement in the illegal drug trade? Does London sit on seven hills as does Rome? How Jeremiah describe London as modern Babylon, and the USA as the "daughter of Babylon"? In 1983, when Queen Elizabeth II toured the USA, why did American Freemasonry address her at a "gala" as "Queen of Babylon?"

Chapter 26: In Search of the Beast Empire. If Rosicrucian English Freemasonry is Mystery Babylon, is there evidence that Templar French Freemasonry plans to inaugurate the Beast Empire of Revelation 17? What biblical requirement must be met for a nation to qualify as "the revived Roman empire"? Why does Germany, France, and Russia not fit the profile? Why does the European Common Market not fit the profile? What Scripture gives the ultimate test to identify the Beast Empire? What prophetic Scripture describes the national emblem of the Beast Empire?

Chapter 27: Headquarters of the Beast Empire. Revived Rome must have the same 13 characteristics of ancient Rome. Ancient Rome: (1) was the melting-pot of the world; (2) was a democracy based on a two-party system; (3) had a divided balance of power; (4) was based on specific laws; (5) protected the rights of its citizens; (6) had a sordid history of slavery; (7) was capitalistic; (8) practiced abortion as a means of population control; (9) loved R-rated entertainment; (10) had a welfare program funded by taxes; (11) had a thriving business in lawsuits; (12) watched sports as a pastime; (13) had as its national emblem a single-headed flying eagle pointing west.

Volume One includes
11 Appendices, Notes, Bibliography and Index — 947 pages.

Vol I: $43 USD (outside USA $48 USD) includes P&H
Vols I, II, & III: $57 USD (outside USA $67 USD) includes P&H

JKI Publishing, PO Box 131480, Tyler TX 75713
If you prefer faster service by Priority Mail or UPS, call for extra cost.
Amex, VISA or MC orders call 1-800/333-5344 weekdays 8-5

SCARLET AND THE BEAST

Volume II

**English Freemasonry, Mother of Modern Cults,
vis-a-vis
Mystery Babylon, Mother of Harlots**

by John Daniel

Table of Contents

281

volume II

god? How did Nimrod attempt to establish world government? What pagan symbol of Nimrod is used by the United Nations as a symbol of world government? Where is this same symbol found in Freemasonry?

Chapter 5: The Female God: Semiramis was the wife of Nimrod. In mystery religions Semiramis was known as the seed bearer of Lucifer. How does Semiramis relate to the Easter Star, the female arm of Freemasonry? What effect did Christ's death on the cross have on the seed of the serpent?

Chapter 6: The Mystery of Secrecy: Rabbinical tradition holds that Melchizedek was actually Shem. What is the Scriptural title given Melchizedek? What is the Hebrew meaning of Shem? How is Shem a type of Christ? What is the relationship between Semiramis and Nimrod and the Egyptian goddess and god, Isis and Osiris? In mystery religions Shem is known as the black god, or evil god. He is also known as God's battle-axe, because he destroyed Nimrod. By what method did Shem destroy Nimrod? How does that relate to the second coming of Christ?

Volume Two includes
Notes, Bibliography and Index — 170 pages.

Vol II: $14 USD (outside USA $17 USD) includes P&H
Vols I, II, & III: $57 USD (outside USA $67 USD) includes P&H

JKI Publishing, PO Box 131480, Tyler TX 75713

If you prefer faster service by Priority Mail or UPS, call for extra cost. Amex, VISA or MC orders call 1-800/333-5344 weekdays 8-5

SCARLET AND THE BEAST
volume III
English Freemasonry, Banks, and the Illegal Drug Trade
by John Daniel

Table of Contents

volume III

Chapter 5: Gradualism: Gold, Dollars, Debt, and Drugs: What was the connection between 33rd degree Freemason John Wilkes Booth and English Freemasonry? What famous Mason founded the Ku Klux Klan? What role did 33rd degree Freemason Jesse James play in funding a second civil war? What was English Freemasonry's role in the Federal Reserve Act of 1913? What was London's role in the 1929 stock market crash? How did London use the Bank for International Settlement (BIS) to loot the gold of European nations during WWII? When did our gold at Fort Knox disappear?

Chapter 6: A Freemasonry of Terrorists: How does English Freemasonry use Right-wing European and South American terrorists? Why was the Italian Masonic banker, Roberto Calvi, ritually murdered by English Freemasonry? What two decisions did JFK make to stop the drug traffic into the USA. What did these decisions have to do with his assassination? Did the Warren Commission "cover-up" have anything to do with the fact that the entire Commission were Masons? What did Pope John Paul I know about the Vatican Bank that led to his Masonic ritual murder? What connection is there between South American drugs and the Falklands War?

Chapter 7: London's Drug War Against America: What is the connection between ethnic Mafiosi and Freemasonry? How is London's Masonic Research Lodge connected to illegal drugs? What novel did Freemason George Orwell write to warn America against London's drug war? How do British rock stars open new drug markets for English Freemasonry?

Chapter 8: Vietnam and the Drug Wars: What is the connection between British Intelligence, the CIA, and Burmese drugs? Why did the CIA use its Air America transport planes to deliver Burmese opium during the Vietnam War? Why was 33rd degree Freemasonry J. Edgar Hoover upset when Castro expelled the Mafia from Cuba? What is the connection between the Mena, Arkansas airport, the CIA, and the South American drug runners?

Volume Three includes
Notes, Bibliography and Index — 220 pages.

Vol III: $14 USD (outside USA $17 USD) includes P&H
Vols I, II, & III: $57 USD (outside USA $67 USD) includes P&H

JKI Publishing, PO Box 131480, Tyler TX 75713
If you prefer faster service by Priority Mail or UPS, call for extra cost. Amex, VISA or MC orders call 1-800/333-5344 weekdays 8-5

SECRET SOCIETIES AND THEIR INFILTRATION INTO THE SEVEN CHURCHES OF REVELATION
7 audio cassette taped messages by John Daniel
— an excellent study in Church history —

The seven churches in Revelation were named after the seven cities in Asia Minor (modern Turkey) where they were head-quartered. First was Ephesus, followed in order by Smyrna, Pergamos, Thyatira, Sardis, Philadelphia, and Laodicea.

Why did Jesus instruct the Apostle John to write to these seven particular churches in this particular order? There were other churches Christ could have selected. South of Laodicea was Colosse. In Greece there were three churches, Philippi, Thessalonica, and Corinth. There were also churches at Galatia, Hierapolis, and Troas.

Why these particular seven?

Many prophecy students agree that these seven churches were selected by Christ because they exemplify seven prophetic periods through which the Church has now historically passed.

First proof. The Greek meaning of the name of each city where the churches were headquartered defines a peculiar charact-eristic that we find in each of seven historic church periods.

Second proof. Each church in Asia Minor was plagued with a pagan problem peculiar to that city in which it was head-quartered. This pagan problem was a mystery religion, or in our modern vernacular, a secret society. Each church in Asia Minor reacted to the secret society in a specific manner. These reactions toward secret societies can also be recognized in seven distinct historic church periods spanning the last 2,000 years.

Third proof. As each of the seven churches in Asia Minor was located in a city with a peculiar characteristic and secret society, so too each historic church period was headquartered within a country having those same peculiar characteristics and secret societies. These countries are Asia Minor, Rome, northern Europe, England, and America.

285

7 Churches

Fourth proof. As did all seven church types exist simultane-ously in John's day, so too were all seven in existence throughout the church age, with one of the seven predominant during each of the seven church periods.

Fifth proof. Each individual Christian will have at least one characteristic, and be confronted by at least one pagan problem peculiar to each of the seven churches.

John Daniel's message to each Christian is that you under-stand what characteristic best fits your spiritual walk with our Lord and Savior, Jesus Christ, because that characteristic is developing you for your eternal vocation — if you overcome the pagan problem.

Christ speaks to you and to your eternal vocation when He says, "To him that overcometh [this particular pagan problem] will I give [this particular eternal vocation]."

$10 USD for each cassette tape
(outside USA $13 USD each cassette tape)
P&H included in price

or

$40 USD for all seven tapes
(outside USA $50 USD)
P&H included in price

If you prefer faster service by Priority Mail or UPS, call for extra cost.

You may order from

JKI Publishing, PO Box 131480, Tyler TX 75713

Amex, VISA or MC orders call 1-800/333-5344 weekdays 8-5

THE MASONIC LODGE: WHAT YOU NEED TO KNOW

17 Spiritual Errors and Dangers of Freemasonry

Compares Masonic teachings with Bible teachings
Errors 1-5: Deity and Worship
Errors 6-11: Oaths and Allegiance
Errors 12-17: Salvation and the Bible

Also includes

THE STRUCTURE OF FREEMASONRY

Auxiliary Bodies
The Structure of American Freemasonry

THE YORK RITE — CHRISTIAN FREEMASONRY?

ONE OR THE OTHER
I Kings 18:18,21
The Need for Fellowship.
Sons of Light?
Do Christians Walk in Darkness?
Come Out from Among Them.

To order this quick reference guide, write:
Ed Decker, Saints Alive, POB 1076, Issawuah WA 98027

To order the eye-popping half-hour video
Freemasonry: From Darkness to Light?
write:
**Marlin Maddoux, International Christian Media
PO Box 30, Dallas, TX 75221
or call toll free: 1-800-347-5151**

287

Jon Kregel, Inc, dba JKI Publishing
ORDER INSTRUCTIONS
To order any of the below items, send your name and address with check or money order to: JKI, Publishing, P.O. Box 131480, Tyler, TX 75713. Allow four weeks for delivery by book rate mail. If you prefer faster service by Priority Mail or UPS, call for extra cost. **AMEX, Visa** or **MC** orders call toll free **1-800-333-5344** weekdays 8 a.m. to 5 p.m.

The Character, Claims and Practical Workings of Freemasonry by C.G. Finney. 1869 reprint with a 1998 Introduction, Epilog, Appendix. ISBN: 1-890913-00-6 **$18 USD (outside USA $21 USD)** — Texas residents add 8.25% sales tax.

Scarlet and the Beast: A History of the War between English and French Freemasonry by John Daniel. 2nd ed. 1995, Vol.1 (27 chapters; 11 Appendices; Endnotes; Bibliography; Index; 947 p.). ISBN: 0-9635079-8-2 **$43 USD (outside USA $48 USD)** — Texas residents add 8.25% sales tax.

Scarlet and the Beast: English Freemasonry, Mother of Modern Cults, vis-a-vis, Mystery Babylon, Mother of Harlots by John Daniel. 1994. Vol. 2 (6 chapters; Endnotes; Bibliography; Index; 176 pages). ISBN: 0-9635079-2-3 **$14 USD (outside USA $17 USD)** — Texas residents add 8.25% sales tax.

Scarlet and the Beast: English Freemasonry, Banks, and the Illegal Drug Trade by John Daniel. 1995. Vol.3 (8 chapters; notes; Bibligraphy; Index; 221 p) ISBN: 0-9635079-4-X **$14 USD (outside USA $17 USD)** — Texas residents add 8.25% sales tax.

Scarlet and the Beast: 3-volume-set. 2nd edition. 1995. ISBN: 0-9635079-9-0 **$57 USD (outside USA $67 USD)** — Texas residents add 8.25% sales tax.

Dealer: Autobiography by Jon Kregel. The true story of a missionary kid and soccer pro and his descent into the cocaine underworld. A must for teenagers. Parents with loved ones in prison — there is hope. You need to read this book, then send it to your loved one in prison. ISBN: 0-8010-5287-4 **$12 USD (outside USA $15 USD)** — Texas residents add 8.25% sales tax.

Drugs: What you need to know to just say NO! by Jon Kregel. A description of street drugs and their symptoms on the user. A must for teenagers and parents. Free with the purchase of **Dealer**, or purchased alone, **$5 USD (outside USA $7 USD)** — Texas residents add 8.25% sales tax.

Illuminati Conspiracy by Myron Fagan (2 cass. tapes). Fagan was a Hollywood playwright who spent most of his professional life researching the Illuminati. In the 1940s he founded the Cinema Educational Guild, which published *The Point*, a monthly exposure of Illuminati influence in America. In 1967-68 Fagan recorded his many years of research, in which he traces the Illuminati's takeover of the media, politics, the financial institutions, and the mainline churches in America. Like most revisionist historians, Fagan is an adherent to the one conspiracy theory of history. His two cassette tapes are an easy and quick way to get an overview of Illuminati-Masonic influence in world affairs. **$10 USD (outside USA $13 USD)** — Texas residents add 8.25% sales tax.

Behold, There Came Wise Men by John Daniel. A 16-page Christmas card of the history of the Wise Men. Who were they? From where did they come? How did they knew to follow a star to Bethlehem? You are carried back 500 B.C. to when a prophecy was given, possibly by the prophet Daniel, "that the wise men would be the first to hear of the birth of the Christ Child." You will follow the starry path they trod. Nice, inexpensive Christmas gift for friends, with a salvation message. **$1.75 USD (outside USA $2.25 USD)** Texas residents add 8.25% sales tax. Send a stamped, self-addressed envelope for quantity purchase prices.

NOTES

NOTES

NOTES

pp. 300